THE OTHER ISLANDS OF NEW YORK CITY

A HISTORY AND GUIDE

Sharon Seitz and Stuart Miller

Third Edition

THE COUNTRYMAN PRESS
Woodstock, Vermont

Library of Congress Cataloging-in-Publication Data
Seitz, Sharon
Miller, Stuart
The Other Islands of New York City: A History and Guide / by Sharon Seitz & Stuart Miller.—3rd ed.
    p. cm.
    Includes bibliographical references (p. 285) and index.
ISBN 0-88150-945-8 (alk. paper)
1. Islands—New York (State)—New York—History. 2. Islands—New York (State)—New York—Guidebooks. 3. New York (N.Y.)—Guidebooks. 4. New York (N.Y.)—History. I. Miller, Stuart, 1966–II. Title.

Text design by Julie Duquet
Page composition by Melanie Jolicoeur
Maps by Paul Woodward, © 1996, 2001 The Countryman Press

Published by The Countryman Press
P.O. Box 748, Woodstock, VT 05091

Distributed by W. W. Norton & Company, Inc.
500 Fifth Avenue, New York, NY 10110

Printed in the United States
10 9 8 7 6 5 4 3 2 1

Dedications

To SGS, for putting up with another one of my crazy plans and going through this all over again.
—Stuart

To all those who have encouraged me on my journey thus far . . . and to Rattsu.
—Sharon

The
Other Islands
of
New York City

0 — miles — 4

1. Governors Island
2. Liberty Island
3. Ellis Island
4. Hoffman and Swinburne Islands
5. City Island
6. Hunter and Twin Islands
7. Hart Island
8. Roosevelt Island
9. Randall's and Ward's Islands
10. Rikers Island
11. North and South Brother Islands
12. Broad Channel
13. Coney Island
14. Prall's Island
15. Shooter's Island
16. Isle of Meadow

Contents

Introduction to the Third Edition

TAKE THE A TRAIN. And be sure to get a window seat, because after the train emerges from the dark subway tunnels of Manhattan and Brooklyn and onto the elevated lines of Queens, the hard-edged cityscape slowly vanishes. Outside your urban porthole, commercial strips beneath the tracks fade into private homes; then the entire landscape melts into an aquatic tableau dotted with boats out for a day of fishing. White-rumped sandpipers, American oystercatchers, and common snipes congregate in marshes and wetlands. Then the subway stops, and its double doors slide open, revealing a weathered fishing village where houses are built on stilts. For the price of a subway ride, you've traveled worlds away from the steamy city in the distance.

You have just entered one of New York City's "other" islands.

Broad Channel, home of the Jamaica Bay Wildlife Refuge and a modest community, is one of dozens of islands within the confines of New York City, a metropolis where even the "mainland" is an island. Manhattan, Staten Island, Queens, and Brooklyn are all either single islands or geographically part of Long Island; only the Bronx is connected to the contiguous United States.

New York's true archipelago, however, resides in its rivers, bays, and other waterways. Some of the city's islands are famous, like Ellis Island, some obscure, like North Brother, and some, like Coney Island, are island has-beens. From Rat Island, a tiny two-acre speck in the Bronx, to Rikers Island, a sprawling penal colony in Queens, the islands of New York City were long forgotten pieces in the city's geographic jigsaw puzzle.

"New York City's smaller islands are our secret treasures," says Mayor Michael Bloomberg.

New York's islands were formed by glacial erosion, most of which occurred twelve to eighteen thousand years ago. As glaciers slowly flowed south, they carved channels in the region's rocky terrain; some sections were so hard that they weren't ground down. When the glaciers melted, they filled in the channels between the landmasses, leaving the hard knobs jutting out as islands.

The isolation unique to islands has endowed them with special purpose and an evocative aura throughout history: from Napoleon's banishment to St. Helena after Waterloo and Charles Darwin's evolutionary theories cultivated in the seclusion of the Galapagos Islands, to the swashbuckling drama of *Treasure Island* and the slapstick comedy of *Gilligan's Island*. Islands are at once forlorn, mysterious, and seductive. "What's so fascinating about islands is that they're just out of reach," says New York historian Joyce Gold.

But the remoteness that fires the imagination also relegates many islands to the recesses of the mind—Woody Guthrie never looked beyond Manhattan when he composed his classic lines: "This land is your land, this land is my land, from California to the New York Island." Even with the benefit of growing up in New York, we too were guilty of the same myopia, having overlooked the city's vast network of islands for years.

Finally, in 1990, while at Columbia University's Graduate School of Journalism, Sharon investigated the curious, often derogatory stories she'd heard as a child in Cypress Hills about the cloistered community of Broad Channel. Her award-winning master's thesis revealed a proud neighborhood of activists determined to safeguard their island hamlet in the face of continuous adversity.

After visiting Ellis Island two years later with Stuart's family—whose roots traced back through the immigrant depot—we chatted casually about the contrast between the Island of Hope and Broad Channel. Thinking we'd stumbled upon a magazine story, we explored further and discovered an entire galaxy of islands, many with a crucial role in New York City's development.

Born a great port city, New York gradually shed its maritime identity as it evolved into a sprawling megalopolis and center for manufacturing, finance, and culture. As New York embraced the modern era—building bridges and tunnels to speed the flow of commerce, and highways like the FDR Drive and the Belt Parkway that cut its citizenry off from the waterfront—its identity as a city of islands diminished.

Many of the city's islands also followed a general pattern of development: Family farms of wealthy merchants were replaced first by forts, then by oppressive government institutions and garbage dumps, and at last by recreational centers and wildlife preserves. According to Russell Gilmore, author of *Forts of New York City*, the islands' most critical role came during their "fort phase" as defenders of America's independence. In the years leading up to the War of 1812 with England, the U.S. government erected a comprehensive defense to protect New York. The outer bastions were on the Brooklyn and Staten Island shores and aimed at The Narrows, while the interior defense was constructed at Castle Clinton and Ellis, Bedloe's, and Governors Islands. While the English invaded and burned Washington, D.C., during the war, their navy, which blockaded New York City, was deterred from entering the harbor. The island forts never had to fire a shot.

By 1820, New York claimed 123,706 inhabitants, surpassing Philadelphia as the most populous city. The number soared to 813,669 by 1860; a quarter of the newcomers were Irish immigrants. A similar boom occurred throughout the rest of the nation, bringing with it an increase in crime and poverty and stirring fears that America's church, family, and social order were in jeopardy. The government, which was run by a handful of wealthy men, turned to newly developed institutions, like the asylum and the prison, to keep the underclass in check. To maximize segregation, municipalities nationwide routinely placed institutions well outside the city limits; for its part, New York City bought up islands, which were nearby, yet isolated. Between 1828 and 1892, the government turned first to Blackwell's Island, then to Randall's, Ward's, Hart, North Brother, Rikers, and Ellis Islands for warehousing the sick, criminal, indigent, and immigrant. Hoffman and Swinburne Islands were built from scratch as quarantines to pacify citizens opposed to a quarantine on Staten Island.

These islands "were waste places that could be spared very readily," John Van Dyke wrote in his 1909 book *The New New York*. However, Van Dyke added, public opinion was changing, and New Yorkers were questioning whether the city had "given up to its crippled and aged, its thugs and thieves, its paupers and prisoners, the most livable and lovable portions of the town." This sentiment, combined with the escalating cost of operating these isolated institutions and revelations about widespread brutality and corruption there, led to a change in policy beginning in the 1930s.

While institutions still occupy some islands, many have been reclaimed for the public good, hosting everything from historic sites to communities to parks and wildlife sanctuaries. Still, when *The Other Islands of New York City* first came out in 1996, many of these islands existed outside the imagination of most New Yorkers. But beginning in the mid-1990s, the city, the state, not-for-profits, and private developers began reconnecting New Yorkers to their 578 miles of waterfront, creating exciting new waterfront parks, walking and bike paths, and water taxi service. Then people began looking beyond the water's edge to the city's intriguing island empire.

In 2002, we created a documentary for public television about the islands; in anticipation of the program, we'd updated the book in 2001. As you hold the third edition in your hands, the logical question is, of course, "Why now?" Well, when a neighbor recently saw a rebroadcast of the documentary he said to Stuart, "That must have been made a long time ago—you looked so much younger."

After absorbing that harsh reality, it made us think about how much time had transpired since the second edition and how many of these islands have experienced transformations large or small. Roosevelt Island has undergone a building boom (for better and worse) while Floyd Bennett Field, on the former site of Barren Island, has received so much media attention that its public campsites—once empty more often than not—now require reservations weeks or months in advance.

The most dramatic change has been at Governors Island, which was closed to the public a decade ago but which is now rapidly becoming a favorite summertime getaway within the city for New Yorkers. But this island is not alone in being rejuvenated for the public's benefit. Randall's Island, with the new Icahn Stadium and dozens of manicured ball fields, has also experienced a rebirth, and Coney Island has seen a revitalization of its amusement area amid concerns about the price of redevelopment. "We've been working hard to increase access to both Governors Island and Randall's Island, and more and more New Yorkers and tourists are discovering all that they have to offer," says Mayor Bloomberg, adding that, "Coney Island is back—and we're going to ensure that the amusement district continues to get bigger and better.

Even the islands that had gone to the birds look different now—Isle of Meadow and North Brother Island, among the most popular nesting sites for herons and egrets in 2000, now sit empty, while others, such as Hoffman and Mill Rock Islands, are the new hot spots for nesting wading birds.

New York City's islands may not be the South Seas, but they offer something singular—proximity to the world's greatest city and just enough isolation to support unique identities. By recognizing how each island has evolved in relation to the city around it, we can better understand New York and even a bit about ourselves.

—SHARON SEITZ AND STUART MILLER

Notes on the Archipelago

When we tell people we have written a book about New York City's islands, they invariably asked, "How many islands are there?"

Well, it depends. Some are islands when the tide is low. Jamaica Bay has many of these "now-it's-an-island, now-it's-not" types, like JoCo Marsh and Pumpkin Patch Marsh. Some were islands long ago. Landfill has fused many of them to the "mainland," changing the city's contours. Berrian's Island is now connected to Astoria, Queens, and is the site of a Consolidated Edison plant, while Crooke's Island has been transformed into Crooke's Point, a peninsula in Great Kills, Staten Island. Some, like Goose Island in the Bronx, are mere bumps in the water with few tales to tell.

For our book, we've profiled forty-five islands and former islands; some offer an engaging anecdote, whereas others have a rich, detailed history to share. There's the tragic plane crash on High Island, the burning of Coney Island's Dreamland, and the failed scheme of Solomon Riley, who wished to build an amusement park for blacks on Hart Island.

The book is organized geographically. For example, the chapter on Hoffman Island can be found in the Lower New York Bay section, while Roosevelt Island is in the East River section. A chapter called Forgotten Islands, a roundup of smaller islands and former islands in the region, punctuates most sections.

Blocked off within most island chapters are stories related to the island's history that warrant their own moment in the spotlight. These Historical Detours feature compelling characters like Nellie Bly and Typhoid Mary and dramatic vignettes like the burning of the excursion steamer *General Slocum*. We've included a brief profile of Robert Moses up front (see Island Emperor), since he influenced the fate of so many islands.

Because of their isolation, islands often exist in worlds of their own, breeding myths and misinformation. Rather than perpetuate fable as fact, we've included various versions when historical accounts are irreconcilable.

Exploring the Islands

While we hope none of our readers has cause to spend time on Rikers Island, many of these islands boast attractions worthy of a day's outing.

We have, in the Exploring the Island and Where to Eat sections, described these experiences—from riding the Cyclone at Coney Island to climbing the Statue of Liberty—in a narrative style filled with historical tidbits that should make the excursions enjoyable even to the armchair traveler.

We have included phone numbers and addresses so you can call ahead to check on prices and hours, since they change so frequently. (If it's free, we let you know.) The Island Hopping section will tell you how to get there, with accessibility icons to tell you at a glance how you can get there.

by boat   by subway

by bus   by tram

by car   by foot

Island Emperor

Robert Moses, who once held twelve city and state posts simultaneously, wielded more authority and did more to shape New York City than any other figure in the twentieth century. Even the islands of New York didn't elude Moses' grasp. His endless drive to add parkland to the city—and bring ever more territory under his control—prompted him to acquire remote spots like Fort Lafayette and Hoffman, Swinburne, and Mill Rock Islands. He also used landfill to connect Hunter and Twin Islands to the mainland Bronx, and joined Randall's and Ward's Islands and Sunken Meadow in the East River.

Randall's Island, with ball fields and the buttresses of the Triborough Bridge (now the Robert F. Kennedy Bridge) dominating the landscape, perfectly symbolizes the master builder's two most significant achievements: the creation of parks and the construction of bridges. During his reign, Moses created more than two million acres of parkland and built twelve bridges.

Robert Caro, in his Pulitzer Prize–winning biography of Moses, *The Power Broker*, depicts Randall's Island as the capital of Moses' empire. Isolated from the city by the moat of the East River, and hidden from public view beneath the Triborough Bridge, Moses wielded untold power from Triborough Bridge and Tunnel Authority headquarters from the 1930s until the 1960s; as appointed head of this revenue-generating public authority, he was not accountable to the public.

Caro wrote that to enter Moses' kingdom, everyone—even top city officials—symbolically paid tribute at the Triborough's tollbooth. Once on the island, visitors were subject to the Authority's rules, not city law. Moses also maintained a splendid dining room with a full-time staff. Businessmen and officials were often kept waiting in an anteroom decorated with pictures of Moses with mayors, governors, and presidents. Once in the dining room, visitors enjoyed a fine repast while submitting to the emperor's monologues . . . and his will.

Born in Connecticut in 1888, Moses moved to New York with his family when he was nine. He studied at Yale, Oxford, and Columbia universities. He was a genius—sharp in intellect and long in vision—who never lost his superhuman capacity for work.

He entered the city's political arena after attaining power in the 1920s as one of Governor Al Smith's top associates. In 1934, Moses became the city's first parks commissioner as well as head of the new Triborough Bridge and Tunnel Authority. He also later held a seat on the planning commission and the all-purpose title of city construction coordinator. In addition to these official roles, Moses controlled both the housing authority and often the mayor's office from behind the scenes.

While he started out as an idealist reformer, politics and an unslakable thirst for power transformed him into a ruthless, autocratic despot. As Moses poured out ideas fifteen hours a day, decade after decade, he shifted sharply right on the political spectrum. His brutal philosophy included maxims like "Nothing I have ever done has been tinged with legality" and "If the end doesn't justify the means, what does?"

His accomplishments were touted as gifts to the masses, yet Moses cared little for the people themselves. Thus the highways he built ushering in New York's automobile age often came at the expense of mass transit, leaving idyllic places like Hunter or Randall's Island inaccessible to poor and working-class folks.

Moses died in 1981, leaving an island legacy that is mixed. He razed historic buildings on Hunter and Twin Islands and helped accelerate the decline of Coney Island's amusement area. His grandiose park plans for Hoffman and Swinburne Islands went unfulfilled, yet his benign neglect allowed them to develop into sanctuaries for migrating birds. He created the Jamaica Bay Wildlife Refuge at Broad Channel, but fortunately he failed in his effort to obliterate the community there.

Part I

Upper New York Bay

GOVERNORS ISLAND • LIBERTY ISLAND • ELLIS ISLAND •
FORGOTTEN ISLANDS OF UPPER NEW YORK BAY

*Hugged by New Jersey and Staten Island to the west and the Battery and
Brooklyn to the east, the five-mile-long and four-mile-wide Upper New York Bay
is the confluence of the Hudson and East Rivers.*

1. Governors Island

*"In 1800, New York magnanimously gave the Island to the Federal gov-
ernment to provide for the Nation's defense. It is only just that Governors
Island now be returned to the people of New York, and that its historic
efforts are protected."*

—SENATOR DANIEL PATRICK MOYNIHAN
MAY 2000

Governors Island

For many New Yorkers, a hassle-free (indeed, totally free) ferry ride to the beach to sip drinks beneath palm trees or take in a concert in a totally car-free environment sounds exotic, like something found in distant destinations. But one of the city's most dramatic real-estate transformations has made this fantasy a marvelous reality at Governors Island.

Long closed to the public, Governors Island has been reimagined as a playground for the people of New York

Islands sit, by their very nature, at a tantalizing remove. For nearly three centuries, no New York island symbolized that notion more than Governors Island. While many members of this archipelago—such as Hart or Prall's Islands—lay unnoticed at the city's periphery, Governors Island is nestled between Manhattan, which grew over those years into the capital of the world, and Brooklyn, which became the most populous borough in the nation's biggest city. And while many of New York City's other islands— such as Roosevelt or Liberty—changed with the times, Governors Island

Governors Island

FERRY

N.J.

N.Y.

Enlarged area

Atlantic Ocean

Carder Road

Hay Rd.

Clayton Rd.

Wheeler Ave.

Division

Early Bird Rd.

Rd.

Craig Rd. North

Gresham Rd.

Enright Rd.

Craig Rd. South

Buttermilk Channel

1. Fort Jay
2. Commanding Officer's Quarters
3. Governor's House
4. Dutch House
5. Blockhouse
6. Chapel of St. Cornelius the Centurion
7. South Battery
8. Liggett Hall
9. Colonel's Row
10. Base Hospital
11. Castle Williams

0 miles 1/4

remained a bulwark of consistency: from the 1630s until the first decade of the 21st century, Governors Island was inaccessible to the public, spending most of that time as one of the nation's longest continuously active military posts.

But Governors Island is getting an extreme makeover. And while the beach is man-made and the palm trees are fake, the island has become perhaps the most welcoming spot in the city. Governors Island offers what sounds like the best of New York in an idyllic environment: historical buildings, a remarkably diverse array of visual and performing arts exhibits, performances and festivals, and a quirky collection of activities ranging from bicycling to miniature golf to trapeze classes, plus lush open space by the waterfront where visitors can picnic amid panoramic views of the city. But there's more to come, with ambitious plans for a $200 million park and public space design that would not only add ball fields and other amenities but also reshape the flat and drab terrain of the island's southern half into a visually sumptuous park of hills, trees, terraces, and lawns.

Resting between Lower Manhattan and Brooklyn—where the East and Hudson Rivers converge and spill into Upper New York Bay on their way past Staten Island—the island has always been centrally located. For centuries, however, the island was off limits to most New Yorkers. When settlers sent by the Dutch West India Company reached New York Harbor in 1624, Governors Island, lush with groves of oak, hickory, and chestnut trees, was known to the Manahatas Indians as Pagganck, or "land of nut trees." The island's locale was so appealing that the Dutch settled here—even before settling Manhattan. The following year, more Dutch pioneers arrived, bringing some 103 head of cattle to what they called Nooten Eylandt, or Nutten Island. Little pasturage was found, however, and the bovines soon joined the colonists eight hundred yards north on Manhattan Island, where newly erected Fort Amsterdam succeeded the Nooten Eylandt fort.

Governors Island's 160 acres were then left to the Native Americans until 1637. In that year, the Falstaffian Wouter Van Twiller, who was governor and director general of New Netherland, acquired it from the Manahatas in exchange for two ax heads, a string of beads, and a few nails. The plump and prosperous leader envisioned lounging in an executive mansion there, a dream that never materialized. Strong tides made sailing to the island difficult, and Van Twiller was damned by his own corpulence—he was too big for the narrow rowboats of the day. A year later, Van Twiller was stripped of his title and properties after being accused of illegal land dealings and extorting money from his employer, the Dutch West India Company.

The British gained control of New Amsterdam and Nooten Eylandt in 1664, renaming them New York and Nutten Island. To protect idyllic Nutten Island from falling into private hands, a decree in 1698 proclaimed it "the Denizen of His Majestie's Governors," thereby granting the island its name.

This rural retreat inspired manorial visions in yet another colonial executive, England's Lord Cornbury, Sir Edward Hyde. Cornbury was a peculiar fellow and a lackluster leader. He was also rumored to be partial to women's clothing, which some say he donned publicly, as tribute to his cousin Queen Anne. A formal portrait of the outlandish governor, which today belongs to the New-York Historical Society, features Cornbury in a cinched blue gown and ladies' gloves, with a bow in his hair—although some historians question whether the drag queen who posed for the painting is indeed Cornbury, and some say this was a political smear job.

In 1703, Cornbury capitalized on fears of a French invasion by instituting a tax to fund fortification of Governors Island. It included levies on people who wore pearl rings, men who donned periwigs, and bachelors twenty-five years of age or older. No fort was built, however, and Cornbury used the money to finance his estate, which, according to legend, was built on high ground overlooking Buttermilk Channel, between the south shore of the island and Brooklyn. He called it "the smiling garden of the sovereigns of the province." When Queen Anne learned of her cousin's controversial financial dealings, she yanked him from office.

Whether Queen Anne's later use of the island is tied to this family feud is speculation, but she nonetheless thought Governors Island the proper place to quarantine thousands of plague-infested Palatine refugees. France's Louis XIV had routed these German Protestants from their homes in the lower Palatinate of the Rhine for religious reasons in 1689. The exiles eventually wandered to England, where they petitioned Queen Anne to send them to the colonies, and in 1710 they were granted land near what is today Newburgh, New York. But when hundreds fell ill aboard ship, the queen quarantined the passengers on Governors Island. Many died and were buried there, but one teenage survivor later played a critical role in American history: John Peter Zenger became publisher of the *New York Weekly Journal* and, in 1735, established the legal precedent for freedom of the press when he was acquitted of seditious libel charges brought by the British government.

When the threat of war with France resurfaced in the mid-eighteenth century, British governors called for the fortification of Governors Island. Again, nothing was built, but in 1755, during the French and Indian War, the Fifty-first Regiment of the British Colonial Militia became the first troops stationed on Governors Island. A British army regiment made up entirely of colonists known as the Loyal Americans, or the Royal American Regiment, Sixtieth Foot later joined them.

Historical Detour: Sub-Par Sub

In September of 1776, with the British commanding New York from Governors Island and Brooklyn Heights, the Continental army summoned an untested, top-secret weapon for a guerrilla attack on the warship of British admiral Richard Howe. Invented by American David Bushnell, the *Turtle* was the first submarine used for military purposes and was designed to destroy hostile ships by detonating explosives under their hulls.

Sitting in the primitive *Turtle* was like being inside a barrel—in the dark. Only six feet wide and seven and a half feet long, the wooden ship accommodated one man, who powered it with a hand-cranked propeller. A brave and adventurous army sergeant, Ezra Lee, left on his mission from the New York shore the night of September 6, and was soon thrown off-course by the tide. Lee cranked the strange vessel for more than two hours until he arrived—going about three miles an hour—underneath Howe's HMS *Eagle* sitting in New York Harbor.

When the sub's detonating device malfunctioned, Lee floated to the top to investigate. Much to his chagrin, he discovered that the fleet hadn't been destroyed, and day was dawning, putting him in danger of being discovered. He quickly descended again and headed back to New York, but a broken compass required him to pop up occasionally to check his course.

His zigzag route brought him within several yards of Governors Island, where he attracted hundreds of redcoats to the parapet. When a small group of these armed curiosity-seekers began rowing out to the *Turtle*, Lee gave the defective magazine one desperate last try. The enemy retreated, and the bomb drifted in the other direction, exploding far from Governors Island in the East River. Lee cranked away at the *Turtle* and made it safely back to New York.

At the start of the American War for Independence, however, the Sixtieth Foot was transferred to British colonies in the West Indies to avert possible allegiance with their colonial brethren. The remaining redcoats, ill equipped to contend with anti-British sentiment, vacated the island and New York on June 7, 1775 . . . with plans to return in force.

In the spring of 1776, General George Washington sent General Israel Putnam and more than a thousand men to erect the first garrison of purely American troops on Governors Island. Other regiments, including the famous Seventh Continental Infantry that fought at Bunker Hill, later aided them. Determined to test the city's defenses, British warships sailed from Staten Island to the Hudson River on July 12 and were met by a barrage of artillery from Governors Island. Although the fray lasted about an hour, and one ship was damaged, the navy proceeded unimpeded north to Westchester.

On August 27, the British army—confident they could overwhelm any American defenses and capture New York—successfully attacked Washington's troops in central Brooklyn, driving them back to Brooklyn Heights. The British could have easily captured Washington and his men—effectively ending the Revolution—if their navy had attacked Governors Island and sailed into the East River to cut off a colonial escape. Modern historians contend that Governors Island was spared this confrontation when strong tides and bad weather prevented an invasion.

In the wee hours of August 30, a beaten Washington and his battered troops withdrew to Manhattan under the protection of nighttime fog. The next day, the British navy, surprised by the maneuver and unsure whether any Continental forces remained, fired on Governors Island from a great distance. The island never felt the attack, and that night the island's Continental troops destroyed the cannons, packed up artillery and provisions, and joined Washington in retreat. The British completed their capture of New York on September 15, 1776, occupying the city and Governors Island until 1783.

During peacetime, the singular purpose of Governors Island was briefly forgotten; it was used as a racetrack, another quarantine station, and, in 1791, an elegant summer resort. But Britain and France were warring, and America's maritime commerce with both countries placed the young nation in the middle—bringing the United States to the brink of war with Britain and France. New York, again feeling vulnerable to attack, begged for protection. Congress eventually appropriated funds for new fortifications on Governors Island, but Governor George Clinton felt the sum was inadequate. He enlisted the help of students and faculty from Columbia College as well as local organizations. Between 1794 and 1798, they erected Fort

Jay, named for John Jay, who had helped negotiate peace with Great Britain and had served as the first secretary of foreign affairs.

The horseshoe-shaped Castle Williams was one of three forts built on Governors Island, a linchpin in New York's coastal defense system.

In 1800, seeking to shore up the nation's defenses, the federal government assumed control of Governors, Bedloe's, and Ellis Islands. During the next decade, while the British attacked American ships and impressed American seamen, fortifications were rapidly erected. Fort Jay was replaced by a more durable structure in 1803; it was later renamed Fort Columbus because of the unpopularity of Jay's treaty with Britain. The original name was restored in 1904. Castle Williams was completed on the island's northwest corner in 1811. Designer Colonel Jonathan Williams of the U.S. Army Corps of Engineers conceived the red sandstone roundhouse to work together with its sister fort, Castle Clinton, at the Battery. Of all the city's defenses, Castle Williams was the most impressive and influential. Based on a French design, it was the first casemated fort in North America—its many-tiered parapets provided greater firepower than earlier forts. In 1812, defenses were strengthened when the South Battery was built to guard Buttermilk Channel. During the War of 1812, the British made no attempt to enter New York Harbor, and the islands' fortresses never fired a shot.

By the middle of the century, the harbor islands were nearly obsolete as forts, since the increased range of ships' cannons required confronting attackers out at sea. Governors Island, however, took on myriad military responsibilities. The local army headquarters in New York was transferred there in 1821, and from 1833 to 1920 the island housed one of the army's most important arsenals. The island was even briefly headquarters for the entire U.S. Army under General Winfield Scott in the 1840s.

The impressive building for the commanding officer was built around 1840 when the island briefly served as headquarters for the entire U.S. Army. Courtesy of the Trust for Governors Island

With the outbreak of the Civil War in 1861, both the Union and Confederate armies thickened their ranks by instituting the first drafts. Understandably, a provision allowing Union men to buy their way out of the war for $300 did not sit well with less fortunate men. More than a thousand men were killed or injured when draft dodgers rioted in New York in 1863. When troops from Governors Island rushed to Manhattan to guard the Sub-Treasury on Wall Street, rioters intent on pillaging the unguarded military post rowed to the island. They quickly reversed course after a group of civilian employees lined the shore brandishing clubs, guns, axes, and knives, while others pretended to make ready at the garrison's cannons.

Far from the bloody battlefields of the Civil War, Governors Island processed and assigned thousands of volunteers and draftees and served as an assembly point for out-of-state militia organizations en route to the South. Castle Williams became a prison for Confederate soldiers; "Johnny Rebs" convicted of espionage and awaiting execution were usually jailed separately in the basement of a building near Fort Columbus.

The crowded brig and barracks on Governors Island bred postwar epidemics, forcing the government in 1870 to destroy contaminated buildings, including a strip of wooden houses nicknamed Rotten Row. In 1878, the War Department relocated army administrative operations to Governors Island and began modernizing the facilities.

By 1900, erosion had reduced the original 160 acres purchased by Wouter Van Twiller to a mere 70 acres. To reclaim the original dimensions, the U.S. Army Corps of Engineers built a bulkhead surrounding some 102 acres of submerged land adjacent to the south and southwest portion of the island and filled it with rock and dirt dredged from channels and excavated during the construction of New York's Fourth Avenue subway.

Even before the project was completed in 1912, the expanded island had become a showcase for daring innovators in the emerging field of air travel. On September 29, 1909, Wilbur Wright took off from the new ground on the first flight from Governors Island, circling the Statue of Liberty before returning. Later that year, he flew from the island to Grant's Tomb in Upper Manhattan and back. In 1910, fellow pioneer Glenn Curtiss landed on Governors Island, completing a solo flight from Albany and winning a $10,000 purse offered by *New York World* publisher Joseph Pulitzer.

With the arrival of World War I, Governors Island reverted to its military role. On April 6, 1917, eighteen minutes after the United States declared war on Germany and the Central Powers, a battalion of the Twenty-second Infantry stationed on Governors Island jumped into the waiting boats of the Revenue Cutter Service (forerunner to the Coast Guard) and sailed across the Hudson to Hoboken, New Jersey. There the doughboys carried out the country's first hostile act of World War I—capturing German steamships berthed in Hoboken and impounding their crews at Ellis Island—all without firing a shot.

For the rest of the war, the island functioned as a military prison, hospital, supply base, and embarkation point for troops, a job requiring new warehouses, barracks, roads, and docks—all told, seventy buildings were erected. To access these scattered structures, the Governors Island Railroad was built. The smallest railroad in the world, it was outfitted with eight miles of track and steam locomotives that operated day and night. The railroad fell into disuse after the war, and in 1921 was sold as scrap metal.

After the war, the Army Air Service encouraged cities to build airports, and by the 1920s sophisticated airfields were needed to accommodate larger, rapidly evolving aircraft. Arguments were made for and against putting the first municipal airport at Governors Island, with certain military kingpins determined to preserve what they called a necessary military presence. One pugnacious New York congressman named Fiorello H. La Guardia called the island a "playground for generals who like to play golf and give garden parties," and accused the military of building new barracks on the island to forestall attempts to build an airport there. In the middle of this controversy, Floyd Bennett Field opened in Brooklyn in 1928 as the city's first municipal airport.

La Guardia's New York City dreamport, however, would not die easily. After being sworn in as mayor in 1934, the Little Flower launched a full-scale effort to build an airfield on Governors Island. He planned to seduce airlines away from Newark Airport and institute express passenger service at Governors Island as a supplement to Floyd Bennett Field. In defiance of critics who said Governors Island was too small, La Guardia proposed using landfill to increase the island by twenty-nine acres. President Franklin Roosevelt even considered a $100,000 survey to study connecting Governors Island to Lower Manhattan, and a local organization called Community Councils advocated constructing a 615-acre airport island just south of Governors.

Well-known aviators like Amelia Earhart supported La Guardia's idea, but many airport operators and other experts insisted that Governors Island, which passengers could reach only by boat, was a poor site. Not only was it near a busy harbor and densely built financial center, but the island, critics argued, was plagued by fog and prevailing winds that would force descending planes to fly dangerously close to skyscrapers. In addition, they felt that with technology constantly producing bigger planes, the island would soon prove too small for a landing field.

La Guardia was unable to effectively counter those arguments, so the flamboyant leader focused instead on countering the army's claim that military readiness was needed close to New York City. (Terrorists, most likely anarchists, had bombed Wall Street in 1920.) To illustrate his point, La Guardia masterminded a fantastic publicity stunt in April 1935. Leading a delegation of the House of Representatives' Military Affairs Committee, La Guardia made an unscheduled stop at the Sub-Treasury, where he asked Deputy Police Commissioner Harold Fowler to turn in a riot call. "I'll show you whether we need soldiers on Governors Island," La Guardia said.

Sirens blared and bells rang in alarm. Thirty seconds later, patrol wagons, radio cars, and 450 city policemen—unaware that this was merely a test—rushed to the scene, only to find La Guardia triumphantly announcing that his point had been proved.

La Guardia's stunt wasn't totally in vain. The House unanimously approved a bill in 1936 to turn Governors Island into an airport, but the bill died in Senate committee. La Guardia then turned his attention to North Beach Airport in Queens (now LaGuardia Airport), and the army remained on Governors Island.

During World War II, Governors Island served much as it had during World War I. New York's induction stations were concentrated there; new warehouses, barracks, and extra hospital wards were erected; and some of the island's historic cannons and cannonballs were thrown on the scrap heap, contributing 2,321,000 pounds of metal to the war effort. Another postwar building program produced new apartments and a strange octagonal tower of white masonry built at the island's northeast tip to provide ventilation for the new Brooklyn-Battery Tunnel. The army called Governors Island home until 1966, when the base was one of ninety-five closed around the country.

With the island declared surplus, developers envisioned building luxury high-rises with sweeping views of Lower Manhattan. But the U.S. Coast Guard stepped in, maintaining the island's military legacy. On June 30, 1966, the solemn music of "Retreat" played as the army bade farewell to the island it had occupied for 172 years. Minutes later, a saluting battery thundered a Coast Guard welcome as the admiral's flag was raised high above Fort Jay, establishing Governors Island as the largest Coast Guard base in the world.

For three decades, Governors Island was home to a multimission base charged with search and rescue, protection of life at sea, environmental protection, port security, and even military readiness, with troops dispatched through the years to Haiti, Cuba, and the Persian Gulf. However, in 1997, the Coast Guard relocated operations, dispersing four thousand members and their families to bases along the East Coast. The closing of the base saved the Coast Guard about $30 million a year—$10 million in housing, fire, and police expenditures, and $20 million in ferry costs.

The Coast Guard departure opened up one of the most exciting real-estate opportunities New York has had in years. Despite its military history and proximity to Manhattan, Governors Island is surprisingly idyllic. Architecturally, it resembles an Ivy League campus, with brick and stone edifices, manicured lawns, and elegant Victorian homes overlooking the stately trees of Nolan Park.

In 1995, President Bill Clinton, sharing a helicopter ride over the city with Senator Daniel Patrick Moynihan, asked about the island's history. Clinton then offered to sell the island back to New York State for $1 if the city and state could agree on a plan that would benefit the public. Despite

Clinton's offer, Congress would have to pass special legislation to allow the transaction before 2002. Most congressional Republicans, however, preferred auctioning the island to the highest bidder. Complicating matters, in 1997, Congress factored a $500 million sale price into its Balanced Budget Act, meaning that it would have to make cuts elsewhere to give New York the island.

New York's initial development proposal got bogged down when Mayor Rudolph Giuliani insisted that only a casino would make access to the island affordable. Historians, preservationists, and much of the public found this outrageous. Additionally, casinos were not legal in New York. Even after Giuliani backed down, he and Governor George Pataki, then bitter political rivals, feuded over how much control the city and state would each have over the project.

Meanwhile, in one of his final acts in office, President Clinton named the island's two fortresses—Fort Jay and Castle Williams—a national monument. The move created a twenty-two-acre national park, thus preventing this swath of land from ever being sold. But it wasn't until Michael Bloomberg became mayor that the island's future finally took shape.

The 150 acres outside the National Park area were finally sold back to the city and state in 2003, but in 2010, Bloomberg, who has actively pushed for more green space in the city, persuaded the state to turn over sole responsibility to the city. The organization overseeing the project was reorganized as the Trust for Governors Island.

The island's rebirth began in low-key fashion in 2003, with reserved guided tours that brought four thousand visitors to the island. Within two years that total doubled. As more of the island was opened to the public and amenities were added—not to mention a ferry from Brooklyn to complement the one from Manhattan—word spread, and New Yorkers quickly embraced this public oasis. In 2009, 275,000 people came to the island. The following year four hundred thousand folks rode the waters for a visit, to sample the Unicycle Festival or the Pig Island festival celebrating pork or to play miniature golf on a unique course designed by an arts group or simply to sit in an Adirondack chair (provided by the Trust) and gaze at the Statue of Liberty.

The Trust has given five-year permits to both the company that operates the Water Taxi Beach (and the concerts there) and the Lower Manhattan Cultural Council, which brings art and artists to the island. It also works year-to-year with a wide array of cultural groups to ensure a diverse audience—for instance, in 2010, the arts group No Longer Empty installed

"The Sixth Borough," a series of site-specific sculptures inside buildings along Colonels' Row, and the Children's Museum of the Arts offered hands-on activities and even a summer-long camp for younger visitors.

Additionally, in the summer of 2010, a selected group of artists worked on the island (occasionally creating their art in view of the public). A public high school focusing on maritime sciences, the Urban Assembly New York Harbor School, moved to the island (from Bushwick, a landlocked neighborhood in Brooklyn). And secured funding promised a new round of visitor amenities and green spaces in and around the northern Historic District.

But hopes for the island are far more complex and ambitious. The master plan, designed by the landscape architecture firm West 8, calls for a 2.2-mile Great Promenade along the waterfront and some yet-to-be-determined developments on the southern end, possibly a conference center, university buildings, or a luxury hotel. (The development could generate revenue to support the other programming but has raised some concerns about the island's identity.)

This artistic rendering shows the ambitious plans for the redesign of the island's southern end.

But the pièce de résistance is the naturalistic landscape proposed on the southern end where ugly old buildings are being demolished. This redesign would become home instead to groves filled with oak and birch trees, wetland gardens, and rolling hills that would create framed views of the city. (The plans go so far as to call for fragrant plants such as sea asparagus and lavender to further delight the senses.) Of course, all this comes with a projected price tag topping $200 million. Skeptics doubt whether all this can or should be fulfilled. The island would need a major infrastructure overhaul (there isn't potable water, and the southern end has no electricity) and greater ferry service to handle growing crowds, not to mention ongoing maintenance to keep everything attractive.

Even if takes years or decades for the grander vision to come to fruition, Governors Island has already been reincarnated in a vital and vibrant way.

Its island location means that it does not belongs not to a particular borough or neighborhood but to everybody.

"It has been reconnected back to the fabric of the city but in a way that will always be different than Prospect or Central Park," says Elizabeth Rapuano, Trust for Governors Island spokesperson. "It is a meeting ground for all New Yorkers to come together."

Quadricycles and bicycles are available for rent to anyone exploring the island.

SHARON SEITZ

Exploring the Island

Visiting Governors Island—which is open Friday through Sunday from late May through mid-October—gives New Yorkers a chance to feel they've escaped the concrete cityscape. "You feel like you're out in the country in some beautiful small town," says Jay Nickerson, a Brooklyn resident who has visited the island on several occasions.

Water Taxi Beach, which sells food as well as the only alcohol on the island, is adjacent to the Manhattan ferry dock. Food carts and concessionaires are scattered around the island, with more to come. There are plenty of beautiful spots to sit and eat, though one highlight is Picnic Point on the southern end. In addition to food concessions it offers a view of the Statue of Liberty as well as hammocks and Adirondack chairs for relaxing.

The island provides reasonably priced rentals for bicycles, tandems and quadricycles (also known as surreys), with five miles of car-free paths. Each season brings a new roster of artists and a new schedule of activities and events for grownups and for kids. (For details go to www.govisland.com.)

A variety of guided tours, demonstrations, and other programs run by National Park Service rangers are available each season. Visit www.nps.gov/gois for current information.

You can, however, take a self-guided tour any time you like, breaking away at any point to sample the artistic offerings or hands-on activities. Begin by walking straight ahead to **Fort Jay** from either the Brooklyn or Manhattan ferry. An elaborate sculpture on the fort's archway depicts the original seal of the War Department with its mortar-cannon-eagle-flag insignia, symbolic of war, peace, liberty and vigilance. A romantic and likely apocryphal story tells that an army prisoner and former stonecutter carved it, earning his freedom during the course of the work. According to legend, the fort commander's young daughter was walking through the main gate when a chunk of red sandstone broke loose. The stonecutter jumped down from his ladder to place himself between the girl and the falling debris, saving her life. For his heroism, he was pardoned.

Southeast of Fort Jay (toward the Brooklyn ferry and away from the Manhattan dock) is **Nolan Park**, which features two of the island's more stately residences: the **Commanding Officer's Quarters** and the **Governor's House**. The twenty-seven-room Commanding Officer's Quarters (circa 1840) was originally home to the ranking officer on the island. Two cannons, cast at the West Point Foundry in the 1840s and typical of those in the island's forts at the time, flank the building. In 1988, a historic diplomatic meeting was held here between President Ronald Reagan and Soviet leader Mikhail S. Gorbachev.

The Georgian-style Governor's House is the oldest building on the island. Purportedly constructed in 1708 as the residence of Lord Cornbury, it was in fact built in 1813 as a guardhouse and later used for the island's

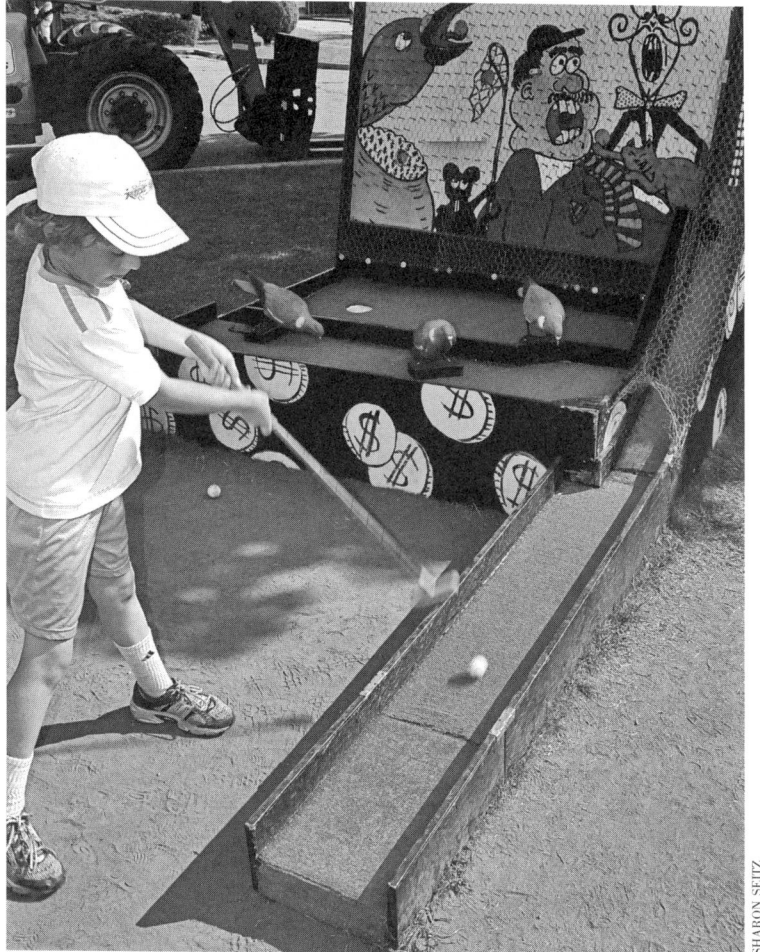

The island's unique miniature golf course features flamboyant designs by different artists.

commanding officer. (There was a legend—without any evidence—that during the American Revolution a house in this area had an underground tunnel large enough for the governor's coach and four horses. The tunnel was connected to a private dock so the British leader could escape the island if attacked.) In between the two estates is the brick **Dutch House** with stepped gables. Built in 1845, it was used as a commissary storehouse until 1920, and, later, as officers' quarters.

Four-acre Nolan Park is also home to a row of butterscotch-colored, high-ceilinged Victorian houses where senior officers and their families once lived. The homes and outdoor space are now frequently used for art exhibitions.

Historical Detour: Great Escapes

Prisons often incite breakouts, and the stockade at Governors Island was no exception. Its island location often enhanced the drama; three escapes are particularly memorable.

Days before the Civil War ended in 1865, Captain William Robert Webb, a Confederate prisoner held in Castle Williams, decided he could wait no longer for freedom. Webb, the first Confederate soldier to escape the island, swam to the Battery, where he emerged wet and disheveled in his Confederate grays. For days, Webb explained his story to anyone who would listen, but nobody believed him. He was left to wander the city and eventually made his way home to Tennessee, where he was later elected a senator.

In 1918, Grover Cleveland Bergdoll, a German American, proclaimed he would never fight against the fatherland and went into hiding. Two years later, the twenty-one-year-old was caught at his mother's mansion near Philadelphia and jailed in Castle Williams as a World War I deserter. Within several months, he escaped by convincing federal authorities he needed to retrieve some money he had stashed on a Maryland farm while a fugitive.

En route to Maryland, Bergdoll persuaded his keepers—two armed military police sergeants—to stop for lunch at his Pennsylvania home, conveniently located along the train route to Maryland. The chaperons were soon puffing on cigars and downing German beer at the family estate while Bergdoll entertained them with readings from Shakespeare. Pleasantly fuddled, the guards thought nothing of Bergdoll going to answer a telephone call. When Bergdoll didn't return to the party, the sergeants realized they'd been duped and took their shameful selves back to Governors Island, where they avoided court-martial only because they hadn't benefited financially.

Bergdoll made it to Germany, where he staved off kidnapping attempts by the United States while his mother tried to effect his repatriation. In 1939, Bergdoll showed up in New York without warning, was court-martialed on Governors Island, and sentenced to seven and a half years in Leavenworth Penitentiary. He was released for good behavior in 1944.

Melvin Blanton, twenty-three, had thrice wriggled out of other disciplinary barracks across the country before being sentenced to Governors Island for desertion and jailbreaking. But the Ohioan didn't stay there long, either. On July 20, 1934, Blanton was working a manual labor detail on the island's south side when a friend, armed with a revolver, came ashore and ordered the only guard—a private on his first hitch—to hand over his weapon. The duo then made their anticlimactic getaway, rowing a mile and a half to Red Hook, Brooklyn. The *Daily News* called the escape "the most spectacular prison delivery in the history of eastern penal institutions," embarrassing the island's army personnel charged with safeguarding the Port of New York.

Blanton and a companion went on a crime spree in Ohio and Indiana, holding up filling stations with a gun stolen from a guard at an Indiana fort. In August, they were in a friend's car in Indianapolis when the driver was pulled over for running a traffic light. None of the three men gave his real name, but Blanton, who was recognized because of his much-publicized escape, was promptly rearrested.

Farther along is the **Blockhouse**, built as a hospital in 1839, which later served as officers' quarters. Lieutenant Ulysses S. Grant lived here in 1852. In a letter to his wife, he wrote: "We can go to the city at almost all hours of the day in small boats belonging to the government which ply regularly for the convenience of us all." But Grant preferred Governors Island to the city, adding: "We get the benefit of the sea breeze here, while in the City we would get but little of it."

The granite church south of the Blockhouse is the **Chapel of St. Cornelius the Centurion**. Of English Gothic design, it was completed in 1906 to replace the original wooden church built nearby in 1847. The church is also notable for its stained glass, artwork, and a credence table carved of stone from the Château de Rouen, where Joan of Arc was imprisoned in 1431.

Across from the church is the **South Battery**, erected in 1812 to defend Buttermilk Channel between the island and Brooklyn. Largely hidden by some of the island's younger infrastructure, it was used as an officers' club by the Coast Guard.

Turning north, back toward Manhattan, it's hard to miss immense **Liggett Hall** on your left. Completed in 1930 as barracks for 1,300 soldiers, it's the largest building on the island, cutting clear across its middle. The hall's classical cupola above the arched passageway is so conspicuous that it shows up as a landmark on nautical charts. Walk through the passageway to find the surreal miniature golf course with flamboyantly colorful sculptures designed by different artists on each hole; the course changes each year.

Then you can retreat to **Hay Road** across from Colonels' Row and on to another set of handsome brick residences now used for art installations. The two-acre green is used for concerts. Continue walking north to **Castle Williams**, a mammoth stone citadel on the island's northern tip known as the cheese box because of its circular shape. Built as a fortification to protect the harbor, it served as a stockade from the Civil War through World War II. The fort's eight-foot-thick red sandstone walls are fitted with three tiers of windows from which nearly one hundred guns once poked their menacing muzzles.

Island Hopping

Free ferry service is available from the Trust for Governors Island, 212-440-2200, in season from Manhattan Friday through Sunday and from Brooklyn on Saturday and Sunday (www.govisland.com/html/visit/directions.shtml). A limited number of bikes are allowed on each ferry.

The Manhattan ferry departs from the Battery Maritime Building located at 10 South Street, adjacent to the Staten Island Ferry in Lower Manhattan. The ferry terminal is accessible as follows:

By car: From the West Side of Manhattan, take the West Side Highway south to West Street, then south to Battery Park and South Street. From the East Side, take the FDR Drive south to South Street. Street parking is close to impossible, but there are several parking lots nearby.

By subway: From the West Side, take the 1 or 9 to South Ferry. From the East Side, Brooklyn, or the Bronx, take the 4 or 5 to Bowling Green. From Queens or Brooklyn, take the R to Whitehall Street.

By bus: From Midtown, take the M6 or M1 to Battery Park. From the East Side, take the M15.

The Brooklyn ferry leaves from Pier 6, Brooklyn Bridge Park, at the foot of Atlantic Avenue.

By car: Take the Brooklyn-Queens Expressway, Route 278, to Exit 27, Atlantic Avenue. Follow signs to Columbia Street

By subway: R to Court Street, 2,3,4,5 to Borough Hall, A,C,F to Jay Street

By bus: B63 to the end of Atlantic Avenue at Columbia Street

2. Liberty Island

"At the threshold of this vast continent, full of new life—where all the ships of the universe arrive—the statue will rise from the bosom of the waves. She will represent 'Liberty Enlightening the World.'"

—FRANCO-AMERICAN UNION, LAUNCHING THE CAMPAIGN
TO BUILD THE STATUE OF LIBERTY, 1875

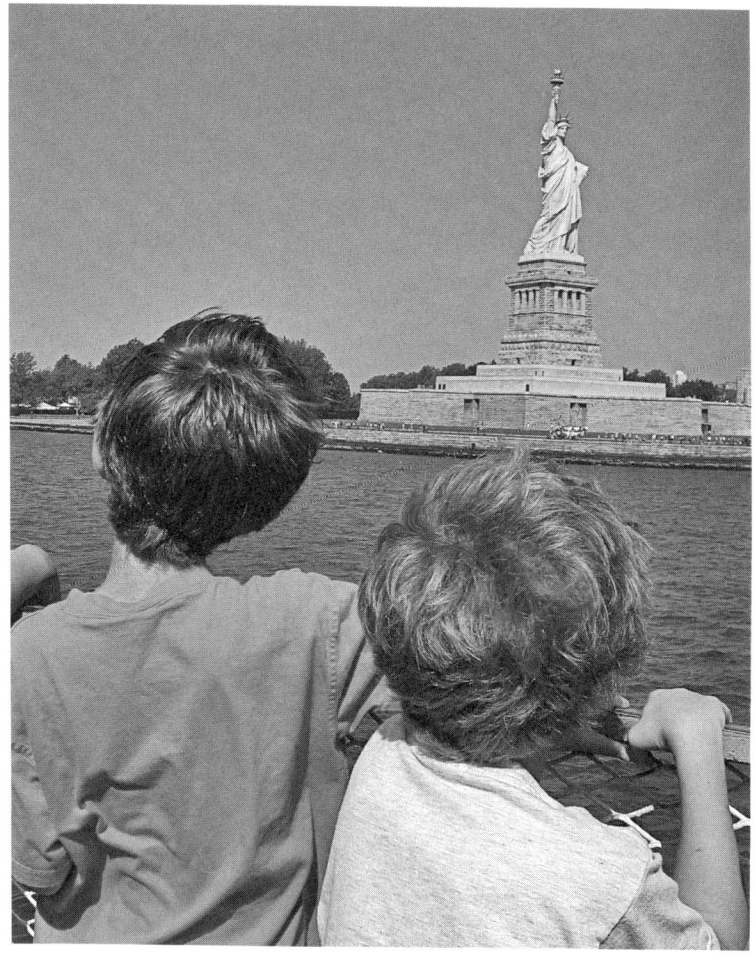

STUART MILLER

Liberty Island

WHEN THE *ISÈRE* ENTERED New York Harbor on June 19, 1885, more than one hundred ships poured out to greet it as guns from Fort Wood on Bedloe's Island and Fort Columbus on Governors Island roared an enthusiastic welcome for this ship bringing from France the long awaited Statue of Liberty. It had taken seventeen days to load the 214 boxes—each weighing between 150 and six thousand pounds—onto the *Isère*, and nearly a month for the ship to travel across the ocean. But New York would have to wait even longer to see the Statue of Liberty emerge from the crates.

Liberty's agonizing journey from conception to completion had taken two decades, yet America was still struggling to finish the pedestal on which she would stand. So, for more than a year, Lady Liberty—a gift from France extolling American ideals—lay in pieces on Bedloe's Island.

The statue was born out of a dinner conversation in 1865 at the home of Edouard de Laboulaye, France's preeminent political thinker. The topic was whether camaraderie could truly exist between nations. Laboulaye said France and America had shared struggles for independence, thus creating an indestructible bond. This notion, sculptor Frédéric-Auguste Bartholdi later wrote, "remained fixed in my memory."

After France's bitter defeat in the Franco-Prussian War (1870–71), Bartholdi's work turned more political. The democracy-minded Laboulaye saw his concept for a Liberty monument as excellent antimonarch propaganda. Laboulaye, however, realized the statue was too potent a symbol to be countenanced in a politically unstable France. The scholar had written extensively on America, using the distant land to convey his views on democracy and individual freedom. So he wrote Bartholdi letters of introduction and sent him to America to propose building the monument there as a symbol of the affinity between the two countries.

Bartholdi wrote that he reached New York, "in the pearly radiance of a beautiful morning." he later wrote. Awed by the harbor—"the gateway to America"—and "the magnificent spectacle of those immense cities" (Brooklyn and Manhattan), he envisioned his statue there, settling upon a twelve-acre site, Bedloe's Island, which he soon learned belonged to "all the states."

The Mohegan Indians called the isle Minnissais, or Lesser Island. Early colonists named it Great Oyster Island, but Bedloe's Island was the name that survived. On December 23, 1667, Richard Nicolls, New York's first British governor, granted the island to Captain Robert Needham, but the next day Needham sold it to Isaak Bedloo. Bedloo, an alderman and wealthy merchant, had been one of 252 Dutch settlers who signed a pledge of loyalty to England in 1664. Rewarded with a string of influential and lucrative political jobs, Bedloo anglicized his name to Bedlow. In the eighteenth century, it was corrupted to Bedloe. (The family battled for more than a century to correct the error, but in 1940 the U.S. Board of Geographic Names rejected the evidence. The island remained Bedloe's until 1956, when it was renamed Liberty Island, belatedly fulfilling Bartholdi's request.)

In 1738, fearful of a smallpox outbreak, New York took over the island, where it established the city's first formal quarantine station. Incoming ships anchored there to wait for a doctor to row out from Manhattan and inspect the passengers and crew. Archibald Kennedy, commander of the British naval station and later the eleventh Earl of Cassilis, bought the island in 1746 and built a summer home. But when the smallpox threat returned in 1758, Kennedy sold the land back to New York City.

On the eve of the Revolution, British troops seized Bedloe's Island, establishing a refuge for Tory sympathizers and setting the stage for an unusual incident. On the night of April 2, 1776, colonists snuck out to Bedloe's to capture the Tories, but found none there. The British either had been tipped off or had heard the boats approaching and removed all their men. With no one to take prisoner, the four hundred rebels instead swiped tools, coats, and poultry and torched the island's buildings. *Asia*, a British warship in the harbor, meanwhile fired two cannon shots at the island, but there were no casualties.

After the war, New York tried renting out the island, but stipulated that it would revert to a quarantine as needed. Not surprisingly, the city found few takers. The French navy leased it as a quarantine from 1793 to 1796, at which point the city turned Bedloe's five buildings over to the state for a quarantine hospital. Four years later, the island was ceded to the United States for the harbor fortification project. A star-shaped battery with thirty guns was completed on Bedloe's Island in 1811; in 1814, it was named Fort Wood after Lieutenant Colonel Eleazer Wood, who died that year in the Battle of Fort Erie. The island served alternately as quarantine and garrison for the next half century, and Fort Wood functioned as an ordnance depot and recruiting station during the Civil War.

After arriving in New York, Bartholdi traveled for five months, meeting both ordinary citizens and power players like industrialist Peter Cooper, President Ulysses Grant, and *New-York Tribune* publisher Horace Greeley. While Bartholdi found this nation of conformists reluctant to embrace his unusual proposal, he felt America's love for the grandiose would ultimately ensure Liberty's success.

On returning home, he minimized his model's sensual contours and, under Laboulaye's guidance, replaced the broken chain in Liberty's left hand with a tablet reading, "July 4, 1776."

Yet Liberty's physical details were shaped by other factors as well. Bartholdi had traveled to Egypt in 1867 and 1869, seeking a commission on a gargantuan lighthouse for the new Suez Canal being built by Bartholdi's friend Count Ferdinand de Lesseps. Bartholdi designed a robed woman carrying a torch, "Progress: Egypt Carrying the Light to Asia." His concept was rejected, but an American newspaper later accused Bartholdi of repackaging this failure into the Statue of Liberty to turn a profit. The sculptor vehemently denied this, claiming, "I never executed anything for the Egyptian ruler except a little sketch which remained in his palace." The subsequent discovery of several "Progress" studies betrays this lie. Nevertheless Bartholdi's fifteen-year commitment to Liberty implies that his was more a labor of love than a moneymaking scheme.

To raise the $60,000 needed to build Liberty, Laboulaye established the Franco-American Union, which launched its campaign in 1875. That same year, the Third Republic restored democracy to France, with Laboulaye co-writing France's new constitution. Liberty was to be presented during America's centennial celebration, but the project was more costly and progressed more slowly than anticipated. Its final cost was four times the estimate, and the subscription wasn't completed until 1880.

Bartholdi believed his career was on the line, and worked doggedly to ensure Liberty's success. If the project failed, he wrote, "I would look like a ridiculous day dreamer and an inefficient man." Under his supervision, craftsmen from the renowned Gaget, Gauthier & Co. toiled seven days a week, ten hours a day before spectators. The public viewing promoted the cause and raised cash; three hundred thousand gazers paid to see Liberty take shape. In October 1881—in a publicity stunt tied to the centennial of the last major battle of the American Revolution at Yorktown—Levi Morton, the U.S. minister to France, drove the first rivet into Liberty's left foot. The following year, Bartholdi invited key members of the press to lunch . . . in the Lady's knee.

When Liberty's old-school engineer, Eugène Viollet-le-Duc, died in 1879, Bartholdi turned to inventive bridge builder Gustave Eiffel (whose Parisian tower was still a decade away). Like his contemporaries— Bartholdi, de Lesseps, and American architect Richard Morris Hunt, who designed Liberty's pedestal—Eiffel was the quintessential impresario of that era: self-confident and ambitious, with a steadfast faith in technological progress as wrought by intrepid individuals.

Several cutting-edge advances, such as reinforced concrete, electric light, and Bessemer steel, were used in the statue and pedestal. Eiffel's own innovation—an iron-and-steel skeleton with a secondary tier of braces attached separately to each of Liberty's copper plates—replaced Viollet-le-Duc's primitive plan to support Liberty by filling her to the hips with sand. Eiffel's idea later influenced the development of skyscrapers.

Laboulaye died in 1883, having lived to see the Third Republic firmly established and the completion of the statue assured. De Lesseps took over the Franco-American Union, but even when Liberty was completed the next year, it remained unclear whether she would ever make New York Harbor her home.

In America, preparations had become mired in divisive controversy. For starters, the United States had a limited cultural history, with a scanty tradition of public monuments, so people were less apt to grasp the significance of such a memorial. But the larger problem was money: Liberty was ostensibly a gift, so Americans were resentful about being asked to pay for the statue's foundation and pedestal, which eventually cost more than $250,000 (as much as Liberty herself). Raising the money proved a monumental task for the American Committee, which was stacked with prominent citizens.

Between 1876 and 1881, little was accomplished. Public sentiment ran from indifference to cynicism; much of the press coverage was sensationalistic,

Constructing the statue was only half the challenge; raising funds for the pedestal took years.

irreverent, and even disdainful. Even when Bartholdi arrived at Philadelphia's Centennial Exhibition with Liberty's right arm and torch, he was met with skepticism. "Had the French sculptor honestly intended to complete the Statue of Liberty," opined an editorial in the *New York Times*, "he would have begun at its foundation, modeling first the boot, then the stocking, then the full leg in the stocking."

Rumors that the French couldn't finish the sculpture without American funding persisted into the 1880s, severely hampering the pedestal drive (although the arm was a popular attraction at Madison Square for several years). That was only the beginning of the committee's tribulations, as everyone found a reason not to contribute. The rest of the country considered it a New York issue. The poor and middle class expected the wealthy to pay, but the upper class disdained the icon's populist concept. Religious conservatives opposed adulating a secular sculpture that, with its torch held high, suggested, "mankind receives true light, not from Christ and Christianity, but from heathens and her gods," according to the *American Catholic Quarterly* in 1880.

STUART MILLER

Star-shaped Fort Wood served as the foundation for the 151-foot tall statue and her eighty-nine-foot tall pedestal.

The island site also hampered fund-raising. Some felt Liberty should be put at Coney Island as a tourist attraction, but most of New York's ruling class and press preferred the tip of the Battery, where Liberty could be easily seen and visited. In fact, many wealthy Manhattanites refused to donate money for a statue in some out-of-the-way spot. However, President Rutherford B. Hayes appointed Civil War hero General William Sherman to choose between Bedloe's and Governors; heeding Bartholdi's advice, Sherman selected Bedloe's, because on Governors Liberty would have had her back to Europe or the Battery.

The debate raged on long after the decision, but some foes were eventually persuaded that Bedloe's would be the ideal spot. In 1884, the *Times*, a late convert, asserted that the statue would indeed be better "where it is not so very easy to reach . . . for, having made the trip, perhaps the visitors are likely to value the wonderful view the more." In this pre-skyscraper era, the paper also said siting "so colossal a mass" at the Battery would "make all the great buildings in the neighborhood look ridiculous."

Despite meager resources and public apathy, the American Committee hired Richard Morris Hunt in 1881 to design the pedestal. One of the nation's leading architects, Hunt had designed the main section of the Metropolitan Museum of Art as well as Newport mansions for society families. Hunt, who shared Bartholdi's love of ancient Egyptian colossi, produced plans for a 114-foot pedestal that threatened to overwhelm both the statue and its paltry budget. He scaled down the pedestal by twenty-five feet, but added more complex stonework that boosted the cost by $20,000.

With the committee scrounging for dollars, newspapers in cities like Cleveland, Baltimore, and San Francisco snidely suggested that New York didn't deserve the statue and claimed they would quickly raise the money and provide a proper home. Such commentary from Philadelphia and Boston in 1882 prompted the *Times* to demean them as "small but ambitious cities . . . jealous of our Metropolitan fame." While the vituperative war of words may have sold newspapers, it did nothing to aid the cause.

With donations trickling in, General Charles Stone, appointed engineer in chief in April 1883, wasn't able to begin work on the pedestal's foundation until October. The foundation was finished in May 1884, but the pedestal's six-ton cornerstone wasn't laid until August. In late autumn, work had to be halted because nearly all of the $182,491 raised had been spent.

Hunt solicited the Belmonts, the Vanderbilts, and the Astors for help, but was rejected. New York State's legislature appropriated $50,000, but Governor Grover Cleveland vetoed the bill as unconstitutional, stating that

New Yorkers shouldn't pay for a national monument. A congressional bill to provide the final $100,000 failed, in part because it was attached to an unrelated, unpopular bill. The press urged the French to pay for the pedestal and publicized Liberty's flaws. The *New York Herald* found her design unappealing, while the *New York Evening Telegram* said the copper was too thin and Liberty balanced in an unnatural position.

In March 1885, only three months before the *Isère* arrived in New York, the project seemed doomed. The American Committee issued a public statement noting that barring an immediate change in fortune, Liberty would be returned to France or given to another city.

Enter Joseph Pulitzer. This Hungarian Jewish immigrant had soared to prominence as a journalistic reformer and spokesman for the masses. Recognizing the promotional value of a good story and the merit of Bartholdi's majestic symbol, Pulitzer had launched a public campaign to fund Liberty's pedestal upon buying the *New York World* in 1883. "The dash of one millionaire merchant's pen ought to settle the matter," he implored. But Pulitzer's paper had a circulation of only fifteen thousand and was among the least popular of the city's sixteen dailies. He raised a meager $135 in the first four days and ended the drive within a month.

Two years and a hundred thousand readers later, Pulitzer launched a second campaign. This was a different story. He encouraged the masses to take custodianship of the statue. "Let us not wait for the millionaires," he proclaimed. "Let us hear from the people." Pulitzer's consistent coverage excoriated the rich and prodded the poor; his shrewdest tactic was bestowing fame on the common folk by printing the letter and name of every one of the countless contributors.

"I am a poor man or I would send more than the enclosed 10 cents for the Liberty Fund . . . You go right on, Mr. World, and make it real hot for all the nobs and snobs," wrote E. James.

"We are twin boys—Yed and Joe . . . Enclosed you will find 50 cents, 25 cents each . . . If we live to be men it will be our pride to say: 'We helped place her here.'"

By May, there was enough money to resume work on the pedestal, and on August 11, Pulitzer triumphantly announced that 121,000 people had donated a total of $102,000; of that, $80,000 had been collected in sums of less than a dollar. The pedestal was finished April 22, 1886, and on July 12, with Eiffel's framework in place, the crates on Bedloe's Island were finally unpacked. "The dream of my life is accomplished," Bartholdi said when the statue was at last erected.

Historical Detour: A Delicate Situation

In April 1954, a man pined to perch on one finger atop the Statue of Liberty as a gesture of international goodwill. Nearly five decades later, his tomfoolery reads like a Dr. Seuss story, yet Viennese circus performer Franz Furtner almost pulled off this absurd and amazing stunt.

The Circumnavigators Club, an organization for people who had traveled around the world, sponsored Furtner's balancing act as "a little something to bring about goodwill and world harmony." Furtner said it would "symbolize the freedom and happiness" he had found in America.

The petition to stage the spectacle was rejected by the statue superintendent, but National Park Service superiors in Washington approved it, erroneously believing the club was a charitable rather than a social organization, and that Furtner was an Iron Curtain refugee. When the government discovered that this Ringling Brothers acrobat had never been behind the Iron Curtain and, in fact, had served in the German army, they angrily revoked permission.

Furtner nonetheless made the papers. The *New York Times* reported that Furtner in fact accomplished his monumental feat during a practice session at the statue, but there were few onlookers that rainy day and no photos taken to validate the stunt.

From the beginning, the statue was a target for art critics, who considered Bartholdi an ordinary talent and Liberty lacking innovation or imagination. (The image of a woman bringing forth freedom could be traced from ancient Rome to Delacroix; before Liberty, America's symbol was a patriotic woman called Columbia.) As recently as 1976, art historian Marvin Trachtenberg referred to Liberty as "presentable but no great sculptural beauty," while Richard Seth Hayden and Thierry Despont, who headed the statue's renovation in the 1980s, wrote that when working on a smaller scale, Bartholdi was an "average sculptor."

However, as Eiffel noted, conventional standards don't always matter: "There is in the colossal an attraction, a particular charm to which the theories of ordinary art are hardly applicable." The Statue of Liberty is today more national icon than revered artwork. While no Michelangelo, Bartholdi should be hailed for realizing his lofty dream using a blend of neoclassical sculpture, high-tech engineering, astute entrepreneurialism, and perseverance. From the moment he recognized the symbolic significance and aesthetic appeal of Bedloe's Island until his tireless efforts brought Liberty to fruition, Bartholdi displayed a keen understanding of the entire artistic process.

When the Statue of Liberty was dedicated on October 28, 1886, "a hundred Fourths of July broke loose . . . to exalt her name," the *Times* proclaimed. The day was wet and foggy, but the celebration's fervor vanquished the elements. Starting at Fifth Avenue and Fifty-seventh Street, the parade's grand marshal, General Stone, led twenty thousand marchers south past one million spectators; at Wall Street, the only area not closed for the holiday, spools of ticker tape spilled from hundreds of office windows, filling the air and the streets with white curlicues. The ticker-tape parade was born.

The celebration moved to Bedloe's Island, where about thirty-five hundred men—mainly the wealthy who had previously snubbed Liberty—beheld the statue's dedication. With the exception of Bartholdi's wife, Jeanne-Emilie, and de Lesseps's daughter, Totote, women were barred from the festivities. The Battery and Governors Island were packed with spectators, and the harbor brimmed with boats—including one filled with women protesting their exclusion, led by Lille Devereux Blake, president of the New York State Suffragette Association.

Bartholdi waited anxiously inside Liberty's crown to pull a cord that would swish away the French flag covering Liberty's face. William Evarts, a senator and respected lawyer who had successfully defended President Andrew Johnson against impeachment, gave a speech on behalf of the American Committee. But Evarts was a long-winded fellow—he'd given eight days' worth of closing arguments in the notorious adultery trial of preacher Henry Ward Beecher—and at one point when he paused for breath, the young man charged with signaling Bartholdi mistakenly gave the sculptor the go-ahead. Bartholdi unveiled his statue. Evarts's oration was drowned out by what the *Times* described as "one thundering paean of acclamations that swept down the Bay on the wings of the northeast gale and smote the hills of Staten Island with a huge shock of sound." (Translation: fifteen minutes of exploding gunfire, blasting whistles, blaring bands, and wild cheering.) The litany of speeches continued until nightfall, when the guests—panicked about being stranded on the island overnight—turned into a stampeding mob in a race to the boats. At least one elegant Vanderbilt was bloodied in the crush.

While Liberty was designed to enlighten the world, financial and technical difficulties often left her in shadows, and even darkness, for the next thirty years. Though Bartholdi wanted a gilded copper torch illuminated by outside lights (as is the case today), the government made an eleventh-hour decision to cut open the torch and install lighting inside. Under the aegis of the Lighthouse Board, the statue's pedestal lights and the torch—to be visible for one hundred miles—were turned on one week after her premiere.

The weak pedestal lights, however, often left Liberty's head and shoulders in semidarkness, while the torchlight's faint glow looked like a faded star unconnected to the statue. And the lights lacked more than wattage—within a week, a money outage darkened the statue completely. Although funding was restored, this embarrassing situation was repeated periodically throughout the next three decades. What's more, when the lights did work, they were often depressingly dim.

Bartholdi, who died in 1904, made one final visit to the United States in 1893. Already distressed that his statue hadn't brought him the prestige, artistic opportunity, or financial gain he had hoped for, he found Liberty's condition disheartening. "I was somewhat disappointed at the effect," he said. "The lights do not show up well at all."

In its early years, the Statue of Liberty was not a major tourist attraction, although twenty-five cents bought admission to the island and a rented bathing suit. The army maintained a presence on Bedloe's Island with soldiers doubling as monument guards, and in 1902 the Lighthouse Board ceded the entire island to the War Department. Four years later a *Times* reporter, whose ferry to Bedloe's included only forty other visitors, found the island's pier and buildings neglected and dilapidated.

Even the indomitable Lady was in poor shape. Her copper skin was green, and there was concern that the salt air had weakened her joints. Plans to paint the statue were met by cries of dismay from artists, who said the patina, or green layer, provided a mellow hue and enhanced the statue's contours. Scientists explained that the patina naturally occurs when copper is exposed to air, and actually protected the metal from erosion. So when Liberty was spruced up in 1907, her exterior was not painted, a strategy adhered to ever since.

The statue's funding and lighting woes were finally resolved in 1916, when the *World* again intervened, raising $30,000. Gutzon Borglum, who later chiseled Mount Rushmore, redid the statue's torch, using translucent amber cathedral glass to allow more light to shine through. Floodlights, the latest technology, replaced the ineffective lightbulbs at the statue's pedestal—although Liberty's face was still haunted by some shadows until more powerful floodlights were installed in 1931.

During a celebration dinner, French ambassador Jean Jules Jusserand toasted the statue, which, unlike most monuments, did not honor a single man or nation: "It was raised to an idea . . . the idea of Liberty." While that had been true at the statue's conception, the French connection was slipping from the public's memory by 1916. Liberty was stepping into a new role, a more assertively nationalistic one. She had developed into America's foremost symbol, a patron saint who represented the country's foundations more clearly than did flag-bearing Columbia, and more majestically than Uncle Sam.

During World War I, as ships set out under this guardian's gaze, Liberty lent her name and image to four bond drives that raised $15 billion—half the cost of the war. Campaign posters touted her as a woman warrior or draped her in the American flag, urging patriotic citizens to "remember your first thrill of American Liberty." In 1924, she was designated a national monument, and in the 1930s—when the army passed the torch to the National Park Service—she began receiving her due as a tourist attraction.

By her golden anniversary in 1936, Liberty's image had been reinvented in the public mind. She had become the "Mother of Exiles." Although few immigrants were arriving—the United States had yanked away its welcome mat in the 1920s—Liberty had beckoned and guided millions of Europeans to this country during the prior half century. These firmly rooted new Americans celebrated Liberty as their guardian angel.

Liberty's association with the "huddled masses" was reinforced in 1965 by the opening of the Museum of Immigrants at the statue's base and President Lyndon Johnson's signing of a new immigration bill there. The law reopened the gateway to America by undoing the bigoted quota restrictions of 1924. Increasingly, other disenfranchised groups have appropriated Liberty's all-embracing symbolism: Vietnam War protesters, Puerto Rican nationalists, Native Americans, Iranians opposed to the Ayatollah, and even Al Sharpton and his disciples have staged freedom protests there.

Although Liberty's reputation remained vital, by the 1980s her body had begun to show its age. A 1981 report by French researchers detailing the monument's deterioration sparked an unprecedented campaign to renovate both the statue and the immigration depot at Ellis Island in time for their centennials in 1986 and 1992, respectively.

While the Statue of Liberty indeed looked resplendent at her rededication, achieving that end involved nearly as much energy and strife as had her construction. With President Ronald Reagan's blessing, virtually the entire restoration was done without the federal government, testing the Republican theory that the private sector can accomplish what the public sector cannot. This proved both the project's greatest strength and its gravest weakness. Without bureaucratic restrictions, a phenomenal amount of money was raised and a staggering amount of labor performed in a short time. However, the lack of government oversight bred bruising behind-the-scenes battles and allowed fund-raisers to mislead the public about the money being donated.

The Franco-American Committee, the Statue of Liberty–Ellis Island Foundation, and several other not-for-profit American fund-raising organizations all vied for the right to oversee the restoration. The Franco-American Committee was done in by its inability to raise money. Meanwhile, the Statue of Liberty–Ellis Island Foundation, headed by Chrysler chairman Lee Iacocca, came up with the cash and demanded more say; it was anointed sole fund-raiser by the government in 1985.

The foundation was accused of egregious commercialism when it licensed dozens of companies to sell Liberty air fresheners, ashtrays, and other dust collectors. Still worse were denunciations that the foundation's fund-raising methods tarnished Liberty's image. In 1985, the *Times* reported that the foundation had solicited multimillion-dollar pledges from major corporations in exchange for official-sponsor status. These "donations," however, often came from consumers who paid to participate in promotions and events thinking they were contributing directly to the statue's refurbishment, when they were actually covering the companies' pledge. Richard Rovsek, the marketing maven and Republican insider who conceived the fund-raising campaign, was fired from his $50,000-a-month foundation job after it was revealed that when he signed up sponsors, he also accepted payment on the side to create their Liberty ads.

Critics questioned the foundation's fund-raising means, complaining that its grassroots efforts had been trampled by deals made with big business. But many felt the end—$400 million in funds—was perfect justification. (Repairing Liberty and her island cost $87 million; the remaining money was used to restore Ellis Island and Castle Clinton and to create an endowment.)

The seamy details surrounding the restoration of the Statue of Liberty were largely hidden from the public, as was Liberty herself. Her makeover required more than a nip and a tuck, and for more than two years, scaffolding screened her. Workers discovered birds' nests, graffiti, busted rivets, and, although most photos hadn't shown them, unbecoming cracks on her nose and chin. (In typical celebrity fashion, Liberty's photographs had been touched up for years.)

On July 4, 1984, Lady Liberty relinquished her torch. The 1916 version had been improperly sealed, and rainwater had corroded the torch and the arm's framework. Twelve French craftsmen, using Bartholdi's original gilded copper design, built a new torch in a Liberty Island workshop, combining the ancient repoussé technique of hammering copper into sculptural form with the latest in computer modeling. American union workers—many ignorant of the statue's French origins—picketed the island, unhappy about foreigners working on an American job. The artisans' expertise, however, eventually won the respect of most Americans.

The restoration team's most surprising discoveries involved discrepancies between Bartholdi's plan and the completed statue. Liberty's right arm, connected at an improper point, was so weak that it swayed in the wind. Because her head tilted slightly to the right, one of her diadem's spikes poked into her right arm. Research traced the irregularities to the original assembly in Paris. After lengthy debate, the team opted to fortify her shoulder and shorten the spike, rather than tinker with history and restructure the statue.

Liberty's refurbishment required imagination as well as research. Removing the seven coats of paint inside Liberty with traditional materials like solvent would have carried the risk of a deadly explosion, so liquid nitrogen—supercooled to minus 325 degrees Fahrenheit—was used. Underneath the paint were two layers of tar. Since most conventional cleansers threatened to scrub through Liberty's copper skin as well, everything from ground walnut shells to corncobs was tried. Finally, workers discovered baking soda; forty tons of it did the trick.

When July 4, 1986, arrived, with a weekend-long celebration that filled New York Harbor with tall ships and fireworks, the Statue of Liberty looked grand. And today, long after the last echoes of ceremonial pomp have faded, the Statue of Liberty still silently exalts the freedoms upon which she and this country were founded.

Exploring the Island

Bartholdi designed the **Statue of Liberty**, 212-363-3200, to be seen from the water, and the boat ride from lower Manhattan allows you to bask in the majesty of his creation. So stand out on deck, because the best view (and photo opportunity) comes as the boat passes around the island to the dock. Liberty's persona changes along with your perspective—on the approach she stands erect, with an indefatigable mien, but as her right side comes fully into view, she appears to stride purposefully forward to enlighten the world about democracy.

It may be tempting to cram Liberty and Ellis Islands into one ferry trip, but each monument is worthy of a separate visit. According to the National Park Service, approximately 85 percent of all visitors to Liberty Island never even set foot inside the main attraction. That is a mistake you don't want to make—the oft-overlooked museum, the pedestal's balcony with its spectacular views, and the crown itself should all be essential ingredients in any visit to the statue for a tourist and a core experience for any New Yorker.

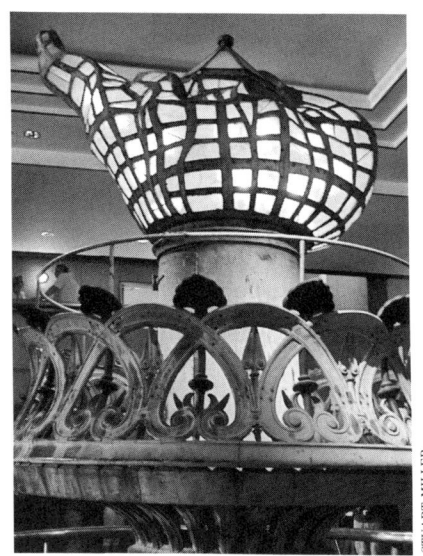

The statue's original amber-glass torch, designed by Gutzon Borglum, greets visitors in the museum's lobby.

Visiting the island once meant navigating huge crowds and endless lines—in summertime, as many as twenty thousand people would enter the statue. Journeying up the narrow winding steps to the crown was particularly excruciating, especially since your time at the top was limited to a matter of seconds to clear the space for the people trudging up behind you.

Tickets are now required for visiting the museum, pedestal, and crown—a maximum of four thousand visitors are allowed in the museum and pedestal per day while a mere 240 tickets are available for the crown each day. While this means you'll need to plan your visit well in advance, the experience itself is far more relaxed and rewarding. The museum, the balcony, and the staircases are far less crowded, and visitors to the crown can spend plenty of time up there, talking to the National Park Service rangers leading their tour. (There are also ranger-led tours of the grounds for those who don't have tickets to get inside the statue.)

There are several tricks to visiting the statue: in addition to buying a timed ferry/access ticket well in advance (especially in summer), you should arrive early and travel light. Since 9/11, the National Park Service has installed dual layers of security. Visitors are first screened before getting on the ferry at Castle Clinton in Battery Park and then again on the island before entering the statue. (Large packages, suitcases, carry-on luggage, and other large parcels are forbidden on the ferry.)

In addition to waiting on two lines for a security check, backpacks and other bags must be put into lockers before you proceed to the statue's pedestal. There are, however, not enough lockers to accommodate everyone, so by midday you must wait for someone to return to their locker and empty one of their belongings. Traveling earlier in the day is also wise because Liberty's interior can be fifteen to twenty degrees hotter than the outside temperature, which becomes more of an issue in the heat of a summer afternoon.

The museum's full-scale copper replica of Liberty's face is a favorite photo op.

The Statue of Liberty is a timeless symbol of America's most cherished virtue, but it is also, from the ground up, a remarkable combination of art, architecture, and engineering. To best experience and appreciate this wonder, spend a half-hour to forty-five minutes exploring the museum before climbing up to the pedestal balcony and the crown. The audio tour is worthwhile, providing a rich layer of details even beyond what you'll find in the museum. (On your way from the ferry dock boat to the statue, take a moment to enjoy Phillip Ratner's five bronze sculptures of the founders—Laboulaye, Bartholdi, Eiffel, Lazarus, and Pulitzer.)

To construct the statue's foundation, Fort Wood's center was filled with 23,500 tons of concrete—then the largest single mass of concrete poured at one time. The stepped-terrace structure you see rising above the fort's walls was added by the National Park Service in 1965 and is home to the statue's engaging museum. This belatedly fulfills the vision of pedestal architect Richard Hunt, who had to scrap his tiered base for budgetary reasons.

The immense bronze doors leading to the lobby were added during Liberty's mid-1980s restoration, with the images on them celebrating the toil of everyone who participated in the project, from plumbers to architects. One panel depicts wrenches and pliers, another features compasses and slide rules; one even shows the scaffolding that caged Liberty during her rehabilitation.

Inside the lobby is the beautiful amber-glass torch designed by American sculptor Gutzon Borglum. It was held aloft by Liberty from 1916 until 1984.

Historical Detour: Emma Lazarus

In the autumn of 1883, Emma Lazarus, whose poetry was praised by contemporaries Ralph Waldo Emerson and Ivan Turgenev, was asked to compose a piece for the Statue of Liberty's pedestal fundraiser. Lazarus tersely replied that she could not write to order. Soon afterward, however, Lazarus visited Ward's Island, where two thousand Jewish refugees from Russia's pogroms were crammed into filthy temporary quarters with no heat, water, or food. Lazarus had no personal connection to the immigrant experience—her Portuguese ancestors were among the first twenty-six Jews in New York in 1649, and her father, Moses, was a wealthy sugar refiner—yet she was appalled by the conditions she encountered. She complained directly to Mayor Franklin Edson—and was inspired to pen "The New Colossus":

Not like the brazen giant of Greek fame,
With conquering limbs astride from land to land;
Here at our sea-washed, sunset gates shall stand
A mighty woman with a torch, whose flame
Is the imprisoned lightening, and her name
Mother of Exiles. From her beacon hand
Glows world-wide welcome; her mild eyes command
The air-bridged harbor that twin cities frame.
"Keep ancient lands your storied pomp!" cries she
With silent lips. "Give me your tired, your poor,
Your huddled masses yearning to breathe free,
The wretched refuse of your teeming shore.
Send these, the homeless, tempest-tost to me.
I lift my lamp beside the golden door!"

That December, a portfolio with her poem and works by Walt
Whitman and Mark Twain brought $1,500 at auction, but "The New
Colossus" slipped into obscurity. When Liberty's dedication-day
parade commenced in 1886 one hundred feet from Lazarus's East
Fifty-seventh Street home, she was in Europe. A year later, she died
at age thirty-eight from Hodgkin's disease. Her obituaries mentioned
many of her poems, but not the one that in 1903 was quietly posted
in Lazarus's memory on a plaque on Liberty's pedestal. It wasn't until
the 1930s, after America had put stringent curbs on immigration, that
Lazarus's poem became heralded as the statue's poignant theme.

Upstairs, at the entrance to the museum, a full-scale copper replica of Liberty's face greets you, providing both an otherwise unattainable perspective of
the statue's mammoth proportions and a perfect photo op. (Go ahead, touch the
nose. Everyone does.) Many historians believe that Bartholdi's widowed
mother, Charlotte, inspired the stoic visage of Lady Liberty.

The museum's first two rooms offer a fairly comprehensive account of the
statue's conception and construction, using models, drawings, written narrative, and video. There are reproductions of Bartholdi's 1869 watercolor and
terra-cotta studies for "Progress: Egypt Carrying the Light to Asia," which
later evolved into the Statue of Liberty, and a series of models depicting Lib-

erty in her various incarnations: In one, Liberty's crown has no diadem; in another, she isn't bearing a flame; in a third, there's no tablet in her left hand. A continuously running video demonstrates the repoussé process, while old photographs, writings, and models depict the entire construction process.

Producing Liberty took more than sculptors and engineers. Raising the requisite funds required an unprecedented marketing and merchandising blitz that was a harbinger of twentieth- and twenty-first-century campaigns. As a licensed logo in France, Liberty's likeness showed up on cognac bottles and Camembert cheese labels, which are displayed alongside criticism of this commercialization. Also on view are satiric attacks on America's uninspired attempts to pay for the pedestal—an 1884 cover of *Life* (not related to the popular twentieth-century periodical) depicts a wilted, wrinkled Lady Liberty, as she was expected to look by the time the funds were raised.

The statue's story doesn't end with her unveiling. In the next room is a compelling textual and audio presentation recounting the reactions of immigrants who, after arduous voyages to America, beheld the Statue of Liberty for the first time. This is a moving reminder that Liberty is more than a statue; she is a symbol of hope, freedom, and opportunity.

"She was a beautiful sight after a miserable crossing that September," wrote Eleanor Kenderdine Lenhart, whose letter about her journey from England in 1921 at age seven is on display. "She held such promise for us all with her arm flung high, the torch lighting the way—opening a new world to those who would accept the challenge."

The wall opposite is covered with posters featuring Liberty hawking everything from war bonds to sheet music for such nationalistic songs as "Liberty Statue Is Looking Right at You," illustrating the patriotism with which she became associated in World War I.

Since then, the Statue has evolved as an American icon—revered and parodied in popular culture and appropriated for political statements and commercial interests. A display case features hundreds of Liberty postcards—from black-and-white classical shots to Liberty with her robe blowing upward à la Marilyn Monroe to a 1918 aerial view of eighteen thousand soldiers at Camp Dodge in Iowa assembled in the shape of the statue. The walls are also lined with Liberty novelties—statuettes, clocks, lamp bases made of copper and jade, and even a Tiffany lamp with a Liberty motif. Photos and posters range from wacky to tacky: the Marx Brothers dressed as Liberty, the Lady wearing a pair of red-white-and-blue jeans in a Levi's advertisement. Although a long way from Bartholdi's lofty vision, these images are testaments to the powerful hold his statue has had on the world.

Now take an urban mountain climb to the top of the pedestal, where you can step outside and marvel at the city's sweeping skyline, stretching from the Empire State Building to the Brooklyn Bridge. If you have tickets to climb to the crown, the odyssey continues skyward, where you experience the wondrous sensation of stepping inside the Lady herself. Looking at the folds of softly illuminated copper, you can appreciate the enormous task that faced the nineteenth-century artisans who pressed and hammered the statue into shape. Although metal casting had long since replaced this ancient sculptural art called repoussé, Bartholdi thought the latter more economical for a job this size. The thin sheets, each hammered to a mere three thirty-seconds of an inch thick, used less copper, saving money and reducing weight for shipping.

Three hundred thin copper sheets were spliced and lapped over one another, then riveted together and fitted to Gustave Eiffel's innovative framework. Each section is supported independently, so the skin "floats," allowing the copper to expand and contract with outside temperature changes. Some 1,799 stainless-steel bars were installed in the 1980s, replacing rusted iron reinforcements. This was a particularly tedious task for the steelworkers, since only four old bars could be safely removed at a time.

The tightly wound spiral staircase can feel claustrophobic near the top, and, if you're tall, be prepared to duck. Also, be aware that the view will not match the pedestal's panoramic vistas. Liberty was designed primarily as a signal to Europe, meant to urge France to pursue democracy. So the windows face south, away from Manhattan, leaving you looking mostly at water.

Still, it is a memorable journey, worth completing at least once. Unfortunately, you can't go any higher since the torch—never open to more than twelve people at once—has been closed since 1916, after several explosions in New Jersey weakened the arm's structure.

The Lady's Figures

Although the Statue of Liberty's history is extraordinarily well documented, some basic data is surprisingly uncertain. Bartholdi wrote that 179,000 pounds of copper were used for the statue, but the National Park Service lists Liberty at 200,000 pounds. A book about the Liberty restoration places her total weight—including framework—at 560,000 pounds, but the park service weighs her in at 450,000 pounds. Liberty's nose is either four feet, six inches long (according to the park service) or three feet, eight inches (per the restoration book). There are, however, a few facts that appear to be as solid as Bartholdi's monument:

LIBERTY'S VITAL STATISTICS
Height: 151 feet
Waist: 35 feet around
Right arm: 42 feet long
Index finger: 8 feet long
Pedestal: 89 feet high
Steps: 354—192 steps to the pedestal, 162 from pedestal to crown

LIBERTY'S SYMBOLS
Shackles: The broken shackles at Liberty's feet signify escape from
   tyranny.
Torch: The flame represents the light of truth and justice illuminating
   the world.
Crown: The seven rays of Liberty's diadem suggest the seven seas and
   seven continents.
Tablet: Held in her left arm, it is inscribed July 4 MDCCLXXVI (1776),
   the date America's Declaration of Independence was signed.

Where to Eat & Shop

Liberty Island is an enchanting picnic spot—cool breezes, magnificent views,
no cars. But the cafeteria has also been vastly improved in the last decade—
the offerings, once limited to greasy fast food, now include paninis, veggie
wraps, and even organic fruit. (The prices are similar to other museum restaurants.) An actor dressed as Bartholdi makes the rounds of the cafeteria's outdoor seating, eager to chat about his work. Next door is a new and grand gift
pavilion offering endless ways to spend your money in the name of Liberty.

Island Hopping

The statue can be reached from both New Jersey and Manhattan. New Jersey
ferry service runs from Liberty State Park in Jersey City, exit 14B on the New
Jersey Turnpike. Manhattan ferry service runs from Battery Park; tickets are
sold in Castle Clinton. A concessionaire, Statue Cruises, 877-523-9849
(www.statuecruises.com;), runs the ferry service. To reach Castle Clinton:

By car: From the West Side of Manhattan, take the West Side Highway south to West Street, then south to Battery Park and South Street. From
the East Side, take the FDR Drive south to South Street. Street parking is
close to impossible, but there are several parking lots by Battery Park.

By subway: From the West Side, take the 1 or 9 to South Ferry. From the East Side, Brooklyn, or the Bronx, take the 4 or 5 to Bowling Green. From Queens or Brooklyn, take the R to Whitehall Street.

By bus: From Midtown, take the M6 or M1 to Battery Park. From the East Side, take the M15.

By boat: From Staten Island, take the ferry to the Manhattan terminal. Follow the signs through Battery Park to Castle Clinton.

3. Ellis Island

"At Ellis Island, I was born again."

—EMANUEL GOLDENBERG, WHO ARRIVED FROM ROMANIA IN 1903 AT AGE
TEN AND WENT ON TO MOVIE STARDOM AS EDWARD G. ROBINSON

STUART MILLER

Ellis Island

ON THE FIRST DAY OF 1892, Annie Moore, a fifteen-year-old Irish lass, entered the United States at the new immigrant depot on Ellis Island. The first one through the gate, Moore—one of 148 arrivals on the steamship Nevada—was presented with a ten-dollar gold piece in a ceremony commemorating the occasion.

And then the jostling began.

For the next sixty-two years, Ellis Island was the sieve in America's immigration process; its Great Hall, brimming with people of many nationalities determined to become Americans, was the consummate melting pot. For the hundreds of thousands of aliens deported from Ellis Island, it symbolized the shattering of a tightly held dream. But for the twelve million foreigners who entered America there—from Knute Rockne to Frank Capra to Felix Frankfurter—Ellis Island was the first step in a new world.

The women waiting in the Great Hall "had expressions of fear on their faces," recalled Raffaele Cotugno, whose account is just one of many preserved in the Ellis Island library. Cotugno, who journeyed from Italy in 1909 at age ten, remembered that children "had streaks on their cheeks where tears had dried on unwashed faces. Buttons were missing on well-worn garments. Belongings were carried in pillow cases, blankets and shawls."

Cotugno's first meal is what lingered longest in his memory, particularly his amazement at the wondrously soft white bread he mistook for cake. "I crammed my pockets full of slices in fear of never getting any again."

Estelle Belford traveled with her mother from Romania in 1905 at age five. She remembered being startled by a big, strange man who came to greet them. "I didn't know him. He picked me up and I started to cry." Then Belford's father put his arms around her mother, and the reunited couple wept with joy.

Manny Steen, who arrived from Ireland in 1925 at age nineteen, remembered Ellis Island as an unsettling place. "The building was grimy and hot as a pistol. . . . All they had was a couple of rotating fans that did nothing but raise the dust. But the worst memory was the physical," he continued. "The doctors testing for social diseases were seated at a long table with a basin full of potassium chloride. You had to reveal yourself right there in front of everyone. This was very demeaning."

But most inconveniences were a small price to pay for a new life, recounted Arthur Tracy, who came to this country from Russia in 1906 as Abraham Tracovutsky, and later became an international star as a radio crooner. His father, Morris Tracovutsky, unable to stay in the family's hometown of Kamenetz after pogroms and the drowning of one son, took his wife and seven children—including six-year-old Abraham—to America. "We left everything as it stood in the house. We took only what we could carry," Tracy said. They bribed guards in every Russian city en route to Hamburg, then journeyed to Liverpool; six long weeks later, they arrived at Ellis Island, where an inspector clucked disapprovingly at the long, unpronounceable family name, and snipped six letters from Tracovutsky. "He performed a little circumcision," quipped Tracy.

With their futures at stake, this vast, impersonal pit stop rife with uncertainty terrified many immigrants. But 80 percent passed smoothly through Ellis Island within five hours. The rest were detained for health or legal reasons; and whereas only 2 percent were sent back to their homelands, that seemingly small number added up to about 240,000 broken dreams.

Only those who couldn't afford a first- or second-class steamship ticket endured the Ellis Island ordeal. Moneyed newcomers received cursory inspections on board ship and were sent to Ellis only if they were seriously ill or lacked the proper papers. Even on Ellis Island, they were kept separate from the masses. The derogatory slur *immigrants* was reserved for the teeming hordes of poor packed into dangerously unsanitary conditions in steerage, the lower decks near the ship's steering mechanism.

Although America had always been a nation of foreigners, most aliens who came through Ellis Island were from markedly different cultures than previous generations of newcomers. During the 1780s, about 5,000 people emigrated to America annually; by the 1820s, some 150,000 were arriving each year. More than 90 percent of these arrivals were from northern or western European countries—England, Ireland, Germany, France, Holland, Belgium, and Switzerland. By contrast, immigrants between 1880 and 1924 were largely from southern and eastern European nations—Italy, Russia, Austria, and Hungary.

Government oversight of the immigration process increased gradually in the years leading up to the opening of Ellis Island in 1892. Until the mid-nineteenth century, ships simply docked at the city's many piers and unloaded passengers. New York State established a board of emigration in 1847, but it focused almost exclusively on quarantining those with contagious diseases. Then, in 1855, the state opened a formal processing station at Castle Garden in Lower Manhattan. During the next thirty-five years, nearly eight million aliens entered America there. Ostensibly a place to check paperwork and provide job, home, and transportation counsel, Castle Garden developed a venal reputation because of corrupt employees and the predatory swindlers and con men lurking nearby.

The federal government established procedural rules in the 1880s—including a head tax of fifty cents per arrival—but the state continued running the show until 1890. Finally, the federal government stepped in, announcing it would operate the depot from one of its harbor islands. The takeover, and the subsequent isolation of immigrants, would help end exploitation and restrict the flow. Many Americans of northern and western European heritage disdained the new immigrants, whom they viewed as poor, uneducated, peasant Jews and Catholics who dressed and spoke strangely, and whom they suspected of political radicalism. The *New York Times* endorsed the takeover, writing, "We want no more immigrants who are fitted for no higher work than digging ditches and paving streets."

William Windom, secretary of the treasury, had three islands from which to choose. His first selection, Bedloe's Island—where the Statue of Liberty had been placed four years earlier—was met by public outrage. U.S. Senator William Evarts and Joseph Pulitzer's *New York World* denounced the idea, as did Bartholdi, who called it a "monstrous plan" and "downright desecration." The military shot down Windom's request for Governors Island. That left Ellis Island, just north of Bedloe's and right off Jersey City, even though Windom deemed it too small and "not a desirable place."

The island Windom scorned was an unimpressive three-acre speck of land. The Native Americans called it Kioshk, or Gull Island, for the birds that loved the water's seafood. It was Oyster Island to Dutch settlers who picnicked there. The English called it Oyster, but also Gibbet Island after several pirates were

The Registry Room or Great Hall, with its majestic tiled ceiling, is a centerpiece of tours today, but during Ellis Island's heyday it was packed with frightened newcomers.

STUART MILLER

hanged there in the 1760s. (Executions were held there sporadically through 1860.) Little else is known about the island before 1785, the year Manhattan merchant Samuel Ellis put it up for sale. Although he also offered "a few barrels of excellent fat shad . . . and a few thousand red herring of his own curing," Ellis found no takers.

Ellis, who also owned a farm in Bergen County, New Jersey, died in 1794, bequeathing the island to his unborn grandchild—if it was a boy named Samuel. When his heir died in childhood, a family dispute ensued. Ownership remained unsettled until 1808, when the federal government, which had built a fort on the private property, paid the family $10,000 for the island. A one-tiered battery built for the War of 1812 replaced the fort; two years later, it was named for Colonel James Gibson, who died in the Battle of Fort Erie. Although the fort was dismantled in 1861, a naval magazine operated there until 1890, when, despite Windom's many objections, Congress voted to double the island in size and replace the munitions with immigration facilities.

After Ellis Island opened, immigration levels plunged from 445,987 in 1892 to 178,748 in 1898. The drop was caused by a cholera scare in 1892, a nationwide economic depression the following year, and a slew of new immigration regulations. The 1885 Contract Labor Law, which prohibited companies from importing cheap labor, was expanded to prevent advertising for workers overseas; steamships were required to pay for the detention and return of any passengers; and the federal government began inspecting immigrants aboard ship for a variety of ailments, ranging from "idiocy" to insanity to contagious diseases. This last change caused friction with New York State, which still inspected all ships entering New York Harbor, quarantining anyone with a contagious disease at Hoffman and Swinburne Islands.

Improvements continued at the Ellis Island facilities, built of Georgia pine with slate roofing, until June 14, 1897, when a devastating fire wiped out seven years of work. While a new station was being constructed, immigrants were admitted through the Barge Office at the Battery in Manhattan. Ellis Island reopened in 1900 with a stylish new French Renaissance building designed by a small firm called Boring & Tilton. The exterior was red brick with ironwork and limestone trim, highlighted by intricate stonework and four towers capped with cupolas and spires. The large Registry Room on the second floor dominated the interior. The Great Hall, as it was also known, was two hundred feet long, one hundred feet wide, and fifty-six feet high, with twelve narrow alleys divided by large iron railings to direct inspection lines. In 1911, wooden benches replaced the railings.

While the building's stately design was visually stirring, it was equipped to administer no more than half a million people a year. The chaos and overcrowding of the next fifteen years—when more than nine million people arrived—proved this a disastrous miscalculation. The government soon used landfill to expand the island for a new hospital and other buildings. By the 1920s, Ellis Island had grown to its present size of twenty-seven and a half acres.

Between 1900 and 1914, three-quarters of all immigrants who reached America came through Ellis Island. In 1907, the busiest year, 1,004,756 people filed through the Great Hall. While the crowds averaged 5,000 a day, the peak that year was 11,747 in a single day. The staff, which ranged in size from 500 to 850, routinely worked twelve-hour days in a vain attempt to keep up. (Immigrants not examined when they arrived had to stay another night on the ship.) The influx continued until World War I reduced arrivals; by 1918, only 28,867 were admitted. After the war, business boomed again, climbing to 315,587 in 1924.

Upon reaching New York Harbor, the immigrants—already dehumanized from having been herded like livestock in steerage—were piled onto barges and then deposited on Ellis Island, where they were funneled into lines for a medical exam and legal inspection.

The medical exam was called a "snapshot diagnosis." After trudging upstairs to the Registry Room, immigrants were glanced at by an exhausted doctor (charged with examining as many as two thousand people a day) who judged whether they suffered anything from lameness to typhus. The line then shuffled to a second set of doctors, who looked for trachoma, a contagious eye disease causing blindness. Those who failed these exams received a chalk mark on their coat indicating the problem and were pulled out of line. Those suspected of feeblemindedness were given a battery of basic puzzles and tests, although many were so culturally biased that the results were absurd. One demonstrated that 80 percent of all eastern Europeans were "morons."

"It is no more difficult a task to detect poorly built, defective or broken-down human beings than to recognize a cheap or defective automobile," wrote Dr. Victor Safford of this assembly-line approach. However, they often made highly speculative diagnoses. Some doctors believed that dull strands of hair hanging on the left side of a foreign woman's head meant she was pregnant. While scientific advances and increases in Ellis Island's medical staff led to more rigorous examinations, these changes also resulted in more medical exclusions. Less than 2 percent of exclusions were for medical reasons prior to 1898; by 1913, the figure had climbed to 57 percent.

Newcomers endured a battery of examinations at Ellis Island, including an eye inspection for trachoma. (Circa 1920.)

After the medical exam, each person waited to see an inspector, who peered at information provided by the ship's manifest and asked questions about age, economic status, relatives in the country, and job skills. With the help of translators who spoke an average of six languages each, the inspectors determined if a person was "clearly and beyond a doubt entitled to land" in America. Immigrants also had to prove they had the then considerable sum of $25, a rule implemented by Commissioner William Williams in 1909 and informally enforced even after it was deemed unfair and repealed. In 1917, the lines slowed down and the number of detainees increased because of the Basic Immigration Act passed by Congress, which required a literacy test and a more detailed exam.

Those who passed went to the railroad and telegraph rooms and then departed Ellis Island. (One-third of the twelve million new residents settled in New York.) Those who failed to meet these standards were stuck in a screened-in area awaiting a hearing before a three-member board of special inquiry.

In the early years, Ellis Island was as riddled with corruption as Castle Garden had been. To rectify the situation, President Theodore Roosevelt appointed Williams commissioner in 1902. A wealthy New Englander who had graduated first from Yale and then from Harvard Law School, Williams was a brilliant administrator and hands-on leader. Although scandals flared up throughout the Ellis Island years, Williams, who served two non-consecutive terms as commissioner, curbed the most egregious excesses. His first report in 1902 decried the depot's "vicious practices" and the way arrivals were "hustled about and addressed in rough language" that left them "bewildered and frightened." To keep out swindlers, Williams forced visitors to apply for passes.

The gravest problems were woven into the daily fabric of Ellis Island life. Inspectors coerced testimony, covered up their own mistakes, and detained immigrants at whim, often trying to extort bribes. The operations contracted out to private businesses were no better. The dining-room floor was often covered with grease, bones, and other debris, while immigrants ate from unwashed bowls without utensils. During one period, the only meal served—day in and day out—was prunes and rye bread. The rates at the island's money exchange were arbitrary and unfair, and phony paper currency was sometimes issued.

Williams replaced corrupt officials and booted out profiteering contractors. These politically connected men took their case to the Oval Office, but Roosevelt sided with the new commissioner. Williams, however, sometimes seemed at odds with himself. While he planted nasturtiums, ferns, and pansies to brighten the dreary facility and posted signs reading ALL IMMIGRANTS ARE TO BE TREATED WITH KINDNESS AND CONSIDERATION, he nonetheless sided with the public regarding the new immigrants.

"Rigid means should be adopted to keep away those who are undesirable," he wrote in an initial report targeted at Russian, Syrian, and Italian peasants. When 6,839 immigrants were deported from Ellis Island in 1903, Williams was accused of operating a star chamber. Roosevelt reminded Williams to be more judicious, writing that to send an immigrant back "is often to inflict a punishment upon him only less severe than death itself."

With the sharp decline in immigration at the start of World War I, a compassionate new commissioner, Frederic Howe, transformed Ellis Island into a welcoming place, offering everything from classes to folk dancing for those confined there. In an effort to give more freedom to immigrants who had been locked indoors for six weeks, he let them out for recreation. "They rolled upon the grass," he wrote in *Survey* magazine in 1916. "Hundreds of them wept at the contact with the earth again."

Howe's reforms, however, made enemies in the bureaucracy. When Howe tried improving food on the island, Congressman William Bennet, who had once been the attorney for the food contractors, called Howe a "half-baked radical with free-love ideas" and demanded an investigation of Howe's leadership.

When the United States entered the war, Ellis Island was mostly used to hold captured German sailors and suspected spies. After the war, anticommunist and anarchist hysteria fueled the desire for increased expulsions of "new immigrants," and Howe found himself more jailer than immigration commissioner. Attacked in Congress as a suspected communist after refusing to deport people without hearings, Howe resigned in September 1919. As the Red Scare peaked that winter, hundreds of immigrants caught in nationwide raids were sent to Ellis Island and deported back to Europe.

The literacy tests and antianarchist laws passed in that era were followed by a 1921 quota rule that had boats racing to New York every month to unload passengers before their nation's quota was filled—a tragedy for those who had given up everything only to arrive too late. Even so, there were too many outsiders for public taste. In 1924, stricter quotas allowed entry to only 2 percent of the total number of people from any one country who had established U.S. residency by 1890. The front door to America was swinging shut.

In addition to the new quota, fewer and fewer immigrants stopped at the island because they were being inspected at their point of embarkation. The huge crowds dwindled to five hundred a day, and the only arrivals were those who were sick or detained for a board of special inquiry hearing.

The final blow to Ellis Island was dealt by a ruling rendered during the Great Depression. Aliens who might take jobs from Americans or become public charges were banned, leaving Ellis Island operating almost entirely as a detention and deportation center. The tide had turned and Ellis Island, once a symbol of hope throughout the world, had come to represent America's disdain for outsiders. As immigration sank to its lowest totals in a century, deportations continued to rise (as did the number of Europeans voluntarily returning home in the face of anti-immigrant sentiments and massive unemployment). In 1932, more than twice as many aliens left through Ellis Island as had arrived.

With the focus of Ellis Island on detention, armed guards and barred windows were installed to control criminal aliens waiting to be kicked out of America. Diminishing government support made the services of volunteer organizations and social workers—who had been helping immigrants for more than a century—even more vital. The General Committee of Immigrant Aid at Ellis Island included groups such as the Belgian Bureau, the National Council of Jewish Women, Daughters of the American Revolution, and the Italian Welfare League. They provided sewing materials, classes, concerts, games, and, most important, friendly faces and familiar languages to ease the immigrants through these difficult times.

The detainees' days were extremely regimented. They were forced to while away the hours on hard benches and were led only occasionally into the courtyard for fresh air, where they walked silently in single file. Paul Laric, a Yugoslavian immigrant, was held with his family there for three weeks in 1940 because his brother's paperwork was not in order. "We spent the entire time in the Great Hall," he later told the island's librarians. "There was a feeling of desperation. The Statue of Liberty was showing us her back as if she was sending us a message."

During World War II, the island was an internment camp for people from enemy countries, be they captured sailors, immigrants, or even naturalized U.S. citizens. Surrounded by barbed wire, Ellis Island held as many as fifteen hundred prisoners; although there were more Germans than Italians or Japanese, the Japanese received the harshest treatment. European prisoners played big-stakes poker and drank Scotch at night, then skipped breakfast in the morning and bought food on the black market later. The Japanese were segregated from the Europeans and had a strict schedule, including earlier wake-ups. They were served meals completely alien to their diet, like pig's knuckles with sauerkraut. (The Coast Guard was also stationed there from 1939 to 1946.)

When the Internal Security Act was passed in 1950, the island again hosted hundreds of immigrant detainees. A response to the new Red Scare, the act demanded that suspected Communists and anyone with past links to fascism be held. Soviet Union propaganda gleefully proclaimed America's Ellis Island a concentration camp, but by material measures life there was more agreeable than ever. Whole families of detainees were given rooms of their own, with fresh linen and cleaning services. Movies, concerts, Ping-Pong, billiards, occasional ball games, and a Salvation Army–run library with twenty thousand books and foreign-language periodicals filled the time.

The officials were "very kindly people" who went to extraordinary lengths, within the system, to make the stay there "as little like a nightmare" as they could, George Voskovec, a Czechoslovakian refugee, told the *New Yorker* in 1951. Although he landed at LaGuardia Field with a valid entry permit, Voskovec was suspected of Communist affiliations, driven to the ferry, and shipped to Ellis Island.

Despite the creature comforts, the experience was psychologically unsettling. Many individuals, accustomed to totalitarian regimes, feared stepping out of line and were preoccupied with self-preservation. There was also little camaraderie because the population was so transient. Voskovec felt "walled in by silence" during his ten-month stay.

Since the war, there had been occasional talk of abandoning Ellis Island, especially with much of it in disuse. In 1951, the *New York Journal-American* made a push for establishing a juvenile drug rehabilitation center there. It ended up on North Brother Island instead. Finally, in 1954, the Immigration and Naturalization Service shifted the island's limited operations to 20 West Broadway in Lower Manhattan. On November 12, the last detainee, a Norwegian seaman named Arne Peterssen, left Ellis Island, and the Great Hall fell silent. Although the island was never forgotten, the thirty-five buildings were left to deteriorate as its fate was debated during the next three decades. Laundry carts, filing cabinets—even an American flag—lay discarded, disturbed only by an occasional vandal.

In 1956 the government put this surplus property up for sale, touting it in newspaper ads as ideal for manufacturing or storage. There were many development proposals in the next decade—a resort hotel, a marina with sail-in movies, a liberal arts college, a school for the mentally retarded, senior citizen housing, and a futuristic city designed by Frank Lloyd Wright just before his death. Some bids were too low; others never got past the talking stage. Concerned citizens, meanwhile, pressured the government to preserve this crumbling shrine to the American Dream.

A monument or museum concept for Ellis Island, in fact, had been tossed around since the compound had first closed. Then, in 1965, President Lyndon Johnson conferred national monument status on the island, allocating $6 million for refurbishing the site. Renowned architect Philip Johnson, who designed the scheme, proposed demolishing some buildings and stripping others down so they could be preserved as "stabilized ruins." He also planned a garish 130-foot circular tower as a tribute to the Ellis Island immigrants. Johnson's concept was forsaken when the money was shifted to Vietnam War spending.

In 1974, Dr. Peter Sammartino, whose parents had come to Ellis Island from Italy, formed the Restore Ellis Island Committee. The head of Fairleigh Dickinson University, Sammartino lobbied Congress, which provided

some preservation funds. In 1976, limited tours of the run-down buildings
began. Finally, in the 1980s, the rehabilitation of Ellis Island was included
in the Statue of Liberty restoration project. Unlike Johnson's abstract con-
cepts, the primary goal this time was to restore the Main Building as a
museum re-creating the immigrant experience.

Unlike Liberty Island, where supplies delivered by barge had to be
scheduled around the tides, Ellis Island was close enough to New Jersey to
permit the erection of a temporary bridge, which saved millions of dollars.
(Although no longer used, the bridge has not been dismantled.) The Ellis
Island restoration was generally more mundane than the Liberty project.
Tasks included repairing the water-damaged Main Building and removing
a piece of anachronistic architecture tacked on by the Coast Guard in the
1940s—an exposed staircase ascending from the Registry Room to its balcony. The most dramatic undertaking required that helicopters set four new
fifteen-hundred-pound spires atop the Main Building's towers.

The Ellis Island project did, however, stir up plenty of controversy. In
1982, the National Park Service endorsed a plan for a conference center
and Sheraton Hotel on the island's southern end. Lee Iacocca, who headed
both the government's advisory committee and fund-raising for the Statue
of Liberty–Ellis Island Foundation, belittled the concept as too commercial
and a tax break for the rich, since finances depended heavily on tax shelter
investments. Iacocca delayed the project and leaned toward an "ethnic
Williamsburg" featuring exhibits, shops, and cultural events highlighting
immigrant contributions to America. Both plans involved razing most
buildings other than the Main Building.

Even after developers erased the hotel from the plan, Iacocca refused to
budge. Then in 1986, Secretary of the Interior Donald Hodel fired him from
the government's committee. Iacocca—who said his firing "borders on un-
American"—averred that the conference center was the reason he was
ousted. But others found his positions on the fund-raising and government
committees (not to mention the Chrysler Corporation) a conflict of interest.
Later that year, Iacocca was bumped up to chairman emeritus of the foundation fund-raising campaign.

At that point, the National Park Service wrested creative control from the
foundation, which still held the purse strings. The two-headed monster was a
disaster for the project's contractors, the *Daily News* wrote in 1990. The architects and engineers reported to the government, but the foundation handled
the contractors, several of whom went bankrupt or needed bonding companies

to complete the job. Although officials denied charges of bad management and undue interference, claiming that restoration work posed special challenges, they approved twenty-five hundred change-orders for tasks as minor as shifting soap dispensers by inches. "No matter what people say, this is not the palace at Versailles," said contractor David Demick of Danaco. "This is a utility building. Restoration should not have been a big deal."

Despite the finger-pointing, the $162 million renovation was an overwhelming success. The Main Building looks as regal and dignified as it had to immigrants in 1900, but the Ellis Island Immigration Museum inside is more welcoming still.

Meanwhile, in the 1980s, record numbers of immigrants began pouring into the United States, reviving xenophobic attitudes about dubious foreigners, who this time were coming largely from Asia and Latin America. The debate over immigrant-related issues remains fierce and divisive in the twenty-first century, even as people journey to Ellis Island to celebrate their own family's arrival in this country. The National Park Service and the Statue of Liberty–Ellis Island Foundation have dedicated more space to telling America's continuing immigration story, not just the one that occurred on the island from 1892 through 1924. They have even renamed the museum "Ellis Island: The National Museum of Immigration," which should help people draw a connection between those whose ancestors arrived in colonial times and during the Ellis Island era with people arriving today.

Exploring the Island

The museum on Ellis Island (www.nps.gov/elis) is a magnificent treasure, blending a meticulous collection of artifacts, text, photos, and oral histories with the Main Building itself to bring the immigrant experience to life. The museum is so packed with stirring, often poignant information that you might feel almost as overwhelmed as one of the twelve million newcomers who trudged through here.

The museum doesn't get as jammed as the Ellis of old, but in summer an early start is advisable in order to reach the smaller rooms on the second floor before they get crowded. Don't rush through everything; you'll need an entire day, with a break for lunch, to absorb it all.

There are several ways to enhance the experience—a film, a live performance, tours, and an audio guide. The half-hour film *Island of Hope, Island of Tears* is screened in two theaters; one show includes a brief overview by a ranger, the other does not. The footage takes viewers from European villages through the arduous trip to Ellis Island. Although not a must-see, the film, especially when interpreted by a ranger, provides a fine visual and factual introduction to the island's history. The **Ellis Island Living Theater** also offers short productions based on immigrants' stories. The hour-long guided tours are lively, although poor acoustics in the cavernous **Registry Room** make hearing the ranger a challenge for those standing in the back. The audio guide tour is the most thorough and can, according to your own time constraints, take you anywhere from forty-five minutes to two hours. Like the ranger tour, it re-creates the tension and drama of the Registry Room in a way that the room's plaques cannot. Many of the voices from the Museum's Oral History Archive are on the audio guide as well as on exhibit phones.

The tour begins with the **Baggage Room**, just inside the main entrance, with a display of original luggage—from wicker handbaskets to

The exhibits at the museum tell the story of the long, often harrowing journey made by millions of immigrants

heavy trunks—toted by some of Ellis Island's immigrants. The striking photos of these immigrants, who brought only what they could carry, accentuates this sculpture of human determination, which symbolizes the fortitude and courage required to leave everything behind for an unknown world. Baggage handlers could often pinpoint an immigrant's country of origin by the style of the luggage or the way ropes had been tied around the bulging caches.

Take the stairs on the right up to the Registry Room, retracing the steps immigrants took en route to their medical and legal inspections. The room today is bright and spacious, so it requires a vivid imagination to visualize crowds of bewildered, exhausted immigrants filling up every inch of it. The elegant vaulted ceiling, design by renowned architect Rafael Guastavino, was installed in 1918 after a 1916 explosion detonated by German saboteurs on Black Tom Wharf in nearby New Jersey damaged the Main Building's interior. Guastavino, whose family had emigrated from Spain, was known for his patented "tile arch system," with interlocking tiles that allowed arches and vaults to be self-supporting. Workers installed the tile by dangling from the ceiling in safety belts but without scaffolding. Their craftsmanship was so superb that during the hall's 1980s renovation only 17 of the 28,282 tiles had to be replaced.

The former processing rooms—now the **Peak Immigration Years** and **Through America's Gate** exhibits—complete the tour of the immigrant's entrance to America through Ellis Island. In the medical exam room, the buttonhook used to lift eyelids in search of trachoma will make your eyes twitch. In the board of special inquiry waiting room, graffiti left by restless immigrants is preserved on the walls. Special tests and puzzles designed to determine feeblemindedness are exhibited as well. The museum also showcases the contributions of charity workers and civil servants, including a most famous alumnus, Fiorello La Guardia, who before entering politics earned $1,200 a year as an Ellis Island interpreter. He spoke Italian, German, and Croatian and often put in eighty-hour weeks.

Now climb to the balcony overlooking the Great Hall to see the dorm accommodations where detainees slept in cots stacked one above the other and suspended from the ceiling.

This is a good time to break for a picnic lunch outside and a stroll around the **American Immigrant Wall of Honor** (www.wallofhonor.org) behind the museum. The 652-foot, double-sided, semicircular wall is inscribed with over 700,000 names, commemorating immigration from its earliest

Historical Detour: The Prince of Ellis Island

Most detainees didn't call New York's immigration center "The
Palace at the Isle of Ellis." And most didn't parlay their illegal
alien status into vaudeville engagements and a friendship with
Frank Sinatra. But most people were not Harry Gerguson.

In fact, by his telling, Harry Gerguson wasn't Harry Gerguson
. . . he was Prince Michael Romanoff.

Gerguson was first detained at Ellis Island in 1922 as a stow-
away from Europe. Gerguson swore he was a New Yorker, but
recalled little about the city, his neighborhood, or his school days.
His excuse? After ten years of solitary confinement in a German
jail for killing a German nobleman, he'd lost his memory. He soon
escaped Ellis Island by stowing away on the Ellis Island ferry,
although he perpetuated a tale that he had been one of the island's
few successful "swimaways," dragging his signature walking stick
with him through the water.

This small, dapper man with a thin mustache and British
accent (he alternately claimed to have attended Oxford,
Cambridge, Yale, Princeton, and Harvard) resurfaced soon after in
Manhattan as Prince Michael Alexander Obolensky, a descendant
of Russia's royal Romanoff family. He later simplified his persona
to Prince Michael Romanoff.

As Romanoff, Gerguson spent the next year persuading the
press and high society from New York to Wichita that he was a
down-on-his-luck nobleman, willing to groom horses for cash. He
mostly lived off the generosity of others and also earned money
lecturing on conditions in Russia. He was subsequently exposed
as a con man and returned to Ellis Island to face deportation.
Immigration officials were forced to free him, however, because
they couldn't prove he was not an American.

Romanoff crisscrossed the United States, living off his forged
identity and periodically landing in jail for writing bad checks. In
1932, he fled to France, where he again ran into trouble with the
law. He stowed away on a boat back to America, but was detained
at Ellis Island, where he charmed officials and even helped run
the island library before engineering his next escape. Four staff
members were suspended for allowing Romanoff to slip away,

although he telephoned Ellis Island brass from his hideout to say his guard should not be blamed. Romanoff was caught two weeks later at one of his regular haunts—an East Side speakeasy—and was shipped back to France to serve the jail sentence he'd left behind. He snuck back into the United States later that year, but ended up again on Ellis Island after the manager of Dunhill's tobacco shop on Fifth Avenue reluctantly turned in one of his favorite customers.

Romanoff was released in January 1933, on the condition that he would relinquish the Romanoff persona. Instead, he capitalized on his notoriety with a brief stint on the vaudeville circuit as the prince. He later went to Hollywood, where an entertaining con was something to be admired. In 1940, after three years of party-hopping, he opened Romanoff's, a restaurant in Beverly Hills, with the financial backing of pals like John Barrymore, Humphrey Bogart, and Charlie Chaplin.

For the next twenty-two years, Romanoff was restaurateur to the stars and big spenders (he also opened eateries in Palm Springs and San Francisco). His celebrity enabled him to finally attain U.S. citizenship in 1958, when President Dwight D. Eisenhower signed a bill written specifically for the occasion. Until Romanoff died in 1971, he had bit parts in many movies, especially anything starring his closest friend, Frank Sinatra.

According to Ellis Island officials, Gerguson was born in Russia in 1890, arriving in New York at age six. When his parents died a few years later, Gerguson became a troubled truant, passing through six orphanages and earning the label "incorrigible." He ran away from his uncle, was arrested for petty larceny, and as a teen was sent with other orphans to live on a farm in Hillsboro, Illinois. This peripatetic soul later returned to New York to peddle newspapers on East Broadway. But the life of a regular Joe held little appeal for Gerguson, so he began trying on new, glamorous identities, eventually settling on the Romanoff persona.

Gerguson built a life around tales so fantastical as to make the most polished fiction writers envious. His most honest comment was, "No one has ever discovered the truth about me, not even myself."

days—from Myles Standish on the Mayflower to Paul Revere's father, Apollos Rivoire, to the ancestors of Stan Musial and Mario Cuomo and thousands of less famous citizens.

The tour resumes behind the Baggage Room, where the Peopling of America Exhibit once was. The Statue of Liberty–Ellis Island Foundation is spending $20 million to transform it into the **Peopling of America Center**, an updated display that expands upon the idea that America's immigration story did not begin with Ellis Island nor stop when Ellis Island closed. (It also expands physically, taking this theme beyond this room and into spaces previously reserved for administrative purposes.) The fact that 30–40 percent of American residents trace their history through Ellis Island is astonishing, but it also means that 60–70 percent of Americans do not. Those visitors will now find their story told here.

The visually oriented displays, which open in 2012, will place a heavier emphasis on interactivity than the rest of the museum, using things like touch screens and electronic maps. There will also be modern first-person accounts and plenty of video, produced by the History Channel. It begins with **Global Migration**, a look at patterns of human migration throughout history. The American portion of the story will begin in an exhibit called **Before Ellis Island** and continue into modern times with the **New Eras of Immigration** displays, such as the **Threads of Migration** exhibit, where visitors can enter their names, hometown, and their family's country of origin, adding their story to a much larger picture. The exhibit will include illegal immigration as an element of contemporary immigration. Finally, in the **Citizenship Gallery**, visitors will explore what it means to be an American citizen.

The final stop is the third floor, where three compelling rooms await. **Ellis Island Chronicles** tells the island's tale from the government perspective. Models and photographs depict how Ellis Island grew from three to twenty-seven acres during the peak immigration years. Mini-biographies introduce commissioners like William Williams, who is quoted as saying, "Aliens have no inherent right to land here." The wheel of the *Ellis Island*, the steel-hulled ferry that traveled nearly a million miles between the island and the Battery transporting immigrants from 1904 to 1954, is on display. (The abandoned ferry sat in its slip after the immigration station closed; it sank in 1968.)

Treasures from Home preserves those belongings immigrants could not bear to leave behind: mirrors and teddy bears; a long-stemmed pipe from Norway; a violin from Ukraine; a cake plate from Italy; and a sewing machine from England.

The final room, **Silent Voices**, recalls the post-1954 years, when the island sat abandoned. Black-and-white photos serve as backdrop to displays of dusty, run-down benches, signs, and other relics—all fitting reminders of what went into transforming this once forgotten building into a tribute to America's immigrants.

In 2001, the Statue of Liberty–Ellis Island Foundation opened the **American Family Immigration History Center**, a repository for more than twenty-five million passenger records dating from 1892 through 1924. Visitors to the island can check the database (which can also be accessed online at www.ellisisland.org) and obtain reproductions of ship manifests and pictures of the passenger ships.

Visitors can also walk over to the **Ferry Building**, restored by the Save Ellis Island organization. There you can view exhibits on the island's hospitals. The building is open only for guided tours offered by the organization's volunteers; make reservations at www.saveellisisland.org or sign up inside the museum.

Historical Detour: The War Between the States

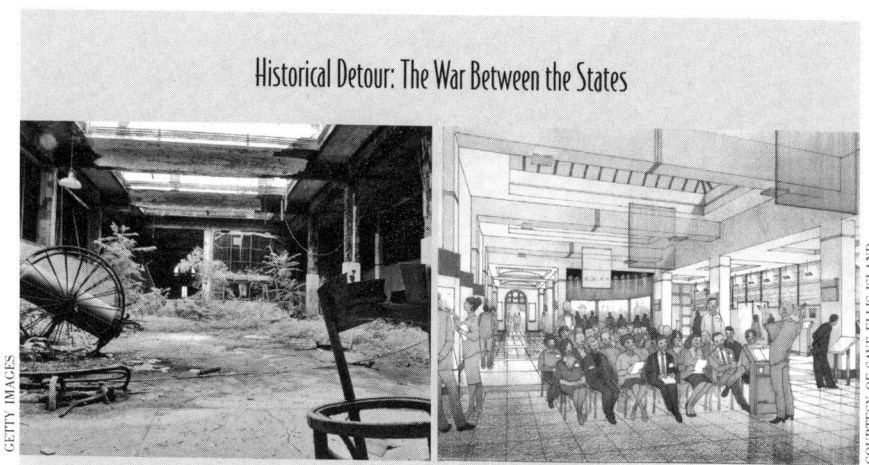

The Baggage & Dormitory Building on the island's south side is one of Save Ellis Island's major projects. The photo on the left is before stabilization began; on the right is an artist's rendering of the planned atrium in that space.

Ellis Island, New Jersey. Historically, it makes no sense. Emotionally, it seems plain wrong. But legally, it is largely true. While the island is actually owned by the federal government, in 1997, the U.S. Supreme Court issued a shocking decision that carved jurisdiction over the land into two chunks. About five acres, including the famous museum, sit in New York, while the remaining twenty-two and a half acres reside in New Jersey. This decision put to rest a battle dating back three centuries.

What are now Liberty and Ellis Islands were formally annexed to New York in 1691, although both islands are geographically closer to New Jersey. The Garden State soon claimed that this was an unjustifiable case of Empire State building. Although ownership was given to the federal government around 1800, the states continued their turf war. In 1834, they signed a compact designed to settle the dispute. It said that New York would "retain its present jurisdiction of and over" the islands while New Jersey kept "exclusive right" to the waters around them. The issue continued to simmer, with court cases occasionally popping up.

Ultimately, New Jersey's main goal was not historical but financial—it wanted tax revenue from concessions and employee salaries, particularly if Ellis Island's south side, home to thirty rapidly decaying buildings, were ever redeveloped. In 1986, the two sides patched up their differences by agreeing to split the revenue and, appropriately, spend it on low-income and homeless housing. The plan, however, was scrapped by the New York State legislature, which was not inclined to give away money to New Jersey or to the poor.

Finally, in 1993, after having lost a Liberty Island battle the previous decade, New Jersey asked the Supreme Court to decide Ellis Island's fate. New Jersey claimed that landfill used to enlarge Ellis Island during the immigration years to twenty-seven acres from its original three acres were in New Jersey's waters as decreed by the 1834 compact. New York emphasized its historical connection to the island, failing to stress strongly enough that the language technically gave it jurisdiction over anything called Ellis Island.

The war between the states grew ugly, with the *New York Times* lambasting New Jersey's efforts as "unfriendly, unbecoming, un-American, untoward, unhelpful, unprincipled, unseemly, unwarranted, and underhanded."

But in the end, New Jersey won. The south side is an important part of Ellis Island's history—home to everything from long, tight corridors connecting the old insane wards, the vaultlike machine used for disinfecting quarantine mattresses, and the commissioner's quarters—yet most of the public doesn't know it exists and thinks the restoration work on Ellis Island has long been completed.

Save Ellis Island, a nonprofit, was born to raise money and help the National Park Service—which retains jurisdiction—devise a plan for preserving and restoring the south side's buildings. In 2000, Hillary Rodham Clinton presented a Save America's Treasures grant of $500,000 to the National Park Service to help stabilize the ruins of what the First Lady called one of the eleven most endangered sites on the Treasures list of 550. New Jersey Governor Christine Todd Whitman kicked in an additional $1 million.

"We want to be respectful of Ellis Island's heritage and history," Save Ellis Island president Judy McAlpin said at the time. "We want to keep the immigrant experience front and center."

The overall plan calls for transforming these buildings into the Ellis Island Institute and Conference Center, with a mission to examine "current immigration and the intersection of world health and human migration in the broadest perspective," says Dorothy Hartman, vice president of programs and planning. There would be spaces for conferences and university classes and possibly overnight accommodations. "Buildings like the hospital and morgue are evocative spaces, and those would be open to the public," Hartman says, while the center green could host ethnic festivals and performances and the Recreation Building, with its 1930 stage and projection booth, could eventually host performances and films.

Work has been painstakingly slow. There are the challenges of navigating the rules and regulations of the federal government plus the enormous amount of work and money needed to complete the job. Hartman likens the challenge to feeling like a hamster racing forever on her wheel.

Still, progress has been made. The signature accomplishment so far is the art deco–style Ferry Building across from the main museum, which opened in 2007 and hosts an exhibit about the island's hospitals. And since then Save Ellis Island has done important stabilization work and begun several other projects. "We are taking incremental steps," Hartman says.

The organization was buffeted by the recession when it had its annual funding cut by the state of New Jersey in 2010; faced with possible extinction, it put out a plea for help, which produced $70,000 in donations by individuals followed by assistance from several New York foundations and finally a pledge of $100,000 by American Express that will allow it to continue. The island has also been buoyed by Ken Salazar, the Secretary of the Interior. "He has come to visit and has spoken publicly of his interest in making this happen, which helped make a lot come together," Hartman says, citing millions steered to Ellis Island from the American Recovery and Reinvestment Act (a.k.a. President Barack Obama's stimulus package). "The previous administration did not take as much interest."

The Laundry and Hospital Outbuilding—which had a collapsed roof—could open to the public with exhibits on the first floor by 2013; the Baggage Dormitory, thanks to the ARRA money, could open a few years later as the first site for conferences and classes, which could also generate revenue. "We're hoping those two buildings could be a tipping point in bringing people on board to help encourage future donations," Hartman says.

Still, hundreds of millions of dollars will be needed, and decades will be required until the project is completely finished. In the meantime, millions of visitors each year converge on the Ellis Island Immigrant Museum. That's Ellis Island, New York.

Where To Eat

Like Liberty Island, Ellis Island is a great place for a picnic. It also has a cafeteria, and, like the one on Liberty, this one has recently upgraded its options, offering more organic and "heart-healthy" options.

Island Hopping

Ellis Island can be reached from both New Jersey and Manhattan. New Jersey ferry service runs from Liberty State Park in Jersey City, exit 14B on the New Jersey Turnpike. Manhattan ferry service runs from Battery Park; tickets are sold in Castle Clinton. A concessionaire, Statue Cruises, 877-523-

9849 (www.statuecruises.com), runs the ferry service.

Since 9/11, the National Park Service has installed extra security before getting on the ferry, so allow extra time. (Large packages, suitcases, carry-on luggage, and other large parcels are forbidden on the ferry.)

By car: From the West Side of Manhattan, take the West Side Highway south to West Street, then south to Battery Park and South Street. From the East Side, take the FDR Drive south to South Street. Street parking is close to impossible, but there are several parking lots by Battery Park.

By subway: From the West Side, take the 1 or 9 to South Ferry. From the East Side, Brooklyn, or the Bronx, take the 4 or 5 to Bowling Green. From Queens or Brooklyn, take the N or R to Whitehall Street.

By bus: From Midtown, take the M6 or M1 to Battery Park. From the East Side, take the M15.

By boat: From Staten Island, take the ferry to the Manhattan terminal. Follow the signs through Battery Park to Castle Clinton.

4. Forgotten Islands of Upper New York Bay

Castle Clinton

Castle Clinton

WELDED TO THE MAINLAND by landfill and dwarfed by skyscrapers, Castle Clinton has been reduced to a bit player, the launching point for the tourist ferry to Ellis and Liberty Islands. Yet it was once a star, a central part of the city's history. Before Ellis Island became America's front door, this fort was the immigrants' gateway to the United States. Long before the majestic Statue of Liberty stood in New York Harbor, the tiny isle of Castle Clinton was the pride of New York City.

The man-made island, constructed from stone in 1807 as a fortress site, was positioned about two hundred feet from the Battery at Manhattan's southwestern tip. The Southwest Battery, completed in 1811, had both the Hudson and East Rivers in its sights. It had twenty-eight cannons and walls eight feet thick, and was connected to Manhattan by a wooden bridge.

The Battery never fired on the British, but during the War of 1812 it went head-to-head with Fort Columbus on Governors Island in annual morale-boosting competitions to blow up old ship hulks. In 1815, the fort was renamed Castle Clinton after Mayor DeWitt Clinton, and remained headquarters for the Third Military District until 1821, when the central offices shifted to Governors Island and the island fort was given to the city.

In 1824, it was reborn as Castle Garden, and during the next three decades it was the city's premier showcase, hosting celebrity galas and concerts, political rallies, and fireworks displays. The fortress was lavishly remodeled to accommodate its new personality. The gunrooms boasted marble busts and painted panoramas. A promenade was constructed along the building's crest, allowing guests a romantic stroll. In 1825, Castle Garden became one of the first public buildings lighted with gas. A massive fountain was installed in its interior in 1843, and the next year a roof was added, turning the former fort into the city's largest indoor concert hall.

Virtually every president from Andrew Jackson to Franklin Pierce was feted at Castle Garden, also home to outstanding assemblies. Daniel Webster delivered some of his greatest orations; Henry Clay, "the Great Compromiser," held conventions intended to defuse growing tensions between the North and South; and Hungarian freedom fighter Louis Kossuth made his celebrated 1851 speech here.

Castle Garden was also home to high culture. It introduced Americans to grand opera performed by supreme Italian vocalists Giulia Grisi and Giuseppe Mario and hosted the first American performance of Beethoven's Ninth Symphony. Indeed, two events were hailed during their time as the social affairs of the century: a grand reception honoring Revolutionary War hero the Marquis de Lafayette on his visit from France, and the American debut of Europe's most popular singer, Jenny Lind, "the Swedish Nightingale."

Castle Garden had been open only a few months when the city's cannons roared one hundred times to welcome Lafayette to America on September 14, 1824. The city was impressed by the Marquis's appearance and awed by the fort's transformation. Reviewing the bash for the *New York American*, James Fenimore Cooper wrote that with its blazing lights and extravagant decor, "the Castle presented a more magnificent spectacle than this country has before witnessed."

The fort was decked out in red, white, and blue and hung with flags depicting the armorial insignias of the thirteen original states. Each of the gala's five thousand guests wore a medallion bearing the Frenchman's likeness. Beyond the pomp and circumstance the party was also a memorable one, with music and dancing continuing until 4 AM.

Jenny Lind's arrival on September 12, 1850, was more demure—the music of flutes, not the blast of cannons, welcomed the soprano. Lind sold out all six thousand seats for six evenings, but there was little chaos thanks to the masterly organization of her manager, the legendary P. T. Barnum.

Barnum auctioned off the tickets. While the average ticket cost about $6, John Genin, a hatter and friend of the showman, was persuaded to pay $225 (over $6,000 in 1999 dollars) for the first seat, A1, a cushioned, crimson velvet chair directly in front of Lind. Barnum assured Genin that the astronomical sum was a good buy, and would reap untold publicity for the hatter. Indeed, "Genin" hats became a fashion statement ballyhooed across the nation.

People traveled from Philadelphia and Boston for the debut, although many ladies, fearing a crush, stayed away opening night. Those without seats took to the water, encircling Castle Garden in their boats. On premiere night, two hundred vessels surrounded the concert hall, filled with fans listening to Lind's voice floating beyond the fort's walls.

"Never did a mortal in this city, or perhaps in any other, receive such homage," proclaimed a front-page story in the *New York Herald*. "From the ceiling to the stage it was one dense mass of human beings."

Lind, whom the *Herald* anointed "the greatest prodigy in song that ever appeared upon the theater of this world," donated her opening-night purse of $12,000 to various New York charities and gave her tour earnings to Swedish schools. Her generosity and talent prompted the newspaper to proclaim her "goddess of the people."

Lind returned to Castle Garden in 1852 for a series of farewell concerts, but the hall's glory days were nearing an end. Three years later, the island was joined by fill to Manhattan and given over to the state, which turned the old palace into a depot for immigrants. When it closed in 1890, Castle Garden's legacy included the admission of 7.9 million newcomers to America. So embedded was the name Castle Garden in the immigrant psyche that for years after Ellis Island opened, many arrivals referred to the new depot as Castle Garden.

In 1896 the building was remodeled and converted into the New York Aquarium. It became the city's most popular public institution, drawing at its peak two and a half million visitors annually. But in 1941, Robert Moses, head of the Triborough Bridge Authority, closed the aquarium and threatened to demolish the building as revenge against upper-crust reformers and politicians who had defeated his proposal for a Brooklyn Battery Bridge.

The aquarium never reopened but Moses' planned destruction of the historic building was thwarted when reformers successfully lobbied the federal government to preserve the site. After several decades without funding, the National Park Service restored Castle Clinton to its original state and opened it to the public in 1975.

In the last decade Castle Clinton has begun enjoying at least a hint of its past glory with a free summertime concert series held inside the fort called Music at Castle Clinton. Performers such as The Hold Steady and Duncan Sheik may not drum up the excitement that Jenny Lind once did, but they do bring people back to this overlooked New York landmark.

Exploring the Island

Although **Castle Clinton**, 212-344-7220, receives three million visitors a year, most merely pass through, stopping only at the Ellis and Liberty Island Ferry ticket gazebo or bookstore. But while the fort may not warrant a separate trip, its dioramic exhibit and ranger-led tours—offered at 10 A.M., 12 P.M. and 2 P.M.—are worth allotting time for on your way to or from the islands. The rangers provide details not found in the exhibit, such as the fact that the fort only had officers' quarters—infantrymen had to commute to the garrison or sleep next to their cannons during emergencies.

The exhibit is in a small room off to the right as you enter the fort and offers an entertaining look at the fort's evolution and how drastically the contours of New York have changed. It features three large models and murals depicting the Castle Clinton area in 1812, 1886, and 1941. The 1812 rendering shows an open fort on a small island connected by a wooden bridge to Lower Manhattan, with the nearby shores of Brooklyn essentially undeveloped. By 1886, Castle Clinton was enclosed, surrounded by Labor Bureau buildings for receiving immigrants, and connected to Manhattan by landfill. An elevated train chugs through Manhattan, which is linked by a magnificent bridge to rapidly developing Brooklyn. The 1941 version shows the castle in its final days as New York's aquarium, now three stories covered by white stucco. Landfill has pushed the fort farther back from the shore, and skyscrapers dominate the skyline.

To complete the experience, step outside: The small fort that may have seemed stodgy and uninspiring upon your arrival now has a stubborn dignity; it is a stark reminder of the country's hard-won independence.

Island Hopping

By car: From the West Side of Manhattan, take the West Side Highway south to West Street, then south to Battery Park and South Street. From the East Side, take the FDR Drive south to South Street. Street parking is close to impossible.

By subway: From the West Side, take the 1 or 9 to South Ferry. From the East Side, Brooklyn, or the Bronx, take the 4 or 5 to Bowling Green. From Queens or Brooklyn, take the R to Whitehall Street.

By bus: From Midtown, take the M6 or M1 to Battery Park. From the East Side, take the M15.

By boat: From Staten Island, take the ferry to the Manhattan terminal. Follow the signs through Battery Park to Castle Clinton.

Part II

Lower New York Bay

HOFFMAN AND SWINBURNE ISLANDS •
FORGOTTEN ISLANDS OF LOWER NEW YORK BAY

*Linked to the Upper Bay by The Narrows, a mile-wide tidal strait, the
Lower Bay borders the eastern shore of Staten Island and the western
coast of Brooklyn, and opens up into the Atlantic Ocean.*

5. Hoffman and Swinburne Islands

"Peopled only by the shades of those who were banished there by disease to die or recover, the isle has held a morbid fascination for occasional visitors curious to see this forsaken spot."

—STATEN ISLAND ADVANCE, JULY 17, 1934,
REFERRING TO SWINBURNE ISLAND

Hoffman and Swinburne Islands

STATEN ISLANDERS HAD had enough. In 1858, after more than fifty years as New York's dumping ground for people with contagious, deadly diseases—yellow fever, typhus, cholera, and smallpox—infuriated mobs burned the New York Quarantine Hospital to the ground. In the face of this unsurpassed expression of NIMBY-ism, the government was forced to create two artificial islands, Hoffman and Swinburne, to house the ill.

Establishing a quarantine had never been an easy endeavor; its location inevitably distressed nearby residents. The first official quarantine was established at Bedloe's Island in 1758, but after a deadly cholera epidemic spread to Manhattan, detainees were shuffled off to Governors Island, and then, in 1801, to Tompkinsville at the northeast corner of Staten Island. (The Seamen's Retreat in nearby Stapleton was used from 1831 to 1882 to separately quarantine seamen and their families.)

Staten Islanders protested vehemently. Their opposition to the Tompkinsville quarantine intensified in 1848, when 180 locals contracted yellow fever. The legislature ordered the quarantine—which detained anyone with a contagious disease, not just immigrants—moved again, this time to Sequine's Point, Prince's Bay, far away at the southern end of the island.

Soon after building began there in 1857, angry residents burned the new structures and piers. Martial law was declared, and the militia patrolled the quarantine site, but another series of new buildings was also razed. Frustrated, the state tried reopening the old quarters at Tompkinsville, but north shore residents proved as furious and destructive as their southern neighbors. On September 1, 1858, lawless islanders armed with fiery fagots of straw broke through the quarantine gates and burned the main buildings. The militia was called in to save what remained, but as soon as rumors spread the next day that the quarantine would be rebuilt, the mob returned, dragging patients onto the lawns and setting the last buildings ablaze.

Desperately, the quarantine commissioners set their sights offshore and established a temporary detention center for yellow fever sufferers on two old ships—the *Florence Nightingale* and the *Illinois*, which they anchored in New York Harbor. Smallpox victims were sent to Blackwell's Island (now

Roosevelt Island), and typhus sufferers went to Ward's Island. The arrangement so effectively restored calm on Staten Island that the commissioners
replaced the ships by constructing two small islands in a shallow area in Lower
New York Bay called Orchard Shoals, about one mile southeast of South Beach
and west of the main channel leading into and out of New York Harbor.

Beginning in the mid-1860s, piles of sand dredged from New York Harbor were heaped into two mounds until they formed the new Quarantine
Islands—Hoffman and Dix Islands—each about two and a half acres in
size. Administrative buildings and a boarding station to inspect incoming
ships were built several miles north, at Rosebank, on Staten Island.

Hoffman Island was named for John T. Hoffman, mayor of New York City
from 1866 to 1868 and governor of New York State from 1869 to 1872. Dix
Island was named for John Dix, a New York senator from 1845 to 1849 and
governor from 1873 to 1875, but the moniker was soon changed to Swinburne Island in honor of Civil War hero and surgeon Dr. John S. Swinburne,
who as port health officer oversaw the development of the islands.

Swinburne Island, or the Lower Quarantine, was completed in 1870.
Hoffman Island, or the Upper Quarantine, was finished in 1873. Immigration at the time was sporadic and manageable. In the beginning, Hoffman's
three two-story brick buildings remained empty, while the hospital at Swinburne adequately cared for people infected with contagious disease. (Treatment for yellow fever included ingesting both iced champagne and spirits
of turpentine.)

In 1880, a great wave of immigration pounded the Port of New York.
Twenty million foreigners immigrated to the United States between 1880
and 1920, and the vast majority of them arrived in New York.

Immigrants were typically packed into steerage, with scant air, bad
water, and decaying food. As a result, many were infected with or exposed
to contagious diseases, putting a strain on the tiny islands, which were ill
equipped for the deluge of human suffering. Those in the private quarters
of first or second class were subject to inspection only if they came from a
port where disease was prevalent.

Voyagers suffering from contagious diseases were hospitalized on Swinburne Island. Passengers exposed to, but showing no symptoms of, the
deadly diseases were detained on Hoffman Island for observation during
incubation periods, which generally lasted from a few days to two weeks.
Immigrants were then sent to the receiving center at Castle Garden in
Lower Manhattan and, after 1892, at Ellis Island; wealthier newcomers
went straight to New York.

By 1884, the quarantine commissioners reported that unhealthy conditions—especially decaying wooden buildings that acted as disease conductors—at Hoffman Island were spreading infections to healthy detainees, who upon becoming ill were sent to Swinburne Island, which wasn't much better. In 1887, Hoffman was tagged "scarcely tenantable" and in need of at least $121,000 in repairs. Staten Islanders, meanwhile, successfully lobbied for a crematorium on Swinburne Island, to stop the burying of diseased corpses at Sequine's Point.

In 1892, as a massive cholera epidemic plagued the world, an average of fifteen ships a day arrived in New York. Between August 31 and October 8, quarantine officers discovered cholera on seven vessels: 914 cabin passengers, 3,405 steerage passengers, and 1,469 officers and crew members were held for observation on Hoffman and Swinburne Islands during those six frantic weeks.

A new three-story dorm was constructed hastily on Hoffman Island, increasing dormitory capacity from 850 to 2,100. Detainees were bathed, and their clothes and effects either disinfected with steam or boiled. The epidemic threatened national security and precipitated hostility among federal, state, and municipal officials, who accused each other of ineptitude. "The recent experience at the Port of New York sent a shudder throughout the whole country," wrote the *New Orleans Medical and Surgical Journal*. The federal government subsequently took over most quarantine stations, although New York State retained control of its facility until 1921.

When it became apparent that Hoffman Island couldn't accommodate the growing numbers of immigrants, the state—after buying Fire Island on Long Island, but deciding not to use it—enlarged Hoffman Island to 9.9 acres. The job was finally completed in 1896, but building didn't begin for several years due to lack of funds. The quarantine commissioners also implored the state legislature for money to improve existing conditions on both Swinburne and Hoffman Islands, but the requests were either denied or appeased with meager allocations.

Immigration peaked in the first decade of the new century. In 1901, 7,801 people were detained on Hoffman Island. While quarantine officials finally received some of the money they'd been requesting, most of the $64,000 allocated for Hoffman Island was slated for a luxury item—a building to segregate cabin-class travelers from steerage. Swinburne, which quarantine officials referred to as a "disgrace to the state," secured only $2,500 for minor repairs.

Despite hard times aggravated by overcrowding and insufficient funding, the islands were effective in keeping major epidemics from breaking out in New York. The good work, however, was overshadowed in 1911 when political maneuvering against the health officer of the Port of New York resulted in a nasty trial rife with accusations of corruption and mismanagement. (See Historical Detour: Tammany Goes Job Hunting.)

New buildings were eventually erected and repairs made to the islands' decaying infrastructures in 1916. Renovations continued through 1923, but few people benefited from the enhancement, since the immigration crunch was ending. Immigration was first interrupted during World War I, and the islands' hospitals were used by the army and navy to care for thousands of soldiers with venereal diseases. Then, in 1921, harsh new laws placed severe restrictions on immigration.

Only three people were detained on Hoffman Island after 1928, and Swinburne Island closed that year. Some adventurous souls contented themselves with nude sunbathing on Swinburne Island. In 1929, a *Daily News* investigation discovered vandals pillaging the buildings, holding "ghoulish orgies," using urns—like the one holding the remains of a five-year-old Austrian girl named Anne Kowrah—for "target practice," and carrying out other despicable frivolities. Fiorello La Guardia, a congressman at the time, arranged to have the remaining urns moved to Hoffman Island. In 1934, a fire, believed to have been carelessly set by a canoeist, destroyed many of Swinburne's buildings.

Hoffman Island's fate was not as forlorn as that of its sister island. From 1931 to 1937, Hoffman was used to quarantine imported parrots as a precaution against psittacosis, or parrot fever.

In 1934, Staten Island Borough President Joseph Palma flirted with the idea of building a summer pavilion, dog track, and amusement park on Hoffman Island. Three years later, then Mayor La Guardia proposed a camp for disadvantaged children, but Parks Commissioner Robert Moses criticized the plan, stating that the polluted water was unfit for swimming. The city did briefly turn Hoffman Island into a picnic ground with a regular ferry run from Staten Island.

Since no one had been detained at Hoffman for years, the quarantine was moved with little fanfare back to Staten Island in 1938. It was sited at Rosebank, about a mile south of Tompkinsville, where eighty years earlier an angry mob had burned the Quarantine Station to the ground.

The U.S. Public Health Service tried relinquishing the outcast islands, but neither state nor city wanted them. Then the government found a new use for Hoffman Island and built a training school for merchant marines there. Operated under the U.S. Maritime Service, with training provided by the Coast Guard, the school opened in 1938 with one hundred students. By 1943, there were twelve hundred enrollees. Students applauded the program, but the National Maritime Union said it fostered antiunionism and created a surplus of labor in a field already suffering widespread unemployment. Swinburne Island was revived during World War II as the electronic control center for underwater mines spread throughout the area to stop enemy submarines.

The Maritime Service eventually outgrew Hoffman Island, moving to Sheepshead Bay, Brooklyn, in 1947. Except for rats, both islands were then deserted. The neglected buildings and piers slowly rotted in the salty air until they were hollow and ragged with time.

Every now and then, an idea came up for the exiled islands. In 1950, Mayor William O'Dwyer rejected suggestions to build a homeless shelter and, later, a drug rehabilitation center there. Five years later, temporary housing for disadvantaged young people was proposed, but the islands failed inspection by city officials. The most grandiose plan was unveiled in 1956 by the most ambitious of planners, Robert Moses. The federal government was trying to sell the islands, and Moses wanted to stop them from falling into the hands of private investors, whom he said would erect massive billboards on the islands and taint the majesty of the bay.

Moses persuaded financier and philanthropist Bernard M. Baruch to donate the $10,000 New York needed to purchase the islands. Moses planned to fill in the one-mile span between Hoffman and Swinburne Islands, creating a giant 250-acre island park with a boat basin, fishing piers, picnic areas, golf courses, and ferry service to and from South Beach and eventually extending to Brooklyn and Manhattan. By using ten million cubic yards of compacted waste to enclose the islands, Moses also claimed he'd extend the life of the Fresh Kills landfill by three years, allowing the city more time to develop a modern incinerator system.

Moses was inspired by an idea promulgated by Cornelius Hall, the Staten Island borough president during World War II. Hall had envisioned connecting the islands to Staten Island via a curved arm of land, thus forging an airport link with Miller Field in the neighborhood of New Dorp. Hall's Breakwater Island was also meant to protect South Beach from erosion.

But Moses' park project never moved beyond the planning stage. Once more Hoffman and Swinburne were left vulnerable to the whims of mischief-makers and the lust of boat-ready lovers seeking privacy amid the ruins. In 1960, a fire destroyed three of Hoffman's sixteen buildings. In

Birds flock to the ruins of the buildings on Swinburne Island.

1965, harbor police arrested three women and eight men shooting pornographic movies on Hoffman Island. A year later, two Wagner College sophomores were ditched there during a prank orchestrated by fraternity brothers, who headed off to the prom. The students were rescued after winds swept their signal fire into a roaring blaze that caused rubbernecking traffic jams on the Belt Parkway and Verrazano-Narrows Bridge.

The Baruch Park plan survived in modified form through 1967. The city, facing a waste disposal problem, then suggested that Hoffman and Swinburne Islands be included in a massive landfill project linking them to Fort Wadsworth Army Base on Staten Island. A concerned public objected to the notion of garbage in the water, as it previously had to Consolidated Edison's proposal to build atomic reactor generating plants on the islands.

In the winter of 1968, the city took a small step toward its original goal of creating a new city park. All the buildings on Hoffman Island were razed, and grass was planted in their place. The city made permits available, concluding that the green space might appeal to day-trippers and overnight campers who could travel there by boat, but virtually nobody took advantage of the opportunity, and by the end of 1969, chatter about a new city park ceased.

The islands, which once figured so prominently in U.S. history—and were so enthusiastically corralled by the city—were deeded back to the federal government in 1972 as part of the twenty-six-thousand-acre Gateway National Recreation Area, the country's first national park system established for urban areas.

While Gateway maintains a popular and active network of recreational areas, including the Jamaica Bay Wildlife Refuge in Broad Channel, Queens, and beachfront in Sandy Hook, New Jersey, Hoffman and Swinburne Islands are off limits to the public. Gateway shot down proposals that would adversely impact the islands, such as Borough President Guy Molinari's 1991 suggestion to move the city's sludge-composting operations there. Since then, the islands have become increasingly popular with herons, egrets, and other colonial nesting birds. Hoffman Island is now the most populated island in the city's fourteen-island Harbor Herons Project, which is monitored by New York City Audubon. (The first waders were sighted in the 1970s on Prall's Island, Shooter's Island, and Isle of Meadow on the northern and western sides of Staten Island.) In the last decade, the total number of nesting pairs here has quadrupled to 621 in 2010. That includes 305 black-crowned night herons, 167 great egrets, 65 snowy egrets, and 77 glossy ibis. Swinburne Island hosts 320 double-crested cormorants, though a handful of waders have been spotted there in recent years

So the islands live on, their histories and current life still virtually unknown to those steering barges and tugs through the bay. Occasionally, a weekend angler will look past rod and reel, pondering the meager remains surviving on Swinburne Island. Or a party will dock its boat alongside the jagged periphery of Hoffman Island, and steal a peek into its jungle wilderness—perhaps unaware of its dark past and the promise of resurrection never realized..

Historical Detour: Tammany Goes Job Hunting

In 1895, when Dr. Alvah H. Doty was appointed health officer of the Port of New York—in charge of the quarantine at Hoffman and Swinburne Islands—he inherited a system close to collapse. The island's facilities were inadequate to accommodate the thousands of immigrants requiring detention, and an emergency three-story frame dormitory constructed in 1893 was still being used, despite a quarantine commissioners' report calling it a "tinder box" and "death trap." Doty repeatedly pleaded with the state legislature for funding to renovate and improve the facilities, but he was largely ignored. Despite the difficulties, Doty prevented infectious diseases from riddling the mainland and received endorsements for reappointment from the medical community and the *New York Times* throughout his tenure.

In 1910, the *Jewish Morning Journal*, on behalf of immigrants formerly quarantined at Hoffman and Swinburne, accused Doty's administration of tolerating overcrowding, filthy conditions, forced manual labor, and attacks on young women. The charges were quietly investigated by Republican governor Charles E. Hughes and quickly dismissed as baseless. It was not long, however, before changing political winds rekindled the controversy.

Later that year, Hughes was ousted by Democrat John Dix, who broke a fifteen-year Republican stronghold on the governorship. Tammany Hall, New York City's omnipotent Democratic political machine, coveted Doty's state-appointed $12,000-a-year position. Tammany persuaded State Senator Thomas F. Grady to introduce a bill transferring the position of health officer from state to city supervision. Tammany also pressured Dix (no relation to Governor John Dix, for whom Dix Island—later Swinburne—was named) to appoint Charles N. Bulger to reinvestigate conditions on Hoffman and Swinburne Islands.

This time, the allegations were scrutinized daily in the mainstream press. The hearings lasted two and a half months during 1911 and included the testimony of some 250 witnesses, many of them former quarantine employees and immigrants who were paid a per diem witness fee by their attorneys to testify.

At first, Doty was so busy containing a cholera epidemic that he didn't attend the hearings. Nor did he retain counsel, since no charges had been brought against him, and the hearing was ostensibly to familiarize the governor with the Quarantine Islands. But the hearings soon evolved into a witch hunt.

On June 27, an immigrant named Freida Alexandrowski detailed through an interpreter the incidents she'd witnessed on Hoffman Island: "I have seen quilts stuffed into the mouths of children by nurses to keep them from crying. I have also seen dying children carried out of the hospital into the open air on cold winter days in their cribs and left there for six hours. The food which the detention station authorities gave us to eat consisted of sour soup, stale, moldy bread which had been cooked in filthy vessels, bad eggs, and rancid butter."

While the practice of exposing to the cold children who suffered from pneumonia complicated by other diseases frightened many immigrants, it was an accepted medical treatment in its day, believed to increase patients' resistance.

Former Hoffman Island superintendent Frank Bartow testified about overcrowding and inadequate sanitary conditions on Hoffman Island. The next day, however, Dr. John W. Brannan of Bellevue and Allied Hospitals cited a letter written by Bartow a year earlier contradicting his testimony and referring to the quarantine as a model place under Doty.

On July 28, Arthur Denyse, a former employee, said he and other employees held orgies and parties in Doty's office after the health officer had left for the night. On one occasion, Denyse said, he emptied the cremated remains of former New York City street cleaning commissioner Colonel George Waring from an urn kept on Doty's mantel and mixed Gin Rickeys in the vessel.

The *New York Times* discredited Denyse's story the next day, reporting that Waring's remains were buried in Stamford, Connecticut. It was also disclosed that Denyse had been fired from his quarantine job after fabricating a cholera scare that had fooled the press.

In August, Doty's friends convinced him to retain legal counsel. But Doty, kept away by a wave of cholera-infected immigrants and his own mental and physical exhaustion caused by the investigation, again failed to testify on his own behalf.

The hearing ended September 1. Awaiting Bulger's assessment, the American Hospital Association lauded Doty for his handling of the cholera crisis and said, "It should be the shame of all citizens to remember the humiliating investigation to which the doctor has been subjected."

Bulger, however, was not to be deterred. On December 5, outlining a litany of misdeeds, violations, and ineptitude, Bulger recommended to Governor Dix that Doty be forced to resign. His final report accused Doty's administration of "gross incompetence and inexcusable negligence," adding that the health officer was "living the social, rather than the strenuous life," while the quarantined immigrants were suffering under inhumane conditions. He also said Doty's bookkeeping practices were "primitive, obsolete, unsystematic, and altogether unreliable." Bulger then recommended thorough reform and renovation of the Quarantine Islands—similar to what Doty had urged all along.

The Times and the Academy of Medicine rebuked the verdict, and an accounting firm countered that Doty's records had been maintained with "scrupulous honor and integrity," adding that the health officer had actually saved the state money.

Doty defended himself in a written statement: "For the past six months I have borne the brunt of this malignant attack upon me at a time when all my days and nights were devoted to a strenuous effort to keep cholera out of this country."

Despite these protests, it was reported three days later that Tammany Hall leader Charles F. Murphy would have final say in naming Doty's successor. On December 29, Governor Dix demanded Doty's resignation. Doty, whose term had officially expired almost a year before, refused to resign, but didn't contest the appointment of a successor.

More than two hundred men applied for the job as health officer of the Port of New York, and on February 14, 1912, Dix nominated Dr. Joseph J. O'Connell for the job. O'Connell moved into the health officer's quarters at Rosebank, Staten Island, on Christmas Eve 1912, the same day that Doty packed his family's belongings and departed.

EXPLORING THE ISLAND

For information on volunteering in the Harbor Herons Project, call 212-691-7483 or go to www.nycaudubon.org/getinvolved/volunteer.

6. Forgotten Islands of Lower New York Bay

Fort Lafayette

Fort Lafayette

ARMED WITH SEVENTY-TWO cannons and standing on Hendrick's Reef—a tiny ledge in The Narrows just four hundred yards from the Brooklyn shore—Fort Lafayette was one of a series of citadels constructed to protect New York during the War of 1812.

While the fort, completed in 1818, was built to keep intruders out, it gained its greatest notoriety for keeping Americans locked up. During the Civil War, this round brick garrison served as a jail for prisoners of war and prisoners of state. (Originally called Fort Diamond, the name change honors Revolutionary War hero the Marquis de Lafayette, who visited in 1824.)

Many of the prisoners came from Washington, D.C., a hotbed of espionage during the war, and Maryland, a crucial Union border state. In April 1861, with Union leaders worried about the capital being cut off from the North, President Abraham Lincoln suspended the writ of habeas corpus, allowing the government to detain people without warrants, charges, or trials. Suspected secessionists were rousted from their beds at night and trundled off to Fort Lafayette and other prisons.

Perceptions of conditions at Fort Lafayette varied wildly, depending on the source. Some captives felt it was among the worst of the bastilles, an overcrowded dungeon where rights were tossed out the window; other prisoners felt they were treated fairly. Many Northerners thought the prison lacked discipline, nicknaming it the Hotel de Burke, after commanding officer Lieutenant Colonel Martin Burke, whose family was living in Maryland. In actuality, it was a perverse mix of harshness and laxity. Burke, who'd earned three citations for gallantry in the Mexican War, cracked down hardest on Union prisoners, but bent the rules for well-connected Confederates.

A member of the Maryland Legislature wrote in 1861 that he and fellow prisoners could purchase good food, liquor, and other provisions from Southerners living in the area. When the men weren't eating, they passed the days reading, writing, and playing cards.

However, the sixty-six-by-twenty-two-foot quarters held thirty-eight prisoners and five cannons, which took up half the space. The group shared one writing table, three washstands, two water buckets, one tin cup, and two candles at night. There were tadpoles in the water, and broken windows weren't replaced when the weather turned cold. Nearby, a roomful of sailors and privateers who had violated the Union blockade were locked in chains and denied beds.

Among the prisoners were many prominent men, including General William Fitzhugh "Rooney" Lee, the son of Confederate army leader Robert E. Lee. (Ironically, in the 1840s, the elder Lee had been assigned to oversee repairs at Fort Lafayette.)

In May 1861, four Baltimore police commissioners were remanded to the one-acre island. Three months later, Kings County Sheriff Anthony Campbell arrived with a writ of habeas corpus ordering Burke to transfer the men to court custody. (Many judges, believing that Lincoln had over-stepped his executive power, continued applying the writ.) Burke wouldn't let Campbell enter the fort, ignoring him for four days until the presiding judge dropped the issue. The commissioners were imprisoned until 1863.

One of the worst railroading cases involved General Charles Stone, com-mander of the Union troops routed at Ball's Bluff, a costly fiasco that fol-lowed the disastrous Battle of Bull Run. The press scapegoated Stone, and later, several soldiers secretly testified before Congress that Stone had met with Confederates prior to the battle. Stone testified at the same hearings without being informed of the accusations against him. On February 8, 1862, he was dragged from his home and locked up for forty-nine days at Fort Lafayette without exercise or outside communication. Stone, never for-mally charged, was acquitted in 1863, but not publicly exonerated. He lived in self-exile in Egypt for many years. His good name was finally restored when he returned to New York in the 1880s as engineer in chief overseeing the design of the Statue of Liberty's pedestal.

In 1863, a group of Confederate prisoners created a handwritten newsletter called the Right Flanker. (They later smuggled it out and pub-lished it as a book in London.) The Flanker detailed how a Confederate prisoner, whose daughter was friends with Burke's daughter in Maryland, convinced Burke to make life easier for Southern inmates. Burke removed prisoners to other forts to relieve overcrowding and asked Southern friends in New York to donate clothing to inmates who wouldn't accept anything from the Union government.

New Yorkers were outraged by the generous treatment afforded these traitors, and newspaper articles sensationalizing the rumors of Burke's lax-ity stoked their fury. One *New York Post* article claimed prisoners were using the fort's roof as a promenade to enjoy sunsets. After citizens and the press clamored for stricter treatment, *the Right Flanker* reported that Burke "tightened the screws," disallowing goods from the outside. Treatment of Northern prisoners also became more severe: one Ohio man was put in solitary confinement for three weeks with no light and no toilet paper.

No one suffered a worse fate than Robert Cobb Kennedy, the final Confederate spy executed before the war ended. In November 1864, Confederate rebels unsuccessfully tried to burn down New York City's major hotels; only Kennedy was apprehended. He was sent to Fort Lafayette, and on March 25, 1865, he was hanged before a crowd of troops, prisoners, and citizens who paid up to $50 for a pass to the island. The unusual gallows lacked a trapdoor; weights and levers violently jerked Kennedy off the ground at 1:16 PM. It took him twenty-nine minutes to die. Fifteen days later, General Lee surrendered, and the war ended. The writ of habeas corpus was restored, but some prisoners were not released from Fort Lafayette for ten months.

On December 1, 1868, the fort made headlines again when a fire started by careless carpenters working on the structure's roof destroyed the garrison and threatened to obliterate a nearby neighborhood (today Bay Ridge in Brooklyn) surrounding Fort Hamilton. Everyone escaped the island unscathed, but fireboats couldn't quell the conflagration. They turned tail as rumors spread that fifty tons of gunpowder were stored in the fort. With a massive explosion apparently imminent, thousands of Brooklynites evacuated in a panic. The front page of the *New York Times* called the fire "an occurrence fraught with so much fear and trembling—so much dread apprehension of terrible calamity." The anticipated detonation never transpired, though live shells were found among the embers the next day.

In the decades after the fire, Fort Lafayette looked deserted but was actually a hub of activity, serving as the navy's loading station and munitions storage facility through World War II. When the fort was abandoned, Parks Commissioner Robert Moses persuaded top brass to lease it to his department, claiming that commercial interests would only create an eyesore like a nightclub, while he intended to transform this small island into a park. Although he prevailed over the American Legion, which wanted to establish quarters there, Moses never bothered developing Fort Lafayette—instead, he obliterated it.

In 1960, nearly 150 years after the brick fortress was built to keep intruders out of New York Harbor, what remained of Fort Lafayette was demolished to allow easier passage between Brooklyn and Staten Island. Hendrick's Reef became the foundation for the massive eastern tower that supports the Verrazano-Narrows Bridge.

Part III

Bronx Waters

CITY ISLAND • HUNTER AND TWIN ISLANDS • HART ISLAND •
FORGOTTEN ISLANDS OF THE BRONX

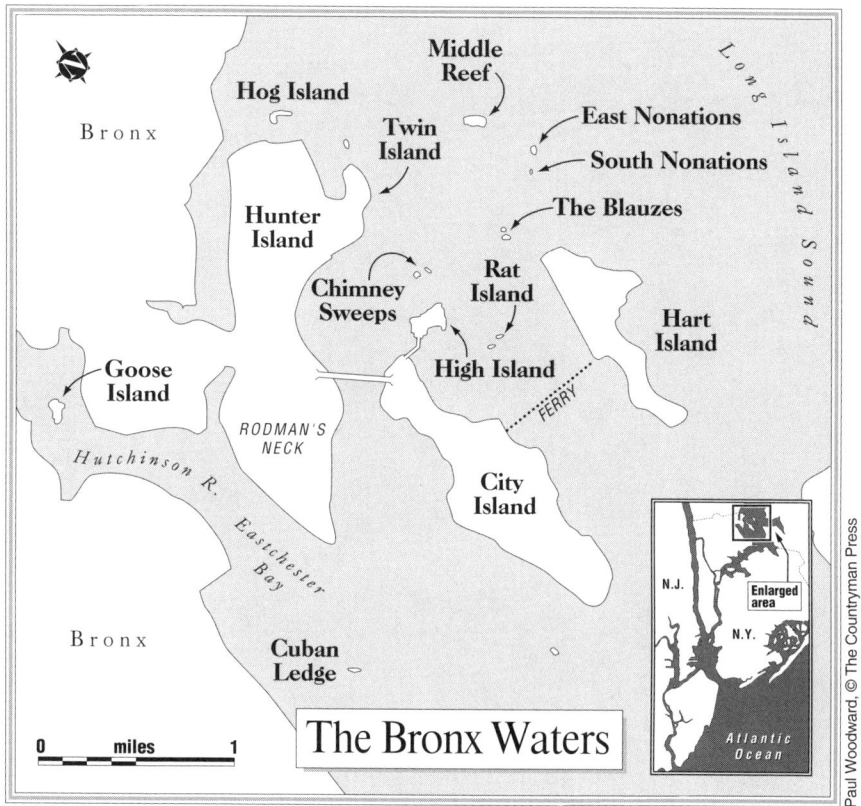

*The spindly Hutchinson River widens into Eastchester Bay, which pours
into Long Island Sound. New York's portion of the Sound is both the
narrowest and the most congested, populated by nearly a dozen islands,
some merely spots on a map.*

7. City Island

"You'd hear the saws going and the intercoms calling different people through the yards. It was like a music around here. And you smelled the varnish and the paints and so forth. It was like a glamorous or romantic thing. Now, there are just as many boats, but the yards aren't like they used to be at all."

—Tom Nye, sailmaker and fifth-generation City Islander

City Island

CROSS THE BRIDGE into City Island and enter a garden of nautical delights. Sailboats, cabin cruisers, motorboats, and rowboats bob in the water in rhythmic symphony. Yacht clubs, marinas, bait shops, boat sellers, and seafood restaurants line the island's commercial strip.

Often compared to a New England fishing village, City Island is more quirky than quaint. There's an urban edge to this island—not surprising since it's in the Bronx and many residents are native New Yorkers—yet it does retain a small-town charm. The pace is easy and familiar. The museum is curated and staffed by residents, the monthly newspaper, right down to the cartoon, is created by local volunteers. And when they share phone numbers, they don't even bother with the exchange: everyone knows that if you're on City Island, it's 885.

With Long Island Sound to the east and Eastchester Bay to the west, the undeniable lure of City Island has always been the water. It keeps the island cooler in summer than the mainland and warmer in winter. Many residents not only own boats but also belong to block associations that maintain private beaches, where they'll often gather to drink coffee or watch sunset together. They emphasize their aquatic connection by decorating their homes with sea paraphernalia—driftwood sculptures, whale weather vanes, seahorse birdbaths. The water is this community's soul.

The first effort to develop this natural harbor did not come for more than a century after Englishman Thomas Pell bought what the native Siwanoy Indians called Minnewit in 1654. But in 1761, a man named Benjamin Palmer purchased the island, then called Great Minnefords Island (also spelled Minniefords), with dreams of exploiting the island's choice location. Surrounded by the Sound's deep water and Eastchester Bay, convenient to both foreign and New England trade, Palmer and his investors believed they could develop a seaport to rival New York. They boasted that their "City Island" commerce center would save ships the hassle of passing through the East River en route to New York. While it now seems laughable to imagine this modest 230-acre island competing with the great metropolis, New York was also young in 1761, developed only about as far as Houston Street.

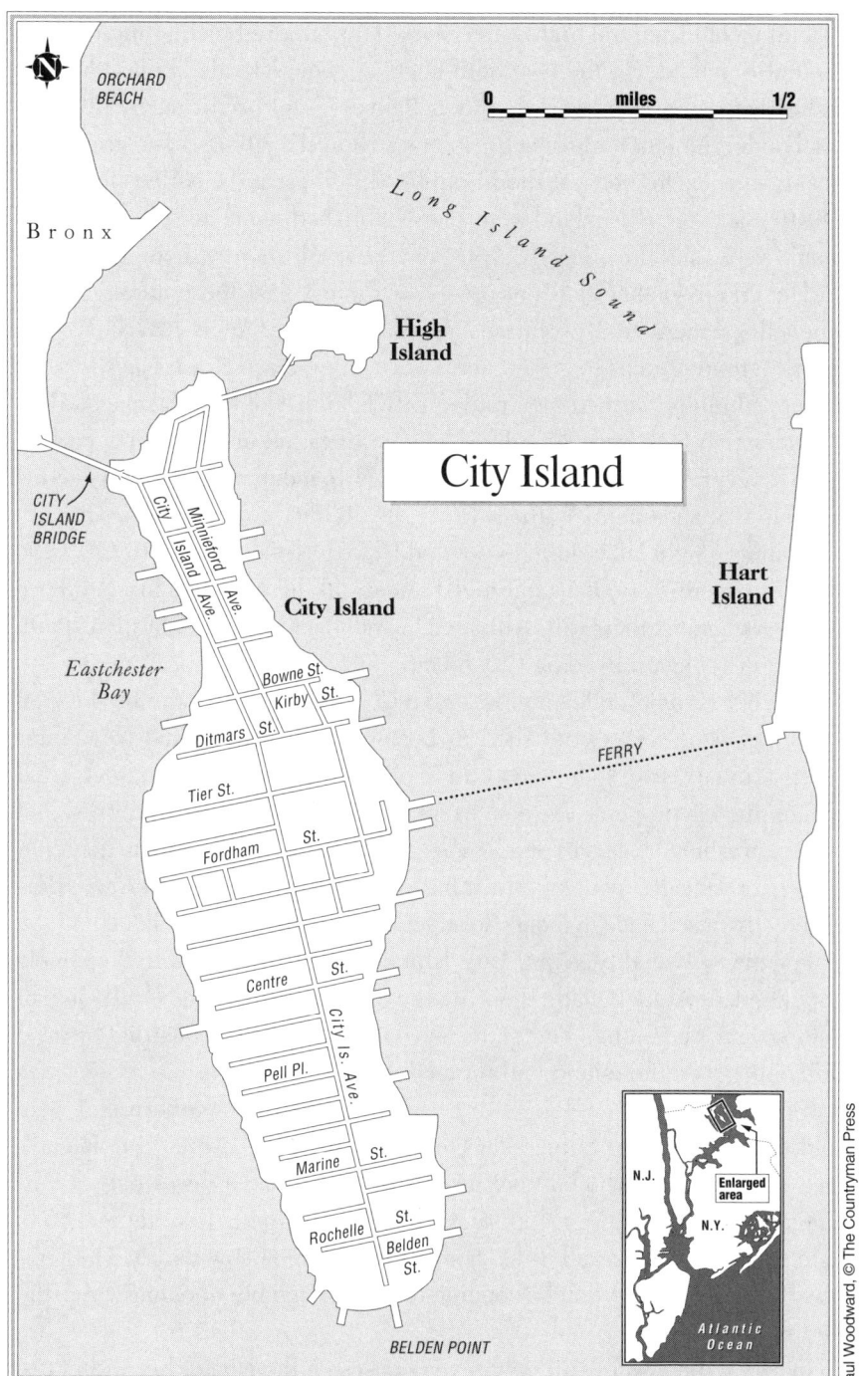

ORCHARD
BEACH

B r o n x

Long Island Sound

High
Island

CITY
ISLAND
BRIDGE

City Island

City Island Ave.

Minnieford Ave.

City Island

Hart
Island

Eastchester
Bay

Bowne St.
Kirby St.
Ditmars St.
Tier St.
Fordham St.
FERRY
Centre St.
City Is. Ave.
Pell Pl.
Marine St.
Rochelle St.
Belden St.

BELDEN POINT

N.J.

Enlarged
area

N.Y.

Atlantic
Ocean

0   miles   1/2

The British Crown subsequently granted the Palmer party title to land extending out from the high-water mark, four hundred feet, around almost the entire island. (In the twentieth century, some islanders, marinas, and waterfront businesses exercised their Palmer Grant privileges by filling in land under the water, altering the island's natural contours.) The group laid out streets, lots for houses, shops, public buildings, and moorings for ships. The first ferries to the island were also established—one in 1763 from Rodman's Neck, and the other in 1766 from the north shore of Long Island.

The grand scheme had not progressed much past the planning stages when the American Revolution cast it adrift. On August 27, 1776, as British ground forces swarmed across Brooklyn, three Royal Navy vessels with one hundred armed men raided City Island. The British troops killed Palmer's livestock and "plundered many things, all of which they carried off and never paid for," Palmer later wrote. Two months later, Palmer sent a letter to British general William Howe, justifying the Revolution. This letter, Palmer would later claim, prompted Howe to seek revenge: In 1779, the British warship *Scorpion* captured Palmer, taking him and his family to New York against their will. Although he found a neighbor to farm his land, Palmer never again lived on City Island.

Talk of a commercial center was revived briefly after the war, but by then ports had been well established in Boston, Philadelphia, and New York. After unjustly losing his land in a war-related lawsuit, Palmer tried reclaiming his property. He also wrote to Governor John Jay and President George Washington as part of a lengthy but unsuccessful attempt to get reimbursed for damages incurred during the war. Future vice president Aaron Burr eventually raised enough money to support Palmer through his old age.

For the next eighty years, City Island remained isolated and sparsely populated. Most men made their living piloting ships through Hell Gate or fishing and clamming. The state legislature approved construction of a bridge between the island and the mainland in 1804, but the project was never funded. In 1819, forty-two acres at the island's southern end were sold to Pelham Town Supervisor George Washington Horton, the island's next entrepreneur, who laid out many streets. City Island was part of Pelham and hosted its town meetings, with Horton charging town fathers $5 to hold their annual council at his house. (His home is now part of The Lobster Box, a restaurant that has operated under a number of names since the turn of the twentieth century.)

In 1847, there were still only seven houses on the island, but within two decades, City Island had grown into a small town. By 1868, eight hundred

City Island's shipbuilding days are gone, but it remains a community with strong ties to the water.

people lived in one hundred houses; the island also boasted three hotels, two shipyards, and two churches. City Island owed its newfound prosperity to the shipbuilding industry and a rough-shelled, highly sought mollusk: the oyster.

Orrin Fordham, an Englishman who moved to the island by way of Connecticut, was the first to cultivate oysters on artificial beds in American waters. In doing so, he made City Island the birthplace of the American oyster industry. "It had been a matter of common observation, that any object tossed into the water in summer, became covered with infant oysters," the *Drift*, one of the island's first newspapers, reported in 1895. Under favorable circumstances, this lasted until spring, when the oysters were large enough to be transplanted: "It was only a short step in logic to conclude, that if objects were thrown thickly into the water, on purpose to catch the floating spawn, a large quantity of oysters would be secured."

The business thrived through the 1890s. Oystermen who earned as much as $1,500 a week selling their catch in places like the Fulton Fish Market became some of the island's wealthiest residents. In the beginning, oystermen made their own sails for their skiffs and sloops, and boats were built by individual boatbuilders. In 1865, with the oyster business already well established, William Darling opened the first sailmaking loft on the island and produced sails for the oyster fleet.

By this time, City Island was establishing itself as a center of commercial shipbuilding. Shipyards designed and produced oyster sloops, schooners, tenders, and, later, luxury and racing yachts. City Island was perfect for shipbuilding for the same reasons Benjamin Palmer thought the island would make a great seaport: extensive waterfront, a well-protected harbor, and deep water right off the yards. The industry eventually attracted "machine shops aplenty, where even a big Diesel engine can be repaired or overhauled, marine railways capable of hauling out all but the very largest yachts afloat, several good yacht clubs . . . awning makers and, in short, every facility and trade which is allied with yachts," wrote *Rudder* magazine in 1929.

David Carll on Pilot Street built the first commercial shipyard in 1862. A native of Northport, Long Island, Carll was known for his three-masted schooners, small sloop yachts, and oyster sloops. Carll also helped build the island's first toll bridge in 1873, using timbers from the battleship USS *North Carolina*, which was dismantled in his yard. (The toll was abolished when City Island joined New York City in 1895.)

The Carll yard changed hands several times early on. Henry Piepgras, a master seaman, boatbuilder, and naval architect from Brooklyn, bought it in 1886 and introduced steel and iron ship construction to the island. "He was one of the pioneers in pouring lead keels, building hollow masts, and developing a strong waterproof glue made out of lime cheese and sour cream," says Tom Nye, a sailmaker and historian whose great-great-grandfather came to City Island in 1869 to work in the Carll yard. (Nye's two daughters are thus sixth-generation islanders).

In 1900, Piepgras sold the yard to businessman Robert Jacob, who brought in expert builders and Ratsey & Lapthorn, a prestigious English sailmaking company. Jacob turned out yachts of all sizes and classes, including the largest one ever built on the island—the 187-foot *Caroline*, constructed in 1914. Frequently, when a boat was launched from the Jacob yard, the buyer treated workers to a bottle of champagne and a big party. Another City Island pioneer was Augustus B. Wood, a Manhattan lawyer, boatbuilder, and yachtsman, who opened his shipyard shortly after Carll. Wood developed a national reputation for building very durable, light boats, including oyster skiffs and the famed Hell Gate pilot boat. Under the direction of Wood and then his son, B. Frank Wood, the yard built both *Feiseen*, which became the world's fastest yacht, and the self-righting lifeboat, which debuted at the 1893 World's Fair in Chicago.

The industry's growth affected the island's development. In 1886, William Belden created an amusement park, picnic grove, casino, and hotel at the island's south end, which soon became known as Belden Point. To attract tourists, Belden advertised in horsecars and elevated trains: COME TO CITY ISLAND, THE COOLEST SPOT WITHIN 100 MILES OF NEW YORK. Some visitors arrived by steamer; others took the railroad to Bartow Station then transferred to the City Island horsecar.

At the turn of the twentieth century, millionaires like Vincent Astor, J. P. Morgan, August Belmont, William Randolph Hearst, the Vanderbilts, and Sir Thomas Lipton traveled to the island in palatial yachts to dine at Thwaites Inn. Boating clubs, restaurants, bathing pavilions, summer camps, and hotels dotted the landscape. At the foot of Ditmars Street, the well-known Macedonian Hotel (later known as the City Island Casino and Beach) attracted political and society figures, while less wealthy urbanites spent summers on the island in bungalow colonies.

August Belmont even began an underhanded effort to transform the island into a vacation spot and racetrack, sending agents posing as regular buyers to snatch up as much property as possible. When news of the scheme leaked out, residents raised their prices, ruining Belmont's plans. Soon after, Morgan financed another major development effort, City Island Homes. This project failed, too.

The islanders were wary of the fancy city folk. "The native City Islander was content with his little world," wrote Alice Payne in *Tales of the Clam Diggers*, "and he hoped, as his ancestors had hoped before him that the invasion, now at flood tide, would never come."

Historical Detour: Linked to the Crime

On March 7, 1932, a retired school principal named Dr. John F. Condon wrote to the Bronx *Home News* offering to be an intermediary between Charles Lindbergh and the kidnappers of the aviator's infant son, forever linking City Island with the Crime of the Century.

The seventy-two-year-old Condon, described by some as eccentric and even senile, owned the Uncas Real Estate office at 313 City Island Avenue and had lived on the island before moving to the mainland Bronx. Some say Condon got involved in the case because he wanted to clear suspect Henry "Red" Johnsen, a yacht hand and boyfriend of the baby's nursemaid, Betty Gow. Others say the zealously patriotic and religious Condon was just angry because America's greatest hero—Lindbergh—had been wronged.

On March 8, the *Home News* published Condon's offer to

intercede in the Lindbergh matter and his promise to donate
$1,000 toward the ransom. While the kidnapping had occurred
more than seventy miles away, in Hopewell, New Jersey, the kidnappers immediately responded to the letter in this small, local
paper, and sent a note the next day accepting Condon's offer.
Condon even convinced Lindbergh to accept his proposal, too. To
hide his identity as go-between, Condon adopted the name Jafsie,
and delivered the ransom money to one of the alleged kidnappers
in St. Raymond's Cemetery in the Bronx.

When the public learned Condon was involved in the case, he
started getting hate mail. The case dragged on for two years, and
authorities even accused Condon of being part of the kidnapping
ring, although he was never arrested. Condon later picked suspect
Bruno Richard Hauptmann, a Bronx carpenter, out of a lineup, and
testified against Hauptmann during his trial. Hauptmann was convicted of the crime and electrocuted in Trenton on April 3, 1935.

It's possibile that Condon simply recognized Hauptmann from
City Island. Hauptmann kept his canoe at Dixon's boathouse on the
island, where Condon rented canoes. Hauptmann had also visited
City Island, where Condon had an office, about three to five times
a week during the summers from 1932 to 1934. "And would I not
have stayed away from City Island because I would have been
afraid of being identified by Condon?" Hauptmann wrote to New
Jersey governor Harold Hoffman in his plea for a pardon.

Condon spent much of the rest of his life lecturing about the
case, particularly about how he believed that Hauptmann had
acted alone. In 1936, he even wrote a book called *Jafsie Tells All*
and sold autographed copies for $2.50 from his City Island office.
The late Skippy Lane, a longtime island resident, recalled Condon
strutting about town in a black derby proclaiming, "You know who
I am? I was the Lindbergh negotiator."

Condon died in 1945 at age eighty-four. In his obituary, the
New York Times reported that "the Lindbergh case lifted Dr.
Condon out of a placid existence and the role of village character
into a complicated and troubled existence . . . with the fierce light
of international publicity focused sharply upon him."

The City Island storefront that once bore the sign JOHN F. CON-
DON is today empty. It was last occupied by a pizza parlor.

Still the residents opted to leave the town of Pelham in 1895 and join New York City. It was a close call, though—with nine hundred votes cast, the city won by only two. The new government replaced the island's deteriorating wooden bridge with a steel structure and built a new school.

To improve transportation and accommodate visitors, a monorail—running from the City Island Bridge to Bartow Station—opened in 1910. Considered experimental, it was one of only two monorails in the country. When it worked, it reduced the fifteen-minute horsecar trip to five minutes. Unfortunately, it was plagued with problems from the first day, when it derailed, injuring several passengers. It often broke down, inciting residents who'd opposed it in the first place to shout, "Get a horse!" The ride was hot in summer, frigid in winter, and there was no ventilation for the hordes of customers shoved into its small compartments. The monorail didn't last long, closing in 1913. (The ruins of Bartow Station, designed by renowned architect Cass Gilbert, remain on Pelham Parkway.)

During World War I, poor access limited the war contracts City Island received, although many shipyards built sub chasers, tugs, and other vessels instead of yachts. After the war, the Henry B. Nevins Shipyard, founded in 1907, built twenty Victory-class sailboats to revive interest in yachting. The boats were named in honor of yachtsmen who had participated in the war. A number of great yachts were even built during the Depression. *Brilliant*, a City Island classic, was built in 1932 by the Nevins yard, and is "probably the best example of a wooden boat ever built," says Nye.

Just as the yards began building smaller boats to adapt to the changing economy and racing styles, World War II arrived. With access to City Island much improved, the shipyards won more contracting work. The yards constructed minesweepers, PT boats, tugs, and landing craft at a pace that necessitated hiring more employees, at least for a while. After the war, the round-the-clock hustle and bustle was gone, and so was the money. "Today, the island economy is struggling for survival," wrote the *New York Herald Tribune* in 1949. "Heavy taxes have discouraged ownership of pleasure boats and cast gloom over the whole nautical scene. Many wealthy families who once regarded yachts as a natural part of summer are doing without them: the yachts lie rusting at anchor or have been hauled up on shore and sit forlornly incased in weather-blackened clapboard with a 'For Sale' sign nailed to the stern."

Postwar America also witnessed a change in building materials and new markets. Fiberglass made it more economical to churn out small pleasure boats coveted by the growing middle class. Some shipyards moved overseas for cheap labor or to inland facilities for lower property taxes. Some City Island yards diversified, but most closed or sold out.

The end of the luxury-yacht era was punctuated by the death of Henry B. Nevins in 1950. One of the nation's most prominent shipbuilders, Nevins never wavered from his origins, working almost exclusively in wood despite technological advances. "And he always stuck to his price," says Nye. "You paid top dollar, but you got what you paid for. He was a fair man, and everyone respected him." Four years after Nevins's death, his widow sold the yard to Carl Hovgard, one of the nation's leading yachtsmen, who bought it as a hobby more than a business. His yard built the *Columbia*, which defended the America's Cup in 1958, but it closed in 1960.

The Minneford Yacht Yard, founded in 1926 by Henry Sayers, saw the changes coming and prospered by being adaptive. In addition to building twelve-meter racing yachts, Minneford offered an extensive marina, boating services, and, eventually, condominium boat slips. Minneford also built yachts that defended the America's Cup six times between 1964 and 1980, becoming the last of the City Island yacht yards to shut down in 1983.

City Island remains synonymous with boating, but today the emphasis is on recreation, not construction. There are nearly three dozen marine-related businesses on the island—bait shops and marinas for fishermen, sailing and scuba schools, party boats, a kayak club, and dock-and-dine restaurants. The Eastchester Bay Yacht Racing Association's Wednesday-night regattas are a staple of spring and summer, with the members of the island's four yacht clubs—the City Island, Morris, Stuyvesant, and Harlem Yacht Clubs—taking to the water. (Independent racers are encouraged to participate; other races are held on weekends.)

But gone forever are the days when the four o'clock quitting-time whistle blew, spilling sailmakers and boatbuilders out onto the streets. UK Sailmakers, where Nye works, is just about all that's left of that life, and its workload and staff have been cut again and again over the last quarter century. "It's changed quite a bit," Nye says.

For decades, City Island was a clannish place—anyone born there was a "clam digger," everyone else a "mussel sucker"—but that has begun to change a bit as the island's population has shifted. When more than a thousand islanders worked in the island's shipbuilding and sailmaking businesses, everybody knew everybody. Today, there is a sprinkling of strangers on most blocks, and many professionals have joined the stew. Once a neighborhood of Victorian homes and bungalows, the island now also has several waterfront condominiums that have attracted New Yorkers—particularly those who work at Fordham University, the Bronx Courthouse, the Bronx Zoo, and the New York Botanical Garden—looking for a safe neighborhood within the borough.

These days, timeworn salts like retired Hell Gate pilot Ed Sadler, whose family moved to the island in the nineteenth century, are a rarity. Sadler, who turned ninety-four in 2010, was born in—and still lives in—the house his grandfather built in 1887. But Patrick Gannon, the Chair of Science Education at Hofstra University's School of Medicine, who was seduced by the sailing opportunities island life offered, said that when he moved here in 2002 old-timers never made him feel unwelcome or like an outsider.

Historical Detour: Go West, Young Man

Riding the horse-drawn trolley his father owned on City Island was perfect training for Harry Carey, star of silent-film Westerns. After local mounted police taught Carey to ride, he often helped his father, Judge Henry DeWitt Carey, operate the horsecar between City Island and Bartow Station. Carey studied law at New York University, but missed his bar exam after developing pneumonia.

Born in 1878, Carey wanted to be an actor, not a lawyer, anyway. He performed at the island's Leviness Hall in productions of *Uncle Tom's Cabin* and *Montana*, a melodrama that he wrote, and kept a small film studio in the cellar of the family home on Carey's Point, opposite High Island. He made a few movies using local talent and sites. *Bride of the Sea* was filmed at Belden Point. He also went on location to High Island, taking palm trees and tropical vegetation for scenery, and was said to have kept some wolves there for his films.

Carey performed in New York, traveled with stage companies, and even took his hit *Montana* on the road from 1904 to 1908. Then he acted in three Westerns filmed on Staten Island. But it wasn't until he met D. W. Griffith at the East Fourteenth Street Biograph studio and lassoed a role in *The Unseen Enemy* with Lillian and Dorothy Gish and Lionel Barrymore that Carey's career took off.

In 1910, he moved to Hollywood, bought a ranch and fifteen hundred acres, starred in *The Sorrowful Shore*, and married leading lady Olive Golden. For the next twenty years, he starred in silent films, primarily horse operas. Although he made the transition to talkies, starring in Westerns like *The Last Outlaw* and *Law and Order*, he had tired of the cowboy stereotype. He broadened his career by taking character parts in other movies including *Mr. Smith Goes to Washington* and *The Prisoner of Shark Island*, and by appearing on Broadway, in *Heavenly Express* in 1940 and *But Not Goodbye* in 1944.

But Carey remained an old cowhand at heart: At his funeral in Brentwood, California, in 1947, Burl Ives sang "The Cowboy's Lament" and John Wayne recited a poem. Then Carey was put to rest wearing a black suit, shoestring tie, and cowboy boots.

The island has not always been so welcoming of strangers, especially when they were of a different color. City Islanders are socially, educationally, and economically a world away from the big city and its Bronx brethren. For generations, the island was nearly entirely white, mostly third-, fourth-, and fifth-generation islanders of Irish, Italian, and German ancestry. This led to racial tensions in the 1960s and 1970s when droves of day-trippers from the Bronx, mainly blacks and Puerto Ricans, descended on the island each summer. They clogged up City Island Avenue, the lone thoroughfare, as they headed to the southern tip, where fishing, a spectacular view of the Sound, and open-air restaurants serving fried seafood awaited.

Traffic choked the island's two-lane main street so badly that frustrated residents stayed home rather than spend more than an hour in traffic just to cross their bridge. Residents cited the volume, not the ethnicity, of the crowds as their objection, but tensions simmered for years. In fact, the community was accused of racism in 1970 when residents petitioned for the rezoning of the southern end to phase out the restaurants that attracted these outsiders. The issue was dropped. The eateries thrive today, and the traffic has abated since concession stands were added at nearby Orchard Beach. While it's rarely smooth sailing on summer weekends, Nye says, "traffic is better here then it has been at any other point in my life."

The island is also more diverse than it ever has been before. As recently as 1990, it was 96 percent white but by 2000, the population was 84 percent white, with Asians and especially Latinos making up most of the newcomers. (It is still a far cry from the Bronx, which was 84 percent black or Latino in 2000.) The island, which grew by nearly 12 percent between 1990 and 2000 to 4,520 people, is now more white-collar than blue-collar and has for several decades been far more prosperous than most New York neighborhoods. The median household income in 2000 was $56,750, with just 4 percent of the households below the poverty line; one-third of the adult population held at least a college degree. (By contrast, Broad Channel, the island community in Queens, has remained blue-collar, with under 12 percent of the population having graduated from college.) In 2010 homes and condos on the island routinely sold in the $500,000–$900,00 range.

The island did weather economic storms in the late 1950s and 1960s when the boating industry sank. In the wake of this demise, storefronts sat empty until antiques shops and art galleries blossomed along City Island Avenue in the 1970s. Frustrated with the Manhattan art world, photographer and sculptor Ron Terner took advantage of the island's cheap rents and moved there in 1974. This Bronx native joined a budding bohemian scene built around a highly successful arts and crafts fair. Terner opened Focal Point Gallery and lived in the back, chopping wood for his potbelly stove and bartering photographic services for meals.

Some islanders were wary of these "hippies," says Terner, "but eventually, the community begins to accept you." He held out against the higher

Artists such as Ron Terner moved to the island in the 1970s; Terner initially lived in the back of his Focal Point Gallery and bartered photographs for food.

rents of the 1980s that chased off much of the artistic community. Terner has become a stalwart of the community—his gallery showcases the artwork of City Islanders twice a year, and he has devoted much of his artistic energy to photographing City Island life, especially the more eccentric and older characters who slowly seem to be disappearing from the scene. (Facebookers can view Terner's evocative images on his Facebook page. The albums are called "Photographs of City Island Past and Present" and "City Island Past and Present II." Accompanying many photographs is a thread of commentary and conversation about his photographic subjects.)

On the bright side, some newcomers are characters in their own right, like Gannon, the doctor, who raises thousands of honeybees in his backyard. He won over his neighbors by inviting them to see his operation—and how his children safely interacted with the bees—and by handing out free honey. Now, he says, his professional accomplishments are secondary in his identity. "They don't call me professor or doctor [here]. I'm the beekeeper."

The 1970s also saw land speculators aggressively pursuing the island's dormant shipyards, marinas, and related businesses. In an attempt to control development and protect the island's seafaring identity, a special zone limiting new buildings to three stories was created in 1976. While modern development has been kept to a minimum on City Island (the six-story Pickwick Arms apartment house built in 1963 is the island "skyscraper"), several condominium complexes sprang up beginning in the 1980s.

There were concerns that condos would change the island's flavor or make life unaffordable for the locals. But Nye, whose wife works a few days a week at the City Island Diner, one of the locals' favorite spots, says gentrification and overcrowding have not become major issues. "And the condos are definitely better than high-rises or empty, decaying waterfront property," he says.

And while "change is inevitable," Nye still counts five childhood friends on his block. "And there are a couple of older ladies there who have been friends going back to the 1930s," he says.

And as city life, with the anonymity it brings, "has crept up here," the local organizations have become more active, Nye says. "There's a lot of community pride."

In addition to repeated efforts through the years to tweak the zoning codes, the community has recently battled the Bloomberg administration's proposal for a new City Island bridge. The city first announced a plan to replace the aging 1901 structure in 2003, but delays have brought soaring costs and unhappiness. The price tag climbed from $32 million to $120 million in 2009, and the residents say the design is a monstrosity. "It is ugly as sin and totally inappropriate," says Barbara Dolensek, vice president of the City Island Civic Association, who also helps run the island's historical society and museum.

City Islanders have fought hard to maintain the community's character—this five-story building, erected in 1910, remains one of the tallest on the island.

Islanders have signed petitions, written letters, and protested on Facebook. They want a bridge similar in style to what they have now—with a peak 20 feet high—but the city designed a cable-stayed bridge with a 150-foot-high tower and suspension cables that the administration claims would evoke a sailboat. The city's claim that this style is more economical obviously looks foolish in light of the current price tag, but Dolensek also says it will look totally out of place next to a community that has changed its zoning so no new construction can surpass thirty-five feet in height. The DOT claims to have factored in the islanders' wishes, but Dolensek says that merely meant reducing the tower from 240 feet to 150 feet. "They have refused to discuss a new design," she says, adding that until construction—now scheduled for late 2011—actually begins, the residents will continue fighting.

Community pride also generated a renewed interest in preserving the details of the island's maritime heritage. Nye, Sadler, and the late Skippy

Lane, a retired tanker captain and longtime local fixture, helped create the historical exhibits at the heart of the City Island Museum, which opened in 1995 and has steadily expanded its collection of documents and artifacts. Sadler, the retired Hell Gate pilot, says the island's shipbuilding and yachting history are vital to its nature. "That's what I look back on, the fact that I was born and brought up in a nautical atmosphere," he says.

Today, of course, the shipbuilding survives only in recollection and culture, yet the community still exerts a special bond. And you don't have to have roots reaching down through City Island history to fall in love with the place, Terner says. "Once you are a City Islander, and you don't have to be a clam digger—you can be a mussel sucker like me—it gets into your blood."

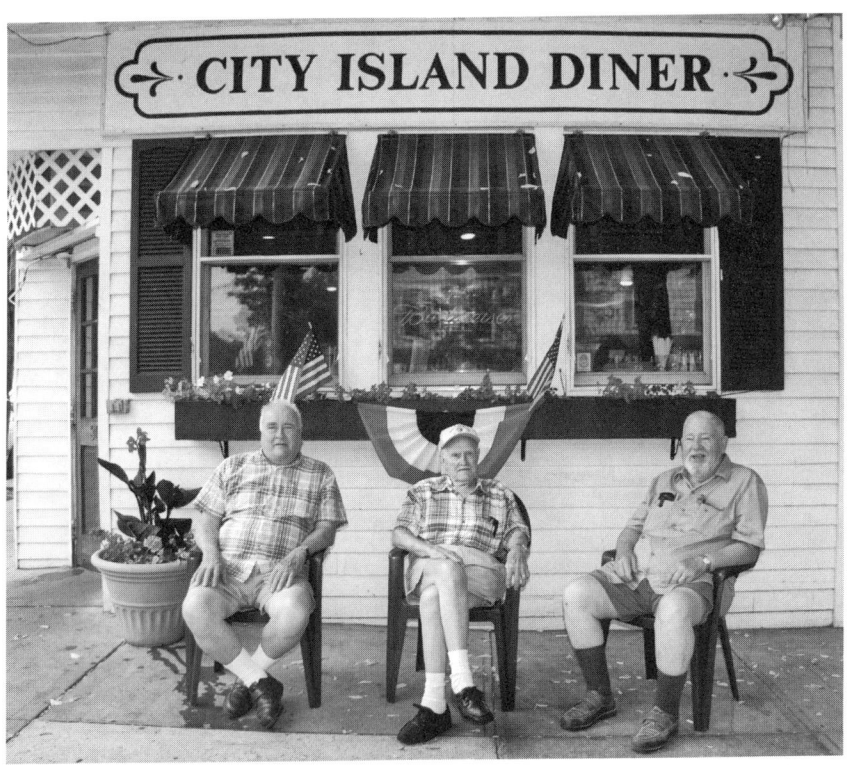

Old-timers Russ Schaller, Ed Sadler, and Stew Hawkins relax in front of the City Island Diner, a favorite of locals.

Exploring the Island

Many visitors to City Island lead with their stomach. And while the community's restaurants cook up plenty of seafood, there's enough to do on the island and in its waters to warrant a full day's outing, especially if combined with a hike at nearby Hunter and Twin Islands.

To experience City Island unabridged, a date with the water is essential. **The New York Sailing Center and Yacht Club**, 190 Schofield Street, 718-885-0335, offers a full range of sailing, navigating, radar, and racing classes as well as captained charters, rentals, a sailing club for people who don't own boats and full-service facilities for those who do.

You can also rent small fiberglass rowboats with an outboard moter from **Jack's Bait & Tackle**, 551 City Island Avenue, 718-885-2042. Jack's, which has been in one family since 1945, is also the departure point for **Island Current**, 917-417-7557, which runs open fishing trips and private charters. Other fishing boats include *Riptide III*, 701 Minnieford Avenue, 718-885-0236, which also runs a four-hour evening cruise under eight bridges en route to New York Harbor and the Statue of Liberty. **Hennessy Yacht Charters**, 697 Bridge Street, 646-363-1968, offers private yacht cruises.

If bobbing on the water isn't adventuresome enough for you, try **Captain Mike's Diving Services**, 530 City Island Avenue, 718-885-1588. Run by Michael Carew, a ten-year veteran of the NYPD Scuba Team, Captain Mike's offers beginner and expert diving, charters and adventures like lobster and shipwreck dives.

To get better acquainted with the community itself, head over to the **City Island Historical Society and Nautical Museum**, 190 Fordham Street, 718-885-0008. (Admission is free.) It's on the main floor of old P.S. 17, which was built in 1897 and closed in 1975. Just inside is a tender built by the Robert Jacobs shipyard in the 1930s. The corridor is adorned with historical maps of the area as well as artwork, including some by Morris Rosenfeld, a renowned nautical photographer and longtime island resident.

The Walsh and Nautical rooms are this small museum's most noteworthy attractions. The **Walsh Room** showcases dozens of watercolor paintings made in the 1930s by former islander Professor Harold Vandervoort Walsh; these depict City, Hunter, and Twin Islands, Orchard Beach, and other local sites. This room is also brimming with oral histories and binders upon binders of City Island history, dating back to the Ice Age and its geologic formation. The **Nautical Room** tells the story of the island's oystermen, shipbuilders, sail makers, Hell Gate pilots, yacht brokers, and America's Cup defenders, and there's plenty of photos of military and classic boats built on the island. Kids will love the display of a large unfinished boat, which was built by islander Adolph Juner, who enjoyed making boats in his basement.

The **Community Room** features lots of then-and-now photos of the island—from Harry Carey (a silent film actor who grew up on City Island) to Andy Garcia (an actor who starred in the 2010 film, *City Island*). Also of interest are arrowheads found in the area, a Revolutionary War cannonball, and a model of the Battle of Pell's Point as well as photos of the City Island monorail, which operated between City Island and the railroad at Bartow Station from 1910 through 1914. Among the curiosities in the School Room are some old desks and the school bell from PS 17. The museum also occasionally hosts talks on local history, such as a recent one on former Parks Commissioner Robert Moses, who was responsible for creating nearby Orchard Beach and developing Pelham Bay Park.

Armchair sailors can also dip into the **City Island Library**, 320 City Island Avenue, 718-885-1703, which has the city's most comprehensive collection of nautical books. Organized in 1969, the Ship Collection contains over a thousand nonfiction and fiction titles on everything from building a ship in a bottle to accounts of old shipwrecks. The building itself has porthole-shaped windows.

Of course, the best way to experience a community is to walk around in it. City Island's architecture is a hodgepodge, but within this miscellany you'll

SHARON SEITZ

Designed in the style of a Norwegian country home, this house from the 1920s is one of four built around a grassy commons.

find three city-designated landmarks and a handful of other notable structures. Start at the southern end of the island and turn right onto Belden Street, a dead-end gravel road. The white house at 175 Belden Street with forest green trim and white picket fence overlooking Long Island Sound was built in 1880. It was designated a landmark in 1981 because of its cottage style, which is rarely found in urban areas.

Back on City Island Avenue, make a left onto Rochelle Street and go to the very end and look to the left. Situated around a grassy common are four Norwegian-style country homes built in the 1920s by boatbuilder Henry Sayers. Head north on the main avenue and then turn left again to 95 Pell Place, a Sears, Roebuck & Company mail-order house called the Osborne. A bungalow with Asian influences, this low-lying structure has a white stucco exterior, maroon trim, a full-width front porch, and a gabled roof supported by stucco-and-wood piers. It was built from a kit in 1930, when Sears was the largest home-building company in the world.

Return to the main drag and continue north to **Grace Episcopal Church** at 104 City Island Avenue. This is a typical New England–style church built in 1861 with timbers hand hewn by employees of the David Carll yard. Adele Bolton, whose father was rector of an Episcopal church in Pelham, founded the church. She regularly rowed over to teach Sunday school and bring "grace" to the islanders. Her brother Cornelius became Grace Church's first rector; another brother, John, made the stained-glass window—a depiction of Palm Sunday—behind the altar. Hanging above the altar are two model-sized, square-rigged ships, one gold, the other silver. Sailmaker George Ratsey and shipyard owner Robert Jacob donated them. Facing in opposite directions, they symbolize birth and death and the belief that God is life's pilot.

The skinny five-story building at 284 City Island Avenue was the island skyscraper before Pickwick Terrace was built in 1963. Built in 1910 by sailmaker Tom Nye's great-grandfather, this black-and-tan building stands out among the avenue's plainer structures with its gambrel roof and Palladian windows.

Make a left onto Tier Street; at the end is a large Victorian house overlooking Eastchester Bay. Built in 1894, this quirky three-story, brown-shingle house with conical roofs was featured in the 1962 film *Long Day's Journey into Night*, starring Katharine Hepburn. The house, which was designated a landmark in 2000, has a large Doric-style porch, inverted and protruding oriels, and intersecting gables.

Return to City Island Avenue and head north to Reville Street. Turn

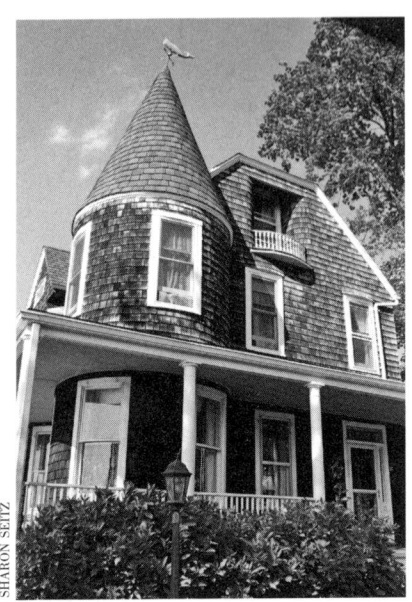

SHARON SEITZ

This New York City landmark is instantly recognizable for its Doric-style porch, conical roof, oriels, and gables, but it is most famous for its role in the 1962 film version of Long Day's Journey Into Night.

right and walk one block until you reach King Avenue. Located here since the 1880s is **Pelham Cemetery**, a picturesque resting place set against Long Island Sound. The headstones read like a Who's Who of City Island history. The cemetery remains anchored to the community: Owner and islander John Ulmer is the fourth generation in his family to oversee it.

To reach the final spot on the tour return to City Island Avenue and continue north until you reach 586 City Island Avenue. This three-story, freestanding Second Empire–style frame house was built about 1876 for leading oysterman Samuel Pell and is indicative of the wealth enjoyed by oystermen. Pell (a descendant of the historic Pell family that had bought what is today City Island and thousands of surrounding acres from the Siwanoy Indians) lived here until 1900. The house became a city landmark in 2002. It was most recently a bed and breakfast and Zagat-rated restaurant, which operated on the island for fifteen years until 2004.

Beyond the architecture, City Island also offers an array of shops and galleries. Ron Terner's **Focal Point Gallery**, 321 City Island Avenue, 718-885-1403, is always a visual feast. **Kaleidoscope Gallery**, 280 City Island Avenue, 718-885-3090, is an artists' collective, featuring everything from ceramics to paintings, plus toys and even Ugly Dolls for kids. It's also the exclusive distributor for City Island Gold Honey, made from Patrick Gannon's bees.

You can also browse for antiques at **Early Ruth Antiques**, 319 City Island Avenue, 718-885-0228, ancient marine equipment and knickknacks at **Trader John's Nautical Equipment**, 239 City Island Avenue, 718-885-1658, or stained-glass and nautical-themed gifts at **Corona's Hidden Treasure**, 329 City Island Avenue, 718-885-1330 (by appointment only).

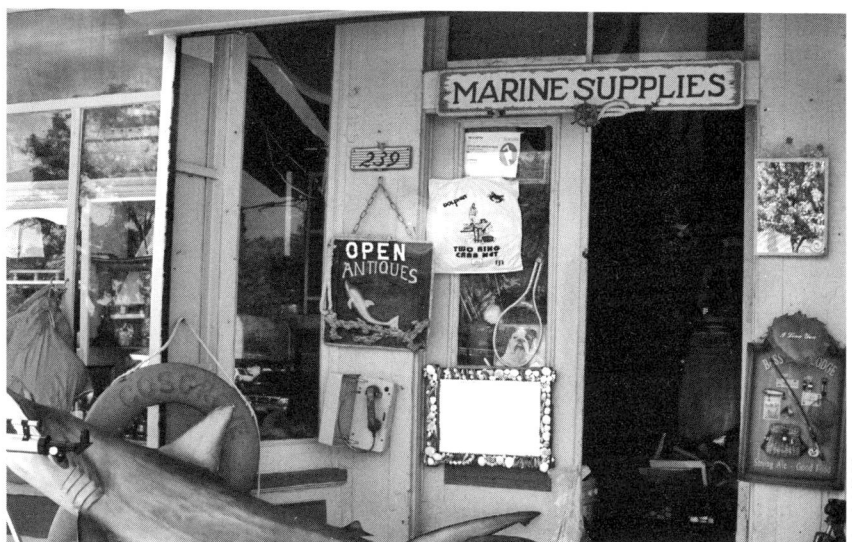

City Island Avenue features an array of quirky and intriguing shops and galleries.

Where to Eat

City Island is best known for its big seafood houses, but there are other more intriguing and affordable options.

If you want to hobnob with City Islanders and enjoy inexpensive home-style cooking, try the **City Island Diner**, 304 City Island Avenue, 718-885-0362. They serve hearty breakfasts, including seventeen omelets with nautical names like Man Overboard, Rigger, and Top Sider. Lunchtime sandwiches, salads, and *Titanic* burgers are similarly satisfying. Look for daily dinner specials and the diner's homemade soups and pies.

The **Black Whale**, 279 City Island Avenue, 718-885-3657, has both a curious history and a delicious menu. The building, according to local lore, was once part of a women's detention center on Hart Island and was brought over to City Island in the late nineteenth or early twentieth century, then plopped down backward with the front of the house facing the garden. From the late 1960s through the early 1980s, this was the place to be for dessert and conversation on Friday nights. Then the restaurant closed. But in 1998, a resident named Bill Kenny revived the Black Whale, with its charming outdoor garden and mouthwatering desserts (including retro treats like hot fudge fondue and the rich but fluffy Black Angel, a hot fudge sundae over angel food cake). He also added a full and well-executed nouveau American lunch and dinner menu, making it the best choice for a moderately priced meal on the island. The Black Whale also screens movies on Tuesday nights, with free popcorn.

The Black Whale serves a delectable orecchiette pasta dish called the Starving Artist in honor of Elliott Glick, who owns the Starving Artist Café and Gallery down the block at 249 City Island Avenue, 718-885-3779. The menu there is secondary to Glick's handcrafted jewelry and the live music he both performs and showcases.

Food is front and center, however, at the **Sugar and Spice Bake Shop**, 536 City Island Avenue, 718-885-9229. Owner Irina Brandler left the publishing industry to study at the French Culinary Institute before opening her shop. Her scones, bread pudding, and creative cupcakes are very popular while she recommends real corned beef hash and sour cream pancakes for breakfast. The shop offers a four-course, prix fixe tasting menu for dinner on the first Thursday of each month. The seats generally fill up months in advance, so reservations are essential. (Cash only and BYOB.)

Another fine alternative to the seafood houses is **Portofino**, 555 City Island Avenue, 718-885-1220, which cooks up northern Italian fare and offers outdoor seating overlooking Eastchester Bay.

If you do crave City Island seafood, follow the locals to **Artie's Steak & Seafood Restaurant**, 394 City Island Avenue, 718-885-9885, which offers fresh ingredients and food that is more about the flavor than the portion size.

Most of City Island's seafood places target the tourist trade and vary little from one to another in their approach. (In fact, one man owns several eateries.) You get a big meal in a big restaurant with big crowds and big prices to boot. You get what you pay for; subtle sauces may not abound, but almost everyone leaves with a doggy bag. Stick with the lobster or the mountainous seafood platters. In general, desserts and side dishes are uneventful. The five hundred seats at **Sammy's Fish Box**, 41 City Island Avenue, 718-885-0920, attract a special-occasion crowd, with a chorus of "Happy Birthday" being sung at any given time. **The Lobster Box**, 34 City Island Avenue, 718-885-1952, has tasteful decor and one of the nicest views of any island restaurant, with a large dining room overlooking Long Island Sound.

You'll find similar fare at the island's other seafood houses, including **The Seashore**, 591 City Island Avenue, 718-885-0300; and the **Lobster House**, 691 Bridge Street, 718-885-1459. Some restaurants offer dock-and-dine facilities, including **Anna's Harbor,** 565 City Island Avenue,

718-885-1373, on Eastchester Bay; and **J.P.'s**, 703 Minneford Avenue, 718-885-3364, on Long Island Sound.

For a fast, cheap seafood meal high in cholesterol and big on panorama try either **Johnny's Reef,** 718-885-2086, or **Tony's on the Pier,** 718-885-1424, both on Belden Point. Johnny's tends to be more popular, but both serve up an endless amount of fried seafood. Beware, however, in the summer, it'll take a long time to reach this far end of the island and then both places will be packed and noisy. So after you get your clam strips, head out to the island's end to enjoy it in the peaceful breeze as you look out on Stepping Stones Lighthouse and, of course, the water.

Island Hopping

🚗 ***By car:*** Take the Throgs Neck, Whitestone, or Robert F. Kennedy (formerly Triborough) Bridges to I-95 North (Bruckner Expressway) to the Orchard Beach/City Island Avenue exit. Follow Shore Parkway into City Island Avenue. The roundabouts on these roadways are confusing, so pay attention. Also remember that driving to the island in summer can be a lesson in patience, as traffic often backs up to the bridge. Once on the island, park on a side street and explore City Island by foot.

🚌 ***By bus:*** Take the 6 train to Pelham Bay Park, then transfer to the BX29 bus to City Island.

8. Hunter and Twin Islands

"It is ironic that there are probably fewer people that actually visit the back parts of Twin Island and Hunter Island, the less improved areas, now than there were in the 1920s. Now that they're accessible and the landmasses are all attached, it is fairly easy to wander up and down these trails, but not that many people do."

—THEODORE KAZIMIROFF JR., NATURALIST AND AUTHOR

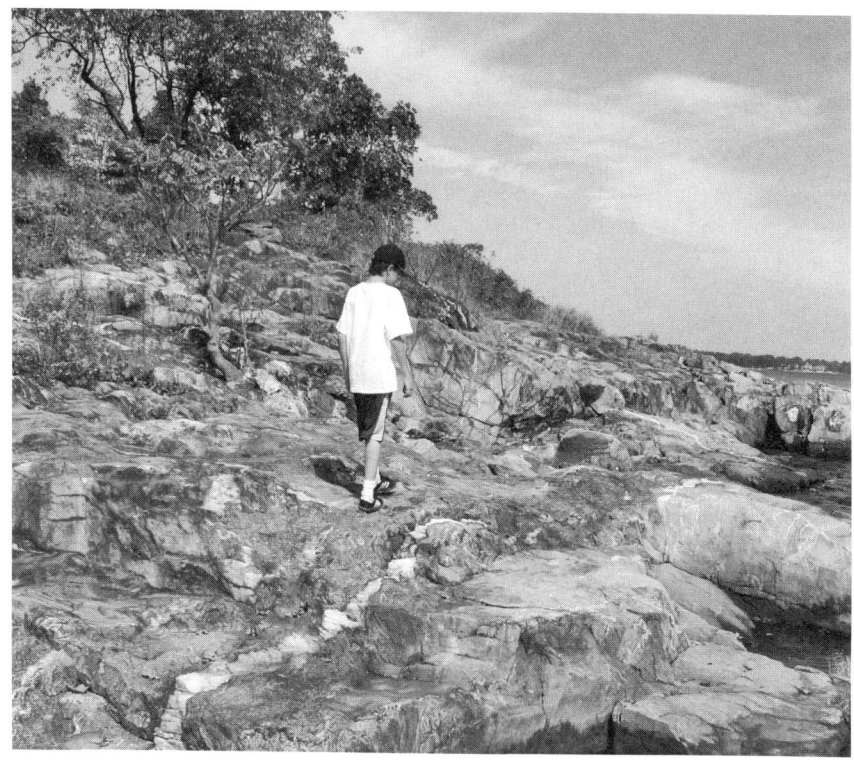

SHARON SEITZ

Hunter and Twin Islands

IN A CITY WHERE CHANGE is the only constant, the northeast corner of the Bronx is an extraordinary reminder of New York as the Native Americans saw it: pristine and picturesque. During the last two centuries, Hunter and Twin Islands have been home to a country squire's luxurious estate, settlement houses for the poor, and campgrounds for working-class immigrants, yet the islands—despite having been connected by landfill to the Bronx—look remarkably similar to the site Thomas Pell bought from the Siwanoy Indians in 1654.

Hunter Island is 166 acres of forest dense with pine, birch, oak, and flowering crab apple trees, as well as wild geraniums, violets, strawberries, and lilies. West of the island is a lagoon separating Hunter from the rest of Pelham Bay Park; to the east is nineteen-acre Twin Island—formerly two small cigar-shaped isles called East and West Twin—and Long Island Sound. Twin features schist rock striped with quartz that was carved out by glaciers thousands of years ago, and is the southern end of a sheet of bedrock that runs up to Maine.

Hunter was called Laap-Ha-Wach King, or "place of stringing beads," by the Siwanoy, who held religious rituals on the island's odd rock formations. In 1654, Pell—for whom Pelham Bay is named—bought the island and became the region's first English settler.

While Hunter Island changed hands several times, all was quiet there until John Hunter bought it for $40,000 around 1810. Hunter had followed his father into business near Wall Street, and he spent another $80,000 building, furnishing, and landscaping an extravagant Shangri-la for his family. Hunter, whose family had emigrated from Ireland, was married to Elizabeth Desbrosses, daughter of James Desbrosses, the warden of Trinity Church and patriarch of one of New York's oldest and wealthiest families. The winged three-story, Georgian-style mansion was made of brick and stone and featured marble front steps, Doric columns, Palladian windows on the second floor, a wide veranda, and terraced gardens leading down to the water. Hunter also cleared many trees for farmland. The mansion's interior boasted extensive wine cellars, imported Turkish carpets, and silk

Remains of the campsites carved from nature by immigrants a century ago can still be found here.

draperies. The highlight was a collection of nearly four hundred paintings by artists like Leonardo da Vinci, Rembrandt, Rubens, and van Dyck—assembled at a cost of $130,000.

Hunter, who also owned part of Hart Island and riparian rights to City Island, moved his family from State Street in Manhattan to their new home around 1813, but their peaceful days soon ended. Shortly after they arrived, Hunter's wife and their son Elias were thrown from a carriage on the island's new stone bridge. Elizabeth struck her head on a post and remained an invalid until her death in 1831.

Hunter, meanwhile, complemented his varied business interests with politics, serving as Westchester County supervisor and, later, a member of the state assembly. A friend of New York governors Silas Wright and DeWitt Clinton, Hunter entertained lavishly. During the most celebrated of these festivities, in 1839, President Martin Van Buren was feted on calf brains au suprême in tomato sauce.

Hunter died in 1852, mandating in his will that his descendants live on the island or sell it. In 1866, Hunter's grandson, John III—a horse racing magnate—sold the property so he could live in Throggs Neck in the Bronx.

To provide parkland for the masses the city bought Hunter and Twin Islands and nearby land in 1888, creating Pelham Bay Park. (Homes in the area, including the Hunter mansion, were leased to charity groups for settlement houses, but were razed in the 1930s by the parks department.) Once the subway reached the region in 1894, German, Scandinavian, Czechoslovakian, and Russian immigrants discovered the islands, building rock shelters and creating summer colonies where they sunbathed and swam. East and West Twin Islands, in particular, attracted boaters and became known as Canoe Beach. After several decades, when vandalism and overcrowding surged, the parks department temporarily banned camping and closed Hunter Island, but the beachgoers kept returning.

In the 1930s, Robert Moses created a magnificent new coastal getaway on Pelham Bay called Orchard Beach. It cost more than $8 million and took four years to complete the project, which joined Hunter Island to Rodman's Neck using two and a half million cubic yards of landfill. The finished beach accommodated two hundred thousand sunbathers, but Moses wanted room for more. In 1947, he linked the Twin Islands to Hunter Island, shifting the focus from the islands' rugged rocks and shady forests to a new sandy shoreline. With tremendous crowds packing Orchard Beach, Hunter and Twin Islands faded into the shadows.

The region's beauty was imperiled when the city turned part of Pelham Bay Park into a garbage dump in 1967. However, a group of local residents led by Dr. Theodore Kazimiroff successfully halted the project. Kazimiroff was a dentist but also a Bronx historian, amateur archaeologist, and naturalist, who was well respected in scientific and academic circles. "Had that been allowed to continue," says his son Theodore Kazimiroff Jr., "Pelham Bay Park would have lost its character, its originality, and its heritage as the home of the former occupants of this country before any European settlers even came here." To prevent further defilement the group pressured the city into creating the Hunter Island Marine Sanctuary.

The younger Kazimiroff says his father's passion for the region stemmed from a childhood friendship he had had with an Algonquin named Joe Two Trees. The native supposedly lived in the Stone Age tradition of his ancestors in the park during the 1920s, where he spent many occasions telling stories to Kazimiroff, then a young Boy Scout. Kazimiroff Jr. popularized this tale in a book titled *The Last Algonquin*. While the younger Kazimiroff claimed that *The Last Algonquin* is a true story, his father never mentioned Joe Two Trees to close friends, and no other Bronx resident ever met the Native American. However fanciful this tale, Kazimiroff's contributions to the region are real and enduring. In 1986, the city established a network of hiking paths on Hunter Island, naming it the Kazimiroff Nature Trail.

Hunter Island's woods and winding nature trails are popular with birders.

Exploring the Islands

Hunter and Twin Islands may be just a few feet from popular Orchard Beach, yet they remain worlds apart. And while the islands have long been connected to each other (and the Bronx) by landfill, they also maintain discrete identities. One park ranger has described them as two unique ecosystems smashed up against each other.

If you prefer a walk in the woods, head over to Hunter Island and its 166 acres of contiguous forest. If scrambling along massive rocks is more your style, Twin Island is for you. Twin is especially beloved by children and makes for a great family outing.

Hunter Island offers an intricate network of trails, including the **Kazimiroff Nature Trail**, John Hunter's old carriage road, and various paved roads. The **Orchard Beach Nature Center**, 718-885-3467 (open Wednesday through Sunday, Memorial Day through Labor Day) has maps available, but don't rely on them too heavily—they don't illustrate every path.

Although the mazelike environment can be frustrating, the island is chock-full of fascinating sights and sounds. Flowers, many originally planted in John Hunter's English-style garden, still flourish here; in spring and summer, orange daylilies, purple wild geraniums, goldenrod, pale blue periwinkles, and grape hyacinth color the woods. Some say a few of the plants are too aggressive, and the city Department of Parks and Recreation has been trying to eliminate the abundance of daylilies in the area.

The parks department took a different role back in 1918 when it planted four acres of Norway spruce to reforest areas Hunter had cleared for meadows. Atop the crest near the center of the island where the mansion once stood, a grove of white pine that Hunter planted as a buffer survives. Owls are fond of these trees, but are difficult to see since they camouflage so well. The brown stone blocks on either side of the trail just northwest of the crest mark the former estate's front gate.

Children love exploring along the rocky coastline of Twin Island (in the foreground) and on Two Trees Island (in the distance).

The island's woods comprise a diverse mixture of trees. Young members include dogwood, crab apple, honeysuckle, black locust, white poplar, and black birch; some of the towering hickory, oak, and tulip trees on the northern end may pre-date the American Revolution. Spring wildflowers include trout lily, Dutchman's breeches, and wood anemone.

From this forest pours forth a wild chorus of sounds. You may hear the call of a red-tailed hawk or the song of a red-winged blackbird. Other members of the choir include wood thrushes, red-eyed vireos, woodpeckers, Eastern towhees, and great horned owls. Rabbits, raccoons, opossums, and wild turkeys may occasionally be found underfoot. And keep an eye out for the coyote found in Manhattan that was released on the island in 2010. Although these animals and birds generally steer clear of humans, the mosquitoes don't. In summer, bring insect repellent or wear long sleeves and pants. Spring and fall are ideal times to visit.

To reach Twin Island, return to the boardwalk and make a left. Walk to the end and step around the side of the fence. There it's easy to give over to the illusion that you're in Maine, not the Bronx. In fact, this metamorphic rock is the southernmost part of the New England mountain range created by glacial erosion. The glaciers polished these rocks, called Hartland Schist, leaving mesmerizing swirls of black, blue, tan, and white; these are garnet and feldspar and thick dikes of quartz.

You may also see traces of long-gone summer colonies—mainly stairs and shelters made from the island's rock and built by immigrants who canoed and played chess and pinochle here. This is a great place to find sea glass and also to explore the tidal pools created by the tide.

The view from this rocky path is glorious: High and Hart Islands to the south, Westchester's David and Huckleberry Islands to the north, and sailboats navigating all around the Sound. The marshland and water attract herons, egrets, osprey, cormorants, and shorebirds in spring and summer and all kinds of ducks, including the bufflehead and goldeneye, in winter. Fishing off Twin Island offers bluefish, bass, and cod.

To your left is a forest with several unmarked trails, and before you, several massive boulders, just before the informal trail bends west toward Hunter Island, where you can walk along salt marshes. Otherwise you can continue to the northern end of Twin Island and cross over at low tide to Two Trees Island. This charming small island is great for exploring with children. (It is, however, common to find a man or two sunning themselves on rocks in extremely skimpy bathing suits.) Litter can sometimes be a problem, but don't let that stop you from combing the area for arrowheads left by Native Americans and artifacts from early European settlers, which are still occasionally found. The mudflat between Twin and Two Trees Island is also a great spot for finding fiddler crabs and tasty, salty glasswort (a seaside herb) and beautiful sea lavender in spring and summer.

The **parks department** offers occasional free tours of Hunter and Twin Islands. For a calendar of events, go to www.nycgovparks.org.

Island Hopping

By car: Take the New England Thruway to the Orchard Beach exit or the Hutchinson River Parkway to the City Island/Orchard Beach exit. Follow the signs to Orchard Beach, and park in the far left corner of the parking lot. There is a fee from the week before Memorial Day to the week after Labor Day. From the parking lot, walk to the boardwalk, and turn left to Hunter and Twin Islands.

By bus: In summer, buses drop off passengers at the Orchard Beach parking lot. From the Bronx, take the BX5 or BX12. From Manhattan, take the 6 train to Pelham Bay Park and change to the BX5 or BX12 bus. From Queens, take the QBX1 to Pelham Bay Park and change to the BX5 or BX12. From the parking lot, walk to the boardwalk and turn left to Hunter and Twin Islands.

Between Labor Day and Memorial Day, you must take the BX29 to the City Island traffic circle and then walk northeast for fifteen minutes to Orchard Beach.

For further travel information, call the parks department at 718-430-1890.

9. Hart Island

"It's an effort to make visible the people who are invisible"
—MELINDA HUNT, FOUNDER OF THE HART ISLAND PROJECT, WHICH HAS
CREATED A DATABASE OF PEOPLE BURIED IN THE CITY'S POTTER'S
FIELD AND SERVED AS AN ADVOCATE FOR THEIR RELATIVES

MELINDA HUNT

Hart Island

AT ITS WORST, NEW YORK can be a cold and anonymous place, where the lonely and unattached can easily get lost in the big city shuffle. In the end, these friendless or destitute New Yorkers may be buried in a long trench, resting alongside with the city's other lost souls. This is Hart Island.

The city has long had a potter's field for burying unclaimed bodies, and this forlorn cemetery has typically been pushed out of sight and thus out of mind. In the eighteenth century, burial grounds for the unknown and indigent were established in Lower Manhattan near what is today the Surrogate Court building on Chambers Street. As the city expanded northward, the potter's field began its procession uptown, first to what is now Washington Square, then to the current sites first of Madison Square, then Bryant Park, and the Waldorf-Astoria, before being pushed off Manhattan Island to Randall's and Ward's Islands in the 1840s. In 1869, the cemetery was sent to its final resting place on Hart Island, the easternmost spot in the Bronx.

On April 20, 1869, Louisa Van Slyke, twenty-four, died without family to claim her body. She became the first person buried on this 101-acre island, a half mile west of City Island. Born at sea, she died in New York's Charity Hospital on Welfare Island. Storytellers often adopt her bare-bones tale as the island's defining symbol, obliging Van Slyke to carry the weight of the 850,000 who have followed.

While many people think of potter's fields as home to John and Jane Does, they comprise merely one-tenth of Hart Island's adult burials. The rest are have-nots who simply couldn't afford a funeral, bodies that have otherwise gone unclaimed, or the remains of people who have donated their bodies to science. The phrase potter's field comes from Matthew 27:3–8 in the New Testament, which describes the aftermath of Christ's crucifixion: "Then Judas, which had betrayed Him, saw that he was condemned, repented himself, and brought again the thirty pieces of silver to the chief priests . . . and they took counsel, and bought with them the potter's field to bury strangers in."

Hart Island's gravediggers are inmates from nearby Rikers Island—only nonviolent misdemeanants are eligible, and the "Ghoul Squad" considers the work, outdoors and away from the jail, a plum assignment. They are

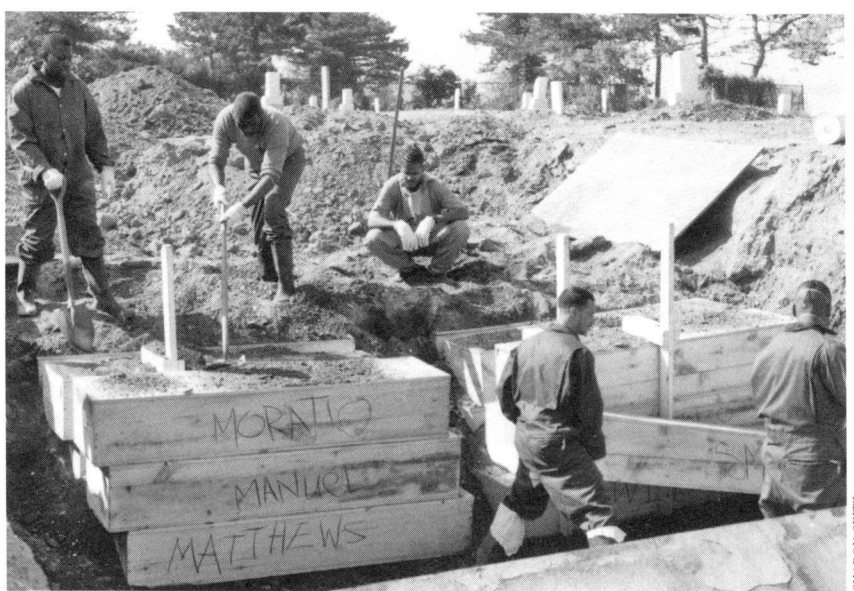

Rikers Island inmates bury the dead on Hart Island.

paid fifty cents an hour for their labor. The dead arrive by truck four times a week and are ferried over from City Island. Inmates in orange and white striped prison jumpsuits, some wearing masks to ward off the fetor of corpses, work seriously and efficiently. (Along with six officers, fewer than twenty-five inmates work on Hart Island, some on this detail, the others on maintaining the grounds.)

In 2009, 1,325 people were buried on the island; in 2008, it was 1,507, and in 2006, the total was 1,428. The young are memorialized by a 1902 granite cross reading HE CALLETH HIS CHILDREN BY NAME. (There are virtually no Jews in the potter's field; local Jewish organizations bury their indigent dead in private cemeteries.)

Burials on Hart Island were once confined to two plots, since bodies like these that have not been embalmed disintegrate quickly. The fields were then turned over and reused to bury a new crop of corpses. In recent decades, the practice was ended. The cemetery today is spreading across the island, with old buildings being demolished and land being cleared for new trenches.

The fields of the dead are dotted with short white markers, each denoting 150 bodies buried three deep in two rows. The plain boxes are staggered in the trenches to make for easier removal, since a body can be disinterred for up to eight years after burial if relatives or friends come forward to claim it. (An average of seventy-two per year were disinterred from 2007 through 2009.) Amputated limbs, gallbladders, and other medical waste are buried in a separate hole.

While most interred on Hart Island took their stories to the grave, some memorable—and possibly apocryphal—anecdotes do survive: The so-called Crypt Swindler, Robert Mowatt, was buried there in 1933, after a life of selling phony deeds for crypts in New Jersey mausoleums; one man was there thirty-three years until his son struck oil, became a millionaire, and had his father's body reinterred in a cemetery; a World War I veteran given a pauper's burial was disinterred after French nuns—to whom he had sent small donations for nursing him during the war—learned of his fate. His body was flown to France and buried in the convent cemetery.

While the morbid details are undeniably compelling, there is more to the history of Hart Island than its potter's field. The Siwanoy tribe sold Hart Island to Thomas Pell in 1654. The name Hart Island began appearing in the 1770s. Over the years, it was often mistakenly called Hart's Island, though a Mr. Hart never owned this one. The name comes either from a mistaken belief by British cartographers that the island was shaped like a heart (and the name was then corrupted) or, more likely, because hart is Middle English for "deer," which once may have lived there.

During the first half of the nineteenth century, the island became "a favorite pugilistic hideaway," according to Elliott Gorn's book *The Manly Art*.

Although bare-knuckled boxing was legal in New York, fights were often subject to raids by policemen searching for gambling, drunkenness, and hooliganism. Hart Island's biggest bout was a grudge match held in 1842 between Irishman James "Yankee" Sullivan and Englishman Billy Bell for a $300 purse.

More than six thousand people sailed out to the island, or, as the *New York Daily Express* put it, "A gang of loafers and rowdies went out of the city yesterday to see a fisticuffins." They witnessed a brutal twenty-four-round, thirty-eight-minute slugfest dominated from start to finish by the 150-pound Sullivan. According to legend, the city's crime rate dropped during the fight.

Part of Hart Island was then bought in the 1860s by the federal government for a Civil War training ground; more than fifty thousand Union soldiers were instructed there, and a full-dress parade was held for the public every day.

Hart Island became the potter's field after the city paid the Hunter family

FROM THE COLLECTION OF MELINDA HUNT

A view of Hart Island in the 1860s before it became the city's potter's field.

(which had also owned Hunter Island) $75,000 for part of the island in 1868. (Oddly, this made it part of New York City before the rest of the Bronx.)

On the remaining acreage, a diverse array of institutions—including an industrial school that took boys off the streets and trained them for the merchant marine and navy, a lunatic asylum, an almshouse, and a school for traffic violators—came and went during the next century.

Life and death peacefully coexisted, albeit in unusual fashion. The *New York Times* wrote in 1880 that when students at the industrial school "behaved themselves well through the week and the weather is fine, the teachers let them have a half-holiday on Saturday afternoons and go out and play among the graves."

In 1895, the Department of Correction established a jail workhouse on the island for aged and infirm inmates, misdemeanants, and drug addicts. A youth reformatory was added a decade later, but was subsequently relocated to prevent youngsters from being corrupted by older inmates.

The oddest potential juxtaposition for Hart Island was shot down in 1925 when the potter's field and the jail were almost joined by an amusement park. Solomon Riley, owner of Spectacle Realty, owned four acres of the island and set about building a playland for Harlem blacks barred from "whites-only" amusement parks in Rye and Dobbs Ferry. Riley planned to bring customers to the island using a fleet of sixty motorboats and to build the park without a fence right next to the prison. This didn't sit well with correction officials, who feared the great influx of visitors and their proximity to the prison would cause a rash of escapes and contraband smuggling.

Riley planned, nonetheless, to open his amusement park on July 4. His workmen constructed two hundred feet of boardwalk, a dance hall, and eight boardinghouses, and began remaking an old iceboat into a bathing pavilion. Newspapers dubbed the affair "Hylan's Folly," because Mayor John Hylan had passed up the opportunity to purchase the tract from the Hunter family when they sold it in 1922. The city ultimately halted the project because of the prison security issue, and paid Riley $144,015 for the land he had bought for $35,000.

During World War II, the 535 workhouse prisoners were moved to Rikers Island so the navy could use Hart for disciplinary barracks. After the war, overcrowding on Rikers Island forced the run-down Hart workhouse—some buildings dated back to the Civil War—to reopen. Except from 1951 through 1954, when the city housed the homeless there over the loud protests of City Island residents, the Hart Island workhouse operated until 1966.

There were two noteworthy additions to the island during the 1950s and 1960s. The army installed its first Nike missile base—the country's principal defense against air attacks—in 1955. The twenty-one-foot missiles traveled at supersonic speeds, and were capable of destroying any plane within thirty miles. They were stored underground and required the installation of a generator powerful enough to provide electricity for a town of ten thousand. Only six years later, the army—in response to rapidly changing technologies and defense strategies—removed the missiles and pulled out.

The other newcomer was far more benign. In 1960, developer Marvin Kratter donated lights and twenty-two hundred seats for a workhouse ball field. These were no ordinary lights and seats. They were historical artifacts salvaged from Brooklyn's Ebbets Field before Kratter's wrecking ball struck. At the May 27 dedication of Kratter Field, 1,340 inmates watched their Wildcats take on soldiers from the missile base. The game ended in a 5–5 tie at 3:50 PM, because it was time for a prison head count.

In 1967, after the prison closed, Phoenix House opened a drug rehabilitation program on Hart Island. In a small way, Phoenix House fulfilled Solomon Riley's dream of entertaining the masses on the island, by sponsoring annual drug- and alcohol-free festivals featuring carnival rides, old movies, and big-name musicians like the Velvet Underground and Janis Ian. The events drew crowds of ten thousand. But in 1976, Phoenix House moved back to Manhattan, a decision based on the cost of ferry transportation and a philosophical shift toward integrating participants in the larger community.

Since Phoenix House's departure, life has been fairly quiet on the island. In 1982, Mayor Ed Koch established a small work camp for misdemeanants, but was unable to persuade judges to sentence enough prisoners there. Six years later, he tried reviving both a prison and a homeless shelter but was shouted down by homeless advocates opposed to the isolation, and by City Island residents who feared more traffic, sewage, and water-pressure woes for their community.

In the meantime, Hart Island remains a paradox: Standing in the green fields flecked with gulls, geese, and wildflowers, surrounded by groves of trees and a spectacular view of Long Island Sound, it is difficult to reconcile the vitality of nature with the constant specter of death.

Death, even symbolically, looms everywhere on Hart Island. An elaborate stone fence surrounds a sixteen-foot obelisk dedicated to Union soldiers who died there. The men perished from disease, not combat. Their corpses were exhumed from the island's graves in the twentieth century and reburied elsewhere in formal cemeteries. The island is also littered with abandoned structures. Gutted jail administration buildings greet the ferry on the eastern shore. A greenhouse once operated by recovering drug addicts is overrun with weeds. A Catholic church, built in 1939 and emptied of its stained-glass windows, altar, and pews, feels cavernous. Empty Nike missile silos on another road sit across from a thirty-foot-high monument erected in 1948, its white paint flaking and its golden inscription, PEACE, fading.

In recent decades the Hart Island dead have had someone to remember them and someone to fight for them. Since 1991, a prayer group affiliated with St. Benedict's Parish in the Bronx has traveled to the island each May, on Ascension Thursday, to say prayers for this city of the dead. Around that same time, a New York artist named Melinda Hunt became interested in the island and its potter's field.

"It says something about America, these people who are invisible but who are part of who we are," she says.

Hunt created a book, a documentary and ultimately, the Hart Island Project (www.hartisland.net); using the Freedom of Information Act, she has begun building a public database of people buried there—something the Department of Correction has never provided. She has publicly taken the DOC to task for their secretiveness—access to the island is extremely limited for the public, and the press is explicitly barred—and for the numerous mistakes made in burials and recordkeeping through the years.

"There has been poor management and poor leadership on the part of the City Council, the Mayor, and the DOC," says Hunt, who has effectively been banished from the island since 2007. "There is no oversight. They are often unable to retrieve bodies."

In recent years, a group called the Interfaith Friends of Potter's Field has partnered with another organization called Picture the Homeless, and together they have also been pressuring the DOC for more access to Hart Island.

The DOC says it is doing more for families. Spokesman Stephen Morello says the correction staff "devotes considerable time to assisting families" and adds that the department has constructed a small gazebo for visitors holding memorial services. Hunt questions why correction officers—who are trained and paid to work with inmates—are handling these jobs and points out that the gazebo is not near where the burials take place. She adds that having grieving parents trying to track a missing child or even the body of a stillborn baby shouldn't be forced to navigate the DOC bureaucracy. (Morello cites "security and liability" as reasons for restricting access to the entire island, though there is no imminent danger that would require such strict security measures.)

Meanwhile, four days a week the ferry never ceases in its deliveries, conveying the plain white truck bearing the words NEW YORK CITY HEALTH AND HOSPITALS CORPORATION. The inmates unload each pine crate from the truck, scrawl a number and surname—Hernandez, Moratio, Smith, Lorenzo—onto the box with black crayon, and then drill the numbers into the wood for good measure. The primitive caskets are lowered into a long mass grave and covered with dirt.

"It's like a warning for people who want to do better for themselves," explained one inmate while working on the island. "I've seen my last name on one box. It's kind of scary, it makes you think. I don't want to wind up here."

10. Forgotten Islands of the Bronx

High Island - Goose Island - Rat Island - Hog Island - East and South Nonations - The Blauzes - Chimney Sweeps - Cuban Ledge - Codling Island - Blizzard Island - Wright's Island

Forgotten Islands of the Bronx

High Island

IT WAS, TO SAY THE LEAST, an inauspicious debut. In 1967, CBS was set to kick off a new venture, WCBS NEWSRADIO 88. The station would transmit from a soaring 541-foot radio tower owned by WCBS and WNBC on tiny High Island, just north of City Island in the Bronx.

The day before the launch, a small, private Piper Cherokee plane crashed into the tower. The plane, flying from East Hampton to LaGuardia Airport in a blinding storm, was unauthorized to fly that day and plunged into Long Island Sound, killing all six on board. The crash demolished all but the bottom sixty feet of the tower's steel frame, squelching transmission. Remnants of the smashed antenna remained strewn about the island for decades.

Fortunately for CBS, several competitors loaned the station transmitters until a two-hundred-foot antenna (now the backup) was hastily erected three days later. Eventually, a 529-foot tower was built as the main transmitter. (Today both WCBS and WFAN 66, a sports station, broadcast from these towers.)

Of course, the tower wasn't the only High Island structure knocked down in the 1960s. To make way for the new radio stations (and their towers), numerous bungalows and trees on the island had to be cleared. The island had housed a small summer community created in 1913 when Nora and Jack Beatty, the island's caretakers, began renting out campsites to earn extra money. (The Beattys lived in a two-story wooden farmhouse on the six-acre island.) In 1925, a new family bought the island and built twenty bungalows, providing summertime refuge to about one hundred people.

The island retreat had none of the luxuries or distractions of the mainland. Before a footbridge was built in 1928, residents walked from City Island to High Island via a sandbar at low tide or took a boat or a ten-cent ferry at high tide. (A steel footbridge was built in the late 1990s when the wooden one burned.) Later, residents parked their cars on City Island, transporting furniture, groceries, and other necessities to the island by wagon. About eight families became so attached to the bungalows that they stayed year-round. In 1960, they unsuccessfully fought a city zoning change that enabled the radio stations to buy the island and relocate their towers from a remote Westchester islet that required costly round-the-clock ferry service.

When the radio station took over, it hired a caretaker live on the island but these days visiting WCBS workers take care of maintenance and security, and High Island sits uninhabited.

Goose Island

Not much ever happened on tiny Goose Island in the Hutchinson River throughout the modern history of New York City. These days, the island is such a happening place—for birds, anyway—that you can follow life there online.

In 2010, the Harbor Herons Project counted 111 nesting pairs on Goose Island: fifty pairs of great egrets, thirty-three pairs of snowy egrets, and twenty-eight pairs of black-crowned night herons. As on some of the other nesting islands, evidence of various threats—raccoon, opossum, and humans—have been spotted here. The first two enjoy dining on eggs, while the latter is simply disturbing and often causes birds to nest elsewhere. To encourage the humans to stay interested but to stay away, New York City Audubon set up a live camera fixed on active nests on Goose Island. The camera operates during nesting season, approximately March through September, and can be viewed at www.nycaudubon.org/projects/harborherons/WebCam.

Most of the information on the tiny isles of the Bronx came from John McNamara, who died in 2004 at the age of ninety-two. McNamara was one of his borough's leading historians, spending decades walking the streets, kayaking the waterways, and researching and writing about the Bronx.

Rat Island

As unlikely as it seems, this two-acre rock halfway between Hart and City Islands was a mini-colony for writers and artists early in the twentieth century. It was also a resting place for convicts escaping from Hart Island, and in the nineteenth century, it briefly hosted a hospital during a yellow fever scare in Pelham.

Hog Island

This L-shaped island just south of the Westchester County border was usually sold as a package deal with Hunter Island. The city bought Hog Island in the late nineteenth century, and a beachcombers' colony sprung up. One woman, Marion Laing, claimed squatter's rights, staying there until her death on September 12, 1930. A tablet to her memory was placed on the island, reading THIS ISLAND WAS HER PARADISE.

East and South Nonations

Legend has it that Dutch and English colonists were unwilling to fight over these two adjoining reefs in the Sound, north of Hart Island, so they became islands owned by no nation. Others say they were originally spelled "Notations," meaning a footnote, or abbreviation.

The Blauzes

The name of these mussel-colored reefs west of Hart Island derives from either the Dutch *de blauwtjes*, meaning "little blue ones," or the Old English word *blazer*, meaning "marker." Early mariners may have used the reefs as guides into City Island; less observant sailors wrecked their ships there.

Chimney Sweeps

Like The Blauzes to their north, these two tiny reefs caused many shipwrecks. Positioned side by side like two stones tied together, these isles resemble a primitive cleaning tool once used by chimney sweeps. Another explanation for the appellation is that the gray humps are as dingy looking as a soot-covered sweep. In the early 1900s, a German family lived on the islands, where they built a tavern attracting boaters eager for refreshment.

Cuban Ledge

South of Rodman's Neck in Eastchester Bay, this islet can be seen only at low tide. Several legends attempt to explain its name, one originating in 1898, when a crew threw its cargo of rocks overboard after learning that the USS *Maine* had been blown up in Havana Harbor. The sailors went ashore and enlisted in the Spanish–American War, leaving the rocks to form a reef or ledge. Others say the islet is cigar-shaped like Cuba, while a different tale says the island was so named when the intoxicated crew of the *Cuban Lady* ran aground there in the 1880s.

Codling Island

This former island, in what is today Eastchester, was created around 1880 when a portion of the Hutchinson River was straightened, severing and isolating a piece of mainland property belonging to George F. Codling. The old channel fell into disuse and silted up, connecting the island to the mainland by 1900.

Blizzard Island

Located in the mouth of the Hutchinson River, this low, rocky ledge was named for David Blizzard, who in the 1860s rented boats and sold tackle directly opposite the island on Tallapoosa Point. Blizzard Island once supported the eastern arch of the original Pelham bridge, built in the late 1880s. The island, eventually joined with landfill to the mainland, is today part of Pelham Bay Park just east of Shore Road.

Wright's Island

Known as Horse Neck in the seventeenth century and Locust Island a hundred years later, the island became known as Wright's Island after Captain George Wright purchased it in 1830. Three generations of Wrights lived on this fifteen-acre island until 1920. The family attached it to the mainland in the 1880s by a narrow causeway. The island was renamed Locust Point (for the swamp trees that grew there) in the 1920s, when it was sold and broken up into residential lots. Marsh draining and landfill operations eventually connected it to the mainland. The approach to the Throgs Neck Bridge, which opened in 1961, is today on what was Wright's Island.

Part IV

East River

ROOSEVELT ISLAND • RANDALL'S AND WARD'S ISLANDS •
RIKERS ISLAND • NORTH AND SOUTH BROTHER ISLANDS •
FORGOTTEN ISLANDS OF THE EAST RIVER

Despite the name, the East River is technically a saltwater estuary or tidal strait, linking Upper New York Bay with Long Island Sound. The sixteen-mile stretch, which separates Manhattan from Brooklyn and Queens, is densely populated. From the Brooklyn-Battery Tunnel to the Throgs Neck Bridge, there are eight bridges, eleven tunnels (for cars and subways), a footbridge, and a tram. Notorious for its roiling currents, the water is home to seven islands. Newtown Creek, which branches out from the East River and ends in Maspeth, bisects Brooklyn and Queens.

11. Roosevelt Island

"Is it possible to rescue Blackwell's Island from prosaic prisoners, unappreciative idiots and small-pox patients, careless of scenery and heedless of aesthetics? Perhaps not within the present decade, but when the population of New York shall have outgrown its present limits, and shall clamor for other islands to conquer, the paupers and convicts of Blackwell's Island will no longer be allowed to monopolize that charming spot."

—*New York Times*, June 1, 1872

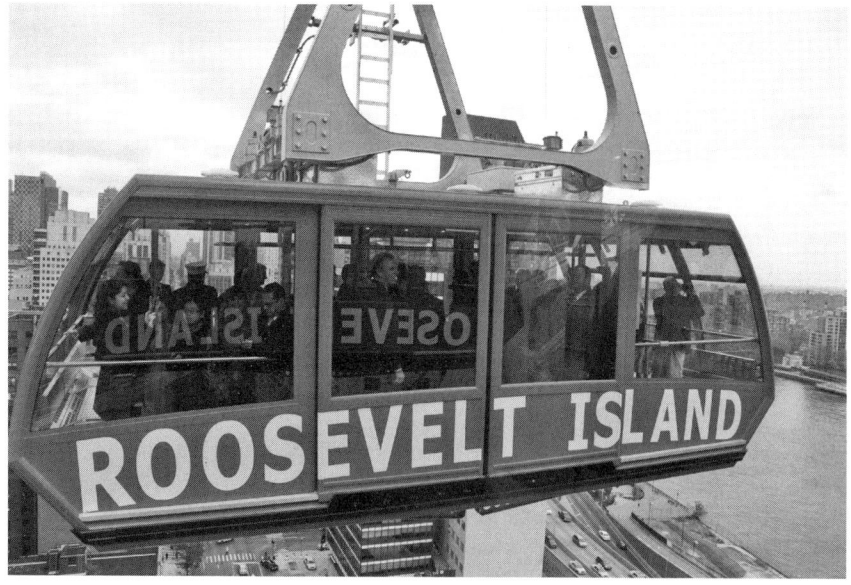

JUDITH BERDY

Roosevelt Island

FOR DECADES, the long, narrow island in the East River was a place no New Yorker wanted to be. Blackwell's Island was a kind of dark inverse to Emma Lazarus's famous poem, a place where the tired, the poor, and the wretched refuse lost their freedom, taken from society and tossed inside impersonal warehouses.

For decades, this East River island was a place most New Yorkers never even thought about. Welfare Island was a failed hospital complex, with unrealized plans, decaying buildings, and underfinanced institutions.

These days, this same island is a place that thousands of New Yorkers love calling home. Sure, Roosevelt Island's Main Street is ugly, and there are only a few shops and restaurants. Concerns about the island's development and complaints about the bizarre bureaucracy that oversees the island are frequent topics of conversation, yet the lush green spaces and marvelous waterfront and skyline views usually outshine the inconveniences and soften the island's dark past.

The aboriginal name of this two-mile-long, eight-hundred-foot-wide strip—which today parallels Manhattan from Forty-eighth to Eighty-fifth streets—is unclear. Many sources call it Minnahanonck, but Stokes's *The Iconography of Manhattan*, perhaps the most comprehensive source on early New York, says Minnahanonck was actually Randall's Island. Dutch settlers referred to Roosevelt Island as Varckens, or Hog Island, and farmed it as early as 1639. After the English captured New York, King Charles granted the island to Captain John Manning, sheriff of New York, in 1668, but this reward for his loyalty later became a hideaway of disgrace.

In 1673, England and Holland were at war, and Manning was commanding Fort James (formerly Fort Amsterdam) when he noticed a fleet of Dutch vessels approaching from Staten Island. With only eighty soldiers available, Manning tried negotiating to buy time, but the Dutch bombarded the fort, and Manning hastily surrendered. The war ended the following year, the English regained New York, and in 1675 Manning was put on trial for giving up Fort James. With his life at stake, Manning pleaded guilty to cowardice and treason, but beseeched King Charles for leniency. At city

Roosevelt Island

1. Smallpox Hospital ruin
2. Strecker Laboratory ruin
3. Tram dock
4. Subway station F
5. Meditation Steps
6. Blackwell House
7. Chapel of the Good Shepherd
8. Octagon Park
9. Octagon
10. Lighthouse Park
11. Lighthouse

Manhattan

East River — West Channel

Island

MAIN STREET

East River — East Channel

36th AVENUE BRIDGE

AERIAL TRAMWAY

Queens

Roosevelt

QUEENSBORO BRIDGE

N.J.

Enlarged area

N.Y.

Atlantic Ocean

0   miles   1/2

Paul Woodward, © The Countryman Press

hall, Manning was publicly stripped to the waist, and his hands were bound with irons. Ten musketeers stood ready awaiting the command to fire. But at the last minute Manning was spared execution. Instead he was condemned to suffer humiliation and disbarment; his sword was broken into three pieces over his head and he was banned from serving the Crown.

The exiled captain lived out his final ten years entertaining friends on his East River island. "His house became a synonyme of hospitality; his wit was a proverb, and he was pronounced the most elegant and agreeable of hosts," wrote Felix Oldboy in 1893 in *A Tour Around New York and My Summer Acre.*

When Manning died in 1685, his island passed to his stepdaughter, Mary Manningham, and her husband, Robert Blackwell, a merchant from Elizabethtown, New Jersey. In 1784, James and Jacob Blackwell, who advertised the island as "agreeably situated," and "one of the most healthy situations in the state," put it up for sale. Fish and fowl were plentiful; there was an orchard with 450 fruit trees, two small houses, a barn, bakery, fowl house, and cider mill.

There were, however, no takers. Jacob tried persuading the city to buy the island for a potter's field in 1797, but couldn't close the deal. The Blackwell family built a house on the island around this time period but finally sold it in 1823. Even this arrangement was short lived. When the new owner died there two years later the island, due to mortgage foreclosure, reverted to the Blackwells . . . until the city found a use for it.

As New York's population exploded and social problems became a pressing issue, the city turned to institutionalization to preserve order in society. Close at hand yet isolated, the city's islands were perfectly suited for segregating outcasts. Authorities emphasized the benevolence of their deed, maintaining that these beautiful islands offered a healing environment for the sick and a place of reflection for the vicious.

The city, which was just developing Fourteenth Street, purchased Blackwell's, its first East River island, in 1828 for a new prison. The island was reached by traveling north on the old Boston Road, which began where Park Row is today, up the eastern side of Manhattan Island. The road was often muddy and inaccessible. Then came an arduous climb down a steep bluff to the river across which a ferry journeyed to the island.

The prison—with 500 cells for males and 256 for females—was built in the center of the island. When its cornerstone was laid on September 10, 1828, there was already talk of adding facilities. "A more eligible spot for health, cleanliness and safety could not have been selected for the erection of all public buildings, which are supported at the public expense," the

Evening Post reported the Committee on the Almshouse as saying. "We hope in a few years to see the madhouse and hospital removed to the island."

The city lunatic asylum opened in 1841, followed by the almshouse in 1847 and, in 1849, the island's first hospital. Penitentiary Hospital treated both law-abiders and convicts, most of them afflicted with infectious conditions, especially venereal disease. The hospital's sinister name was changed to Island Hospital in 1857. A workhouse was added to the prison in 1850.

City Hospital, also called Penitentiary Island and Charity Hospital, served both Blackwell's Island prisoners and the city's poor.

But the government's claim of an island oasis for the needy proved hollow. In 1842, Charles Dickens visited several of the institutions, including the lunatic asylum. While impressed with its "handsome" architecture, especially its octagon tower and elegant five-story spiral staircase, Dickens was disturbed by the disorder and overcrowding.

"The moping idiot, cowering down with long disheveled hair; the gibbering maniac, with his hideous laugh and pointed finger; the vacant eye, the fierce wild face, the gloomy picking of the hands and lips, and munching of the nails: there they were all, without disguise, in naked ugliness and horror," he wrote in *American Notes*. "The terrible crowd with which these halls and galleries were filled so shocked me, that I abridged my stay within the shortest limits, and declined to see that portion of the building in which the refractory and violent were under closer restraint."

The island's rural character had evolved into a nightmarish netherworld crowded with institutions built by inmate labor from granite quarried from the island's bedrock. And there was more to come. In 1858, Charity (later City) Hospital opened, replacing the flimsy Island Hospital, which had been destroyed by fire. James Renwick Jr., architect of the island's Small-pox Hospital and St. Patrick's Cathedral in Manhattan, designed City Hospital. Built in the French Second Empire style with a distinguished mansard roof and two wings flanking the center, City Hospital was the largest hospital in the country—three stories high, 354 feet long, and 122 feet wide, with a capacity of twelve hundred patients.

Despite its magnificent architecture, City Hospital added to the island's ugly reputation. The nurses and servants were mostly workhouse prisoners who often stayed after their terms ended, "receiving no wages but a pretty liberal allowance of whiskey, the bung of the whiskey barrel being under the control of the physicians," according to a City Hospital history published in 1904.

Among the other hospitals opened between 1856 and 1867 was one each for the treatment of fever, smallpox, epilepsy, paralysis, and "incurables." All told, there were eleven institutions by 1872. Patients were often referred to as inmates, although their only crime was being poor or sick. Many were foreign-born and from the city's ghettos, where disease, poverty, and crime prevailed. Women in the insane asylum outnumbered men two to one, in part because husbands frequently punished insubordinate wives by having them temporarily committed.

It was no secret that Blackwell's Island was a rude purgatory of sorrow and suffering. In 1878, a city investigation revealed severe overcrowding in many of the institutions. A year later, after a probe into mistreatment of patients by nurses in the lunatic asylum, the board of physicians and surgeons called for a complete reorganization of the asylum. But little changed.

Blackwell's Island "is a city in which all the misery, despair and vicious-ness of the metropolis are epitomized," wrote the *Daily News* (no relation to the current tabloid) in 1884. "Within its granite walls the pauper and mad-man, the wrecked creature whose life is wasting on a hopeless sick-bed and the moral leper, who were better dead, lie cheek by jowl, wards of the community which casts them out but cannot rid itself of them."

Three years later, some reforms were made after fearless reporter Nellie Bly exposed abuses in the asylum (see Historical Detour: Nellie Bly—Committed to the Truth). In 1890, a follow-up investigation by the city found the asylum orderly, but still overcrowded. (It also discovered prison inmates sharing cells a mere three and a half by seven feet in size.) The asylum was moved to Ward's Island in 1894, and a year later Metropolitan Hospital occupied this magnificent building with the octagon tower.

By the time the Strecker Memorial Laboratory—the country's first center for studying pathology—opened on the island in 1892, most of Blackwell's older buildings were antiquated, especially the crowded penitentiary. To improve prison conditions and remove the unfair criminal stigma borne by patients in the charitable institutions, the city planned to relocate the new penitentiary to Rikers Island and turn Blackwell's Island into a hospital compound. The talk produced little action, however, and in 1921, with the hospital park still not built, the city changed the island's name to Welfare Island in an effort to erase its horrific reputation.

Before the prison was finally shoved off to Rikers in 1935, one last showdown at the penitentiary uncovered a tightly guarded Pandora's box of graft and corruption. When reform-minded Fiorello La Guardia became mayor, ending Tammany Hall's reign, he appointed Austin H. MacCormick commissioner of correction. On January 24, 1934, MacCormick and his men made a surprise raid on what MacCormick called "the worst prison in the world," cracking a highly organized system of drug smuggling and mob domination. "Boss gangsters lived in luxury, swaggered around, and at the same time there was an almost incredible condition of misery and degeneracy," wrote the New York Herald-Tribune.

Racketeers and their cronies—about 500 out of the prison population of 1,658—feasted on steaks, chops, and fine desserts in relatively lavish cells. Joseph Rao, the Italian leader, Harlem racketeer, and alleged henchman of "Dutch" Schultz, ruled from headquarters he had established in the administration building's hospital quarters, where only six of fifty "patients" were actually ill. Rao had a garden and pet milk goat and enjoyed expensive cigars, silk robes, lilac toilet water, and monogrammed stationery. The Irish mob leader, Edward Cleary, was less ostentatious. He kept a German police dog he called Screw-Hater (slang for "guard hater") in his dormitory hospital cell, along with a cache of smuggled goods, including fresh cranberries, pickled herring, potatoes, milk, and liquor. Both kingpins kept large cotes filled with homing pigeons believed to have trafficked notes and drugs into and out of the prison. Cleary's cote was built right into his hospital room. The bulk of the prisoners were forced into servitude. They often waited on the big shots, were fed bland stew in the mess hall, and shared cells because of overcrowding.

The two mob leaders and sixty-six cronies were arrested in Mac-

Cormick's sweep and put in solitary confinement. Warden Joseph McCann was suspended, but permitted to resign without facing a departmental trial. The court dismissed criminal charges, ruling that McCann's incompetence and neglect of duty did not constitute a crime.

Historical Detour: Big Guns in the Big House

One was corpulent, the other voluptuous, but both did time in an island prison. Tammany Hall leader William Marcy "Boss" Tweed went to the Blackwell's Island Penitentiary in 1874. Actress Mae West was confined to the Welfare Island workhouse in 1927. Neither personality lived the rigorous life of a convict, however. They were jailed in style.

After Tweed and his ring defrauded the city of millions of dollars, the 280-pound politician was sentenced to twelve years in the Blackwell's Island Penitentiary. He was furnished a room away from the main cellblock—a relatively luxurious "apartment" with a desk, library, and other frills, including a six-by-eight-foot window facing south, from which Tweed observed the city he had plundered. He received many visitors, including his private secretary, who continued working for him. The apartment entrance was unlocked, and there was rarely a guard within fifty feet of the front door.

Even after newspapers reported Tweed's preferential treatment, little changed. Six months later, the warden ordered Tweed to wear prison garb and suffer the same food and lodging as the other prisoners, but he was released soon afterward, having served only one year. He was later arrested on civil charges and sent to Manhattan's Ludlow Street jail, where—except for an escape to Spain—he again enjoyed a privileged existence until his death in 1878.

Mae West was jailed for ten days for obscenity after starring in a play she had coauthored called *Sex*. She was spared from dormitory life and given a private cell and a job sweeping and making beds—a relatively easy assignment. Her biggest complaint, however, was with the clothes she had to wear.

"For Miss West the change from the silks and crepes and sheer stockings of the average well-dressed woman about the city to the prison outfit was a shock," wrote the *New York Times*, "but she suppressed her instinctive recoil and resolutely slipped into the uni-

form." West wore the coarse blue cotton dress and heavy cotton
stockings, but eventually purchased a pair of white stockings at the
workhouse commissary. She wrote a poem about the uncomfortable,
fuzzy prison underwear and dedicated it to Warden Harry Schleth.

When she was released, West donated to the workhouse
$1,000 she had earned writing a magazine article about her expe-
rience. The money went to the Mae West Memorial Prison Library.

Before the penitentiary was demolished in 1936, a debate ensued over
the island's future. Parks Commissioner Robert Moses advocated utilizing
the land for a public park, a concept that dated as far back as 1867, when
the *New York Herald* recommended razing the buildings to create an
"island paradise." Dr. S. S. Goldwater, commissioner of hospitals, however,
supported the old hospital park idea and called for a much-needed centralized care facility for the chronically ill. He planned to double the
island's bed capacity by knocking down the five old institutions remaining
and replacing them with seven modern ones. Since Moses was already
building parks on Randall's and Ward's Islands, Goldwater won the debate.

Once again, the hospital park didn't fully materialize. A nurses' residence opened in 1938, and Welfare Hospital for Chronic Diseases (later
Goldwater Memorial Hospital) opened the next year. World War II post-
poned further construction, and afterward, priorities shifted. While the
hospital shortage continued, the city poured its money into housing, mass
transit, schools, and—out of proportion to actual needs—into the roadways
and spans designed by Robert Moses and his Triborough Bridge and Tunnel Authority. Only one more chronic-care facility opened on the island,
Bird S. Coler Hospital, in 1952. (Goldwater and Coler merged in 1996,
forming what is now called Coler-Goldwater Special Hospital & Nursing
Facility.) The city finally abandoned the hospital park concept and closed
or relocated Welfare Island's ancient institutions—Metropolitan Hospital
moved to Harlem and City Hospital to Elmhurst, Queens, leaving the forsaken asylums and hospitals to decay.

With most of Welfare Island lying fallow, architects and city planners
searched out a constructive use for the neglected 147-acre strip. Numerous
plans were proposed in the 1960s, including a twenty-thousand-unit residential community of fifty-story buildings. The American Institute of
Architects, influential urban writer Lewis Mumford, and Parks Commis-

sioner August Heckscher advocated preserving the space as a park. In 1965, after the Metropolitan Transit Authority promised to link the inconveniently located island to the subway system within ten years, new suggestions flooded in, including one proposing to reconstruct the Metropolitan Museum of Art's Temple of Dendur on the island's southern tip. Even more unusual was a plan to dig up bodies from Queens and Brooklyn cemeteries and reinter them on Welfare Island, freeing up borough land for housing.

Mayor John Lindsay established a committee of citizens and city officials, who ultimately recommended a multiuse plan designed by architects John Burgee and Philip Johnson. The plan was socially idealistic—a mixed-income, mixed-race, handicapped-accessible new town of twenty thousand. The community was to have two neighborhoods—Northtown and Southtown—with low-rise apartment buildings tightly clustered to allow for ample park and recreational space and water views. It would be a walking and cycling town, with a four-mile promenade along the island's perimeter and a pedestrian Main Street, from which cars would be banned. (They'd park in a garage near the Thirty-sixth Avenue Bridge linking the island to Queens.) The project promised to restore seven historic landmarks, retain Coler and Goldwater Hospitals, and build facilities like a school, a hotel, shops, and an office building.

In 1969, the city leased the island to the state for ninety-nine years, allowing the new Urban Development Corporation (UDC) to take control of this "New Town in Town" as it came to be known. Created by Governor Nelson Rockefeller to expedite housing renewal, this public authority was given power to float bonds and override local zoning regulations. UDC installed its own team of architects, each working on a separate segment of the project. However, it also altered the original plan, creating fewer but significantly taller buildings.

With the name Welfare Island having lost its appeal, the island was renamed in 1973 to honor President Franklin Roosevelt. But the UDC design teams didn't communicate well with each other, and the city's fiscal crisis delayed construction of a promised subway stop. The state did come up with an alternate means of transportation, a commuter tram to Manhattan. But UDC found itself operating in the red and unable to repay loans and bonds, so when Roosevelt Island welcomed its first tenants in 1975, only 40 percent of the project was completed. UDC subsequently left the housing business, passing responsibility for Roosevelt Island on to the state division of housing and community renewal.

Roosevelt Island's earliest residents possessed a frontier spirit. Paul Claudato was the first tenant, moving into Island House from the Bronx in May 1975. Although there was a buzz of activity from construction workers and hospital employees, the island's first fifty families enjoyed a "glorious isolation," recalled Claudato before his death in 2008. Main Street wasn't finished, and there was no shopping. To keep new residents happy, a stretch limousine took Island House tenants to a supermarket in Queens. It was three months before Claudato even heard a noise in the hallway. A neighbor! "I felt like Robinson Crusoe finding the footprint in the sand," he said.

Once the tram arrived in 1976, the island evolved into a full-fledged small town, albeit with New York diversity. In Genesis-like fashion, islanders created what had not existed before—a library, Little League, garden club, theater troupe, and other volunteer organizations. (Today, the island has dozens of volunteer groups, most surviving since the early days.) Shopkeepers moved in, parks were built, and some landmarks were restored or stabilized. By 1980, seven thousand people lived on the island. In 1984, the Roosevelt Island Operating Corporation (RIOC) was established, becoming the first independent agency charged with developing and operating the island. Development stalled until 1989—the same year the subway finally opened—when a high-rise luxury rental with free-market units and a smaller subsidized building for low-income, disabled, and elderly residents opened.

Roosevelt Island has long attracted United Nations employees, who like the island's relative quiet and the easy commute, and these days it is drawing more young singles who can't afford "mainland" Manhattan. The island is part of Manhattan even though the only bridge access is from Queens. By train or tram, it's Bloomingdale's in five minutes and Lincoln Center in twenty minutes. "My broker usually takes out-of-towners to Roosevelt Island because you can get more square footage for a price you are more used to," says Eric Andersen, thirty-four, who moved in 2010 from Wilmington, Delaware, to New York to work as a Wall Street lawyer. "And now I'm looking across the river at apartments that cost $1,000 more a month for the same unit."

Nisha Shandal, who moved to the island from Toronto in 2010, loves the proximity of Manhattan and the ability to escape from it. "It is just peaceful here," she says. "There is a greater sense of community here. [In Manhattan] everyone is in a rush. There are more people who say hello here." Still, Judy Berdy, president of the island's historical society, says younger, more affluent tenants live in the new buildings near the island's subway station and are more oriented toward Manhattan. "There is not much integration of the communities," she says. Roosevelt Island is unlike City Island and Broad Channel not just because it lacks the deep roots and the sense of permanence home ownership provides—89 percent of its units are rentals. The city's other inhabited islands are largely white, but Roosevelt Island has delivered on its promise to be both economically and racially mixed. According to the 2000 census, nearly one-third of the island's 9,520 residents were foreign born; approximately 45 percent of the population was white, one-quarter was black, another quarter either Latino or Asian. Green signs on lampposts declare "Welcome" in seven languages. The island had both a high median income ($49,976 in 2000, with nearly a quarter of the households earning over $100,000) and a relatively high number of residents living in poverty (one in six, with nearly one-third of the households earning below $30,000).

Horrific conditions at the city's notorious lunatic asylum were exposed by pioneering undercover journalist Nellie Bly in 1887.

Historical Detour: Nellie Bly–Committed to the Truth

In 1885, when she was about to turn twenty-one, fortune smiled on Elizabeth Cochrane. Raised in Pennsylvania mining towns and frustrated by her inability to find employment in Pittsburgh, Cochrane had written a blistering rebuttal to a chauvinistic Pittsburgh *Dispatch* columnist's pontifications on women and work. Her letter caught editor George Madden's attention, and he asked Cochrane to write a story on the subject.

After the success of that piece and another on the taboo subject of divorce, Madden offered Cochrane a full-time job . . . and a pseudonym, since journalism wasn't considered a proper vocation for a lady. The name they chose, from a well-known song, was Nellie Bly. Bly wrote features about the Pittsburgh slums and women in factories before traveling to Mexico, where she sharpened her skills as a muckraker by reporting on poverty and corruption. Bly's talent and instinctive sense of adventure proved indispensable for the story that would earn her national recognition—an inside look at life in the dreaded lunatic asylum on Blackwell's Island.

It wasn't easy being a "girl reporter" in the nineteenth century, and when Bly moved to New York in 1887 looking for a job, she found journalism's boys' club closed to her. She got her foot in the door after interviewing all the top editors for a Pittsburgh *Dispatch* story about women in journalism; their shameless sexism created quite a stir and won Bly an interview at the *New York World*. Impressed by her moxie and anxious for an extraordinary probe of the notorious bedlam on the East River islands, the *World* assigned her to an undercover investigation of alleged abuses at the asylum.

Bly checked into the Temporary Home for Women at 84 Second Avenue, claiming to be Nellie Brown from Cuba. She jabbered nonstop and feigned irrational behavior; the police were eventually called in, and Bly was sent to court. A few reporters on the court beat took notice of the attractive, well-dressed redhead and filed stories. The *New York Sun*'s front-page headline asked, "Who Is This Insane Girl?" while the *New York Times* described Bly as the "mysterious waif" with a "wild, hunted look in her eyes." The *World* remained silent as Bly was remanded to Bellevue Hospital for an examination and, finally, ferried to Blackwell's Island.

Bly was appalled by the detestable conditions she found there, and when a *World* attorney obtained her release ten days later, Bly wrote a series of stories detailing her harrowing experiences. The first ran on October 9, 1887, and Bly was given a byline—a rare honor in those days. She told of inedible food, insensitive doctors, nurses who savagely beat patients, and foreign women committed to the asylum because nobody could understand them.

"We were taken into a cold, wet bathroom, and I was ordered to undress," described Bly. "I noticed one of the craziest women in the ward standing by the filled bathtub with a large, discolored rag in her hands. She was chattering away to herself and chuckling in a manner which seemed to me fiendish. . . . They began to undress me, and one by one they pulled off my clothes. . . . I gave one glance at the group of patients gathered at the door watching the scene, and I jumped into the bathtub with more energy than grace.

"The water was ice-cold, and I again began to protest. How useless it all was! I begged, at least, that the patients be made to go away, but was ordered to shut up. The crazy woman began to scrub me. . . . From a small tin pan she took some soft soap and rubbed it all over me, even all over my face and my pretty hair. . . . My teeth chattered and my limbs were goose-fleshed and blue with cold. Suddenly I got, one after the other, three buckets of water over my head—ice-cold water, too—into my eyes, my ears, my nose and my mouth. I think I experienced some of the sensations of a drowning person as they dragged me, gasping, shivering and quaking, from the tub. For once I did look insane. I caught a glance of the indescribable look on the faces of my companions, who had witnessed my fate and knew theirs was surely following."

The *World* hammered home Bly's reportage with front-page commentary about the despicable abuses. The story of her escapade caused a national sensation and ushered in a new era of crusading investigations into sensationalistic topics. When Bly returned to the island later that month with the assistant district attorney and grand jury, many of the violations had been tidied up.

The jury nonetheless recommended reforms and increased funding, which was approved by the city. Already starting to face up to the island institution's problems, the city had been contemplating change. Bly's in-depth exposure ensured there was no turning back.

In 1895, Bly married seventy-year-old millionaire Robert Seaman just days after they met on a train to Chicago; a year later she gave up her career. After Seaman died in 1904, she ran his Iron Clad Manufacturing Company until it went bankrupt in 1912—in part because Bly was robbed by employees. She then lived in Europe for six years, occasionally working as a war correspondent for the New York *Evening Journal*. She returned to New York as a *Journal* columnist in 1919, but died of pneumonia three years later at the age of fifty-seven. Bly was honored in her *Journal* obituary as "the best reporter in America."

But the island is changing. In 1997, Governor George Pataki cut all funding to the island, forcing it to become self-sufficient. With infrastructure suffering, RIOC sought new capital by pushing the Southtown development. A surge in construction led to dramatic growth and a shift in the population. By 2007, RIOC estimated there were twelve thousand residents on the island and that the number would soon reach sixteen thousand. The days of every face seeming familiar if not friendly are fading fast. "I used to know everyone on the island, but now I can't say that," says Ronald Syperreck, who moved here in 2002 from Glendale, Queens. "It's crowded."

Worse, while the new Riverwalk buildings in Southtown are more attractive than the island's older buildings, they are altering the island's dynamic. Two of the new buildings were sold to two Manhattan hospitals, who rent the units to about two thousand doctors and nurses. The developer has counted the hospitals' subsidized apartments to count toward affordable housing requirements, which has angered some longtime residents, especially since most of these tenants are there for a limited time and thus less invested in the community.

"Their community allegiances tend to be to those institutions during their stay here," says Dick Lutz, editor of the *Main Street WIRE*, the island's newspaper.

That change has been compounded by the luxury condos and market rentals at Riverwalk, the development of the old Octagon building from the lunatic asylum as upscale rentals, and a push from some other buildings to leave the Mitchell-Lama program that provides below-market rentals. (The program gave developers financial incentives to guarantee caps on rents or, with the island's co-op, purchase and resale prices.)

"There has been a profound change," says Matthew Katz, three-time president of the Roosevelt Island Resident Association. With the Eastwood Building, which was home to seniors and the disabled, leaving Mitchell-Lama, Katz says the shift will become even more pronounced as each unit gradually converts to fair market rates. "A fundamental premise of the island was as a sanctuary for low-to-middle income New Yorkers and for the disabled and seniors," he says. "It has been ignored." (The number of disabled residents dropped from two hundred in 2005 to eighty in 2007.)

Roosevelt Island features beautiful views, lush green spaces, and a peaceful lifestyle, but its Main Street is drab and has long been plagued by limited shopping.

The thousands of newcomers have also made the morning commute unbearable, with subway cars so crowded they can't be boarded, Lutz says. And Katz says that with the Coler-Goldwater chronic care hospital on the south end of the island likely to close in the next decade, there'll be another ten acres to develop. He's concerned about maintaining the proportions of people to parks and also about what a population of twenty thousand might mean for the subway and the island's other infrastructure.

Riverwalk has brought new upscale residents and retailers to the island but has raised concerns about overcrowding and a fraying of the sense of community.

On the bright side, Riverwalk has also sparked some investment, with a Starbucks, a Duane Reade, and several new dining options opening. But Lutz says the Southtown development has not helped Main Street, which has long been a disaster. "You'd think the addition of well over one thousand apartments would provide a critical mass of consumers for island businesses," he says. But just as old-timers view the new development as "'down there,' away from our daily life," Lutz says, "folks in Southtown, hard by the subway station, don't come north much." (He believes some sort of local transportation connecting the north and south could solve many of the island's problems.)

With limited competition and a captive but limited customer base, Main Street merchants have never had an incentive to compete, sending irked islanders to Queens and Manhattan to shop. (The local Gristedes has improved in recent years, Berdy says.) Additionally, the strip is plagued by empty storefronts. Lutz says bureaucratic bungling has made even opening a new store an arduous task most merchants aren't willing to endure. "Why cope with the paperwork, the proof of economic readiness, the waiting, and the hassle when all you want to do is open up and start selling pizza," he says. "A merchant will go to Queens where he can shake hands with a landlord and be in business tomorrow."

Trying to navigate governance on an island ruled by a state agency is a form of madness that once would have sent residents to the local lunatic asylum. "They're a state bureaucracy, that's incurable," says Berdy. For years, the RIOC presidency—at $150,000 per year—was a patronage perk for cronies of the governor, which was especially problematic under George Pataki's indifferent rule. At one point, residents even held a Roosevelt Island Tea Party, ceremonially pouring tea into the East River to protest, among other things, the appointment as president of Jerome Blue, a former staff member to Pataki's political patron Senator Alfonse M. D'Amato. Blue was considered among the worst of the RIOC bosses—and was finally forced out by Pataki after D'Amato lost his Senate seat—but even when the presidents were better suited to the job, friction remained.

Finally, an Eliot Spitzer appointee, Stephen Shane, agreed to let the residents create an election to recommend members for the unpaid, part-time board and to invest it with more clout. (Direct elections are the next step, Katz says.) The 2008 election had a higher turnout than the Obama-McCain presidential vote, and the result was a board suddenly featuring seven residents. Ironically, in 2010, the RIOC board—which oversees development and operations on the island—flexed its political muscle by ousting Shane, the man who had empowered them. Lutz felt that while the decision "appears an error" it was at least done by the residents. "Democracy is messy and imperfect," he says, but "a strong and assertive board of directors is a plus." (Shane's overall tenure got mixed reviews. Some praised him for being engaged, but his outspoken style reportedly rubbed residents the wrong way.)

Governor David Paterson then angered island activists by ignoring a bill passed by the legislature that would have given the board a say in the selection of presidents. He appointed a new president, Leslie Torres, without even considering other candidates. Katz says that while he believes Torres is qualified for the job, the move smacked of the totalitarian approach that has continually angered locals.

That disregard for public input flared up again with the revival of a memorial for Franklin Delano Roosevelt on the island's southern tip. The plan was first designed by renowned architect Louis Kahn in 1972 but then shelved during the city's fiscal crisis. Recently the 4.5-acre Four Freedoms memorial has been revived, much to the consternation of some locals.

"When Kahn designed it nobody lived here to have an opinion," Katz says. "We're not opposed to a memorial for Roosevelt, but they never asked us for approval [for this plan]. We get tuned out."

And while Kahn's plan has its ardent supporters, many residents loathe the design, which will have huge concrete walls blocking the view. "It is awful, ugly and stark," says Berdy. (The city and state are also contributing about $10 million toward the $50 million price tag, despite Governor Paterson's 2010 suspension of state-funded construction projects due to the recession.)

By contrast, plans for the ten acres of parkland known as Wild Gardens/Green Rooms near the ruins of the old Smallpox Hospital just to the north of the FDR memorial have received more enthusiastic approval.

And for all the issues Roosevelt Islanders face—including concern that the pioneer spirit has dimmed and that expansion has undermined the island's intimacy—they still feel passionately about their home. "This is the best place I've ever lived, and I am both eager to share it and eager to protect it, even as it changes," Lutz says.

While there are plenty of people who never get involved, Lutz believes that being "clearly defined by the surrounding water, there is a strong identity here."

"Roosevelt Islanders tend to be more interested in their community than people in the average community," he adds.

Lutz and Katz both define themselves the same way, using similar language: "I am a Roosevelt Islander first, a New Yorker second, then an American, then a citizen of the world," Lutz says. Katz echoes that thought, "I'm a New Yorker, but I'm a Roosevelt Islander."

Exploring the Island

A unique residential community, Roosevelt Island offers five public parks and six New York City–designated landmarks, four of which can be seen during a leisurely stroll. The island is ringed by a paved esplanade, which provides a four-and-a-half-mile scenic loop for walkers and cyclists.

Near the tram and subway station is a new **visitors' center**, a beautiful terra-cotta and cast-iron kiosk with a copper roof and Guastavino tile ceiling. It was one of five original kiosks that stood at the Queensboro Bridge Trolley Station at Second Avenue and 59th Street, but was moved to the Brooklyn Children's Museum in 1970 and served as the museum's entrance until a museum expansion in 2005. When Judy Berdy of the historical society heard the museum was getting rid of the kiosk, she sought funding, rescued the 210-square-foot, 86,000-pound building, and had it brought to the island.

From the visitors' center, walk north, veering right onto an artery of Main Street. The **Blackwell House** to your right was built in 1796 by James

Blackwell and is the sixth oldest house in New York City; it is the sole surviving building on Roosevelt Island from the days when the island was still privately owned. When the island was developed, the building was restored, but tenants let it fall into disarray. The exterior has been renovated, but it sits empty, with plans for a community center unrealized.

While most residents are less concerned with the island's aesthetics than its atmosphere, outsiders are often struck by Main Street's gloomy and monotonous architecture. These older buildings tier down to the water, providing many residents with river views, but the tallest portions flank Main Street, making it dark and dreary. Generic red-and-white signs identifying shops heighten the downtown's drab appearance.

Continue north on Main Street to the **Chapel of the Good Shepherd**, the only refreshing piece of architecture in the town center. This stone-and-brick Victorian Gothic church was built in 1889 by English architect Frederick Clarke Withers, who was one of the first members of the American Institute of Architects. The church was commissioned by the New York Episcopal Mission Society to minister to residents of the island's institutions; it was renovated in 1976 and is now called the Good Shepherd Community Ecumenical Center. The church's bronze bell, cast in 1888, is exhibited in the plaza.

Farther north on Main Street is a flourishing community garden to your left. Past Octagon Park is **Octagon Tower**, which is all that remains of the lunatic asylum. The tower's two wings were demolished in 1970; in 1982, a fire destroyed the tower's Victorian cupola, exposing the inside to the elements. Then, in 1999, yet another fire demolished much of the building's upper portion and severely damaged the interior.

But the tower—made of blue-gray Manhattan schist quarried on the island—has been reopened as the crowning touch of a 500-unit luxury

Once the centerpiece of the lunatic asylum, the Octagon Tower is now part of a luxury rental complex.

SHARON SEITZ

rental complex, complete with a private outdoor swimming pool, fitness center, and a billiards room. The rotunda lobby is open to visitors. Here you can see the famous spiral staircase and enlarged black-and-white photos of the old Octagon, including the ruins before its restoration.

The new wings, sitting on the footprint of the asylum's wings, were built of gray stone to match the rotunda. The refurbishing included the building's transformation into a green building (LEED Silver certification) with the largest number of solar panels on any building in New York City; it is one of only two large-scale residential buildings in the region switching from conventional power to fuel-cell energy for all heat and electricity.

Head to the west side of the esplanade with the East River on your left, then veer north until you reach **Lighthouse Park**, the island's most picturesque spot, with views of Mill Rock and Ward's Island, the Robert F. Kennedy (formerly Triborough) Bridge, and Manhattan's Upper East Side. A fifty-foot Gothic lighthouse sits on the northern point. Designed by James Renwick Jr. in 1872, it replaced a fort constructed in the previous decade by a patient in the lunatic asylum who feared a British invasion. According to an 1866 *Harper's New Monthly Magazine* article, officials let the patient—who styled himself "Thomas Maxey, Esq., architect, mason, carpenter, civil engineer, philosopher, and philanthropist"—build the four-foot-high clay and grass garrison with a house inside the parapet because, in the adrenaline rush of his work, Maxey also cleared acres of marsh, making the land useful. Officials even gave Maxey some old Civil War cannon, which he stuck through the walls of his fort.

On your way back to the tram or subway, you may want to relax at the observation pier or meditation steps along the esplanade and contemplate Manhattan's skyline, including the UN, Chrysler, and Empire State Buildings.

Two other landmarks, the gothic ruins of the Smallpox Hospital and Strecker Memorial Laboratory, stand at the island's southern end. The Smallpox Hospital has deteriorated badly over the years, although the Trust for Public Land has helped stabilize the remaining façade. The castlelike hospital is fenced off, but at night it is bathed in floodlights. RIOC hopes to allow access when the ruins are stabilized as part of the Southpoint development. The Romanesque Strecker Memorial Laboratory, built in the 1890s, had been empty for nearly half a century, but the Metropolitan Transportation Authority recently restored the exterior as part of its process of converting the interior into a subway electrical substation.

Eventually, this southern end of the island will be redeveloped with a green space, Wild Gardens/Green Rooms park, and an FDR Memorial, opening up vast new spaces for visitors to explore.

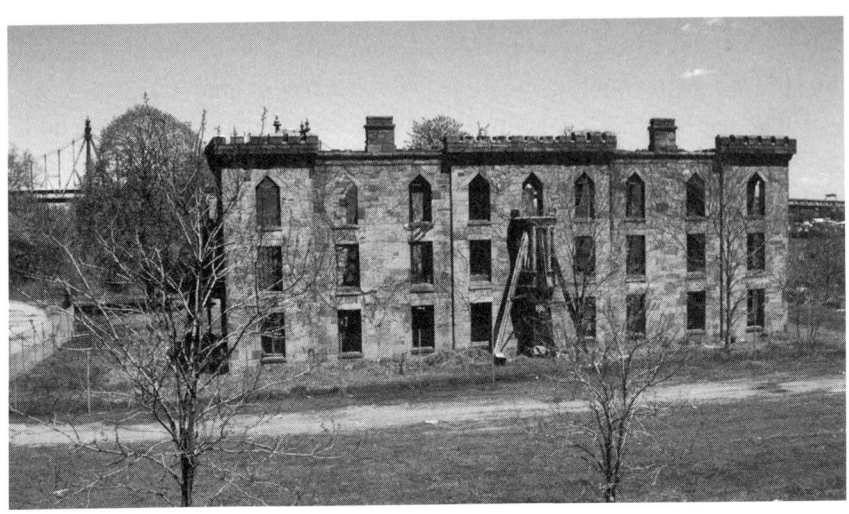

The ruins of the Smallpox Hospital are a ghostly reminder of the island's past.

Island Hopping

By tram: More than a mode of transportation, this urban gondola is a tourist attraction in itself, affording dazzling views of Manhattan, the island, and the East River. After leaving the tramport at Second Avenue and Sixtieth Street, the Swiss-built machine, which accommodates 125 people, is the only mass-transit tram in the country. At its peak, it climbs 250 feet above the river. A $25 million renovation in 2010 smartly reconfigured the operations to enable one side to stay in service while the other is repaired. (Previously, any problems resulted in a total shutdown.) It also shortened the ride from Manhattan to the island—a whopping thirty-one hundred feet—cutting it from five to three minutes. The hostage scene in Sylvester Stallone's movie *Nighthawks* was filmed on the tram, as was the climactic battle between Spider-Man and Green Goblin in the first Spider-Man movie. A red Roosevelt Island bus meets the tram and takes passengers throughout the island. For information call RIOC, - 212-832-4540.

By subway: From Manhattan or Queens, take the F train to Roosevelt Island.

By bus: The Q102 to the island can be caught at Queensboro Plaza.

By car: Take the Thirty-sixth Avenue Bridge from Queens, and park in the Motorgate garage on the right as you enter the island. Private vehicles are restricted. If you want to save money, park on the Queens side of the bridge and walk over.

12. Randall's and Ward's Islands

"I never visit these islands without a sentiment of admiration, excited by the beauty of their position and adaptedness to the purposes to which they have been appropriated."

—ROBERT KELLY, PRESIDENT OF THE SOCIETY FOR THE
REFORMATION OF JUVENILE DELINQUENTS,
WHICH RAN THE HOUSE OF REFUGE IN 1869

LAUREN PRIMERANO

Randall's and Ward's Islands

EVERY NEW YORKER looks at some part of life in this city and thinks, "This shouldn't be that way," but few actually set out to fix the problem and fewer still succeed. The recent rejuvenation of Randall's and Ward's Islands is one of those rare sagas where the dream of a single New Yorker gave rise to a successful transformation of a significant slice of city land.

For years, New Yorkers experienced the islands only peripherally, by train whooshing across the Hell Gate Bridge, or by car inching toward the toll plaza of the Triborough Bridge. Travelers weren't drawn to explore beneath those massive spans, because the islands were plagued by an incoherent and unappealing identity.

Arches and abutments dominated the landscape, casting long shadows and dividing a hodgepodge of poorly maintained recreational areas and government institutions into large chunks and narrow slices. Sure, there were ball fields, tennis courts, soccer fields, a driving range, and a stadium, but much of the space was occupied by a slew of city agencies: the Department of Parks and Recreation garage and maintenance area, Triborough Bridge and Tunnel Authority headquarters, training facilities for the fire and sanitation departments, the police harbor division, a separate detective unit, a sewage disposal and sludge treatment plant, a psychiatric hospital, and a homeless shelter. Overgrown shrubbery and public drug dealing and other unsavory activities that went hand in hand with the homeless shelter lent an air of menace to the place.

Further confusing the situation was the fact that Randall's and Ward's maintain distinct names even though the Little Hell Gate waterway between them has been mostly filled in, creating a single island between East Harlem and Astoria, Queens. Randall's Island is just south of Mott Haven and Port Morris and segues into Ward's Island at a point parallel to Manhattan's 115th Street; Ward's continues down to Ninety-ninth Street.

After nearly twenty years, this 486-acre mass has finally been reborn, home to brand-new athletic fields, a tennis academy, a beautiful new track stadium, natural areas for educational programs and spaces for circuses, concerts, and other events. There is even a new exit ramp off the Triborough

Bridge (now renamed for Robert F. Kennedy) for easier access from the Bronx and a new pedestrian ramp off the bridge from Queens.

"We've been a little busy," says Aimee Boden, executive director of the Randall's Island Sports Foundation (RISF), the public-private partnership that operates the island's parkland. "Now Randall's Island is where New York City goes to play."

When the athletic fields opened in 2010, the *Daily News* called the island a "great new athletic and recreational resource" and "a destination like no other in the five boroughs."

This complex of artificial-turf soccer fields is just one major addition from the Randall's Island Sports Foundation.

The island owes much of its new lease on life to the dreams and persistence of one visionary woman. Karen Cohen, a former interior designer who has served on numerous philanthropic boards, spent years watching her own children play on the island. Each round of city budget cuts in the 1970s and 1980s brought "more garbage and more condoms and more drugs" to the islands, she says. Finally, this well-connected Upper East Sider was impelled to action, not only for her own kids but also for those in neighborhoods like East Harlem just across the river, which lack proper recreational spaces. "This is their backyard," she says.

In 1992, frustrated by the city's unwillingness to spend on its parks and its children, Karen Cohen founded the Randall's Island Sports Foundation. By blending public and private funding while working with the parks department, the Foundation aimed to recast the island as the center of the city's sports and entertainment scene. Raising money for the Randall's Island Sports Foundation initially aroused different reactions than, say, the Statue of Liberty–Ellis Island Foundation. Common responses to early pleas for support were "You mean Rikers Island?" or "What are you talking about?" Despite the island's identity crisis, Cohen and the foundation persevered, though early progress was halting and incremental.

Cohen gradually stepped back from day-to-day responsibilities as the foundation's staff and board came into their own. One important board member was a wealthy philanthropist who went on to become mayor. While progress still came slowly, Cohen says, "having Michael Bloomberg, who was truly on our side, as mayor helped us forge ahead."

Even with nearly two decades of accomplishments more work remains, yet the island's rebirth is finally secure. Cohen says seeing the new ball fields gave her chills. "It made me so happy. To be able to create something so wonderful for the children of New York gives me great hope." That is a Herculean accomplishment that even Parks Commissioner Robert Moses couldn't fully achieve in a twenty-year battle at the height of his power.

Before Moses became parks commissioner in 1934, these lush green islands had never been available to the public as a communal backyard. Between Dutch governor Wouter Van Twiller's 1637 purchase of Minnahanonck (Randall's) and Tenkenas (Ward's) from Native Americans and the end of the American Revolution, several owners established homes on these islands, located near the village of Harlem but far removed from New York, which had not yet developed past Canal Street. Ward's was known as Great Barn Island, Randall's as Little Barn, Barn probably being a corruption of Barendt, a former Dutch owner's name. The most notable event of these early days occurred in 1696 when stones for the original Trinity Church were quarried on Little Barn and hauled by sloop to Lower Manhattan.

In 1772, Captain John Montresor bought Little Barn and settled in with his family. Prominent in the British military, Montresor secretly surveyed New York and the harbor islands before the Revolution and advised British army chief General William Howe on New York invasion sites. (Montresor also inadvertently helped make a hero of spy Nathan Hale. Montresor witnessed Hale's execution and recounted it to Hale's friend Captain William Hull, whose memoirs made famous Hale's last words, "I only regret that I have but one life to lose for my country.")

Early in the war, the colonists controlled New York, and General George Washington established a smallpox quarantine on Montresor's Island in the spring of 1776. In early September, after triumphing at the Battle of Brooklyn, the British, who viewed the islands as key strategic points, drove the Americans from nearby Blackwell's, Montresor's, and Great Barn Islands. Great Barn became an army base, while an officers' hospital was established on Montresor's Island, with Montresor's wife, Frances, serving as matron.

The Americans, meanwhile, held positions in what is now the south Bronx, just across a narrow kill north of the island. Skirmishes broke out between American and British sentries. When a British officer was shot, the redcoats threatened to bomb the Yanks. Instead, the two sides agreed to a cease-fire and became so friendly that they traded tobacco and other goods. Hostilities recurred once, at dawn on September 22, when American General William Heath sent 240 men in three flatboats to attack Montresor's Island. The offensive failed when many soldiers refused to attack. Heath court-martialed the insubordinates.

Montresor later blamed the Americans for burning his house and barns in early 1777. Heath contended, however, that after the British witnessed Yankee troops faking preparations for a large-scale invasion, the British panicked and set fire to their countryman's island before fleeing. Montresor moved back to England the following year.

A farmer named Jonathan Randel bought the island in 1784 and tilled the soil there until he died in 1830. His heirs sold the island, along with Sunken Meadow, a sandy fifty-acre isle just to the east, to New York City in 1835. (Randall's current name derives from a spelling error by the city.)

Meanwhile, Jaspar and Bartholomew Ward bought Great Barn Island to the south. The brothers' efforts to develop a farming community there around 1807 failed, but they later operated a cotton mill on the island. The Wards, along with a man named Philip Milledoler, also built the first bridge from Harlem to the island—wooden in some accounts, stone in others. Neighbors across the river hated it, claiming its pilings created dangerous obstructions and currents in the water. A storm destroyed the bridge in 1821.

After the city established a penitentiary on Blackwell's Island, government officials vigorously pursued the strategy of turning more of the city's islands into dumping grounds for social outcasts. In 1843, a new potter's field opened on Randall's Island. Some one hundred thousand bodies were also exhumed from a Manhattan potter's field and reburied on Ward's Island. Then in 1845, an almshouse opened on Randall's, followed by a children's hospital three years later. The State Emigrant Refuge, for "sick and destitute aliens," opened on Ward's in 1847, after officials rejected Ellis Island as a site. The busy facility also supplemented the oft- overwhelmed Castle Garden immigration station from 1860 until Ellis Island opened in 1892.

During the nineteenth century, Randall's and Ward's Islands, along with Blackwell's and North Brother, became home to numerous government institutions for isolating the poor, sick, and undesirable.

In 1854, the House of Refuge, run by the Society for the Reformation of Juvenile Delinquents, became Randall's most prominent resident after outgrowing its East Twenty-third Street site. Randall's was also eventually burdened with the Idiot Asylum, while Ward's subsequently accommodated a homeopathic hospital, the Inebriate Asylum, a rest home for Civil War veterans, and the city's insane asylum.

Much of the architecture, especially at the House of Refuge and the insane asylum, was impressive in a forbidding way. In 1880, the *New York Times* described the asylum as "one of the ornaments of the City. It looms up like a mountain. It is built of brick, with stone trimmings, and has a great many wings all highly ornamented."

But inside, these intimidating institutions were impersonal at best, tyrannical at worst. Discipline at the House of Refuge was extremely strict. "The boys have a cowed way about them that is anything but pleasant," wrote the *Times*. Criminals were housed separately from street urchins.

Both groups consisted mainly of teenage Irish boys (and a few girls) with little schooling. The average number of children there through the end of the century was between five and six hundred, although in the 1860s and 1870s, nearly a thousand were often crammed in.

Children spent four hours a day in religious and secular instruction and six and a half hours in industrial employment, caning chairs and making shoes for outside contractors. After their stay, some were released to family or friends, but most girls were indentured as housekeepers and most boys as farmers. (This practice gradually died out after the immigration flood of the 1880s supplied even cheaper labor.)

While society officials nobly proclaimed this ascetic lifestyle the path to salvation, they were oblivious to the reality at the refuge, where taskmasters inflicted a pitiless sweatshop existence, savagely beating children who couldn't keep up and hanging any child who misbehaved by his or her thumbs.

There were periodic state investigations, and longtime superintendent Israel Jones was accused in an 1872 state report of being "a man wholly unfit and unworthy of the position and whose administration is characterized by brutality and neglect." Yet nothing was done until 1887, when businesses forced the state to prohibit their competition from using refuge inmates for cheap labor. Military drills replaced work; beatings lessened, and overall conditions improved slightly. But investigations at the turn of the twentieth century still revealed underfed, poorly clothed boys who were often mistreated by drunken officers. Boys were subjected to such discipline as weeks of standing handcuffed to a cell for up to nineteen hours a day. Not surprisingly, the refuge was beset by armed revolts and arson throughout its existence.

Treatment was not much better elsewhere on the islands. An 1887 state investigation declared that the insane asylum "should be condemned as uninhabitable." It was operating at twice its thousand-person capacity, its patients huddled together in filthy wards. The dismal conditions attracted only the least qualified attendants, exacerbating the situation. In 1896, the city turned the asylum over to the state, which simply continued the warehousing policy. By 1899, the Manhattan State Hospital had become the world's largest mental institution, with 4,393 patients; the state continued piling more people in until the population peaked at 7,000 in 1926.

In 1934, Robert Moses took over the parks department and the Triborough Bridge Authority (now the Triborough Bridge and Tunnel Authority). For Moses, Randall's and Ward's Islands were vital to a long-unrealized plan linking Manhattan, the Bronx, and Queens by bridge, which would provide city dwellers access to Moses' new system of parkways on Long Island.

To this project Moses added a sports complex featuring a stadium, ball fields, and parks for Randall's and Ward's Islands. (The parks department had been contemplating the concept since 1916.) However, the islands were still monopolized by various government institutions. To achieve his goals, Moses had a bill rammed through the state legislature forcing the institutions out within a decade. The House of Refuge and most of the others were demolished by 1937. In some cases, patients were forced to transfer to overcrowded institutions.

As head of the Bridge Authority, Moses also snagged federal funding for his parks department project by claiming that the new recreational facilities would attract toll-paying drivers across the new bridge and to the islands, which had previously been accessible only by ferry.

By 1936, the Triborough Bridge—more than seventeen miles of four connected bridges supported by Randall's and Ward's Islands—was complete. An engineering marvel, the twenty-five-cent toll bridge, designed by O. H. Ammann and Aymar Embury, opened to gushing admiration on July 11. Within six weeks, drivers taking the bridge from the city and Westchester were causing the worst traffic jams in Long Island history. (To relieve the crush of cars, Moses, who disdained mass transit, later built the Long Island Expressway.) The Triborough Bridge carried eleven million vehicles over the islands in 1941. That total more than doubled by 1949 and again by 1960. In 2008, 59.7 million vehicles drove across the bridge.

Although unable to fund his envisioned seventy-thousand-seat arena, Moses did build the twenty-one-thousand-seat Municipal Stadium, which opened the same day as the Triborough Bridge. (The stadium was renamed in 1955 in memory of John Downing, a former recreation director who worked forty-one years for the parks department.)

Over the next three decades, Moses had the land between Randall's, Ward's, and Sunken Meadow filled in, allowing him to build dozens of ball fields and tennis courts. Moses also built a footbridge connecting Ward's Island to 103rd Street in East Harlem. While it had been planned since 1938, Moses didn't follow through until 1949, when he helped Mayor William O'Dwyer defeat Newbold Morris, who was championing new parks for the poor neighborhoods of Harlem. Moses, uninterested in creating parks for the poor, defused the issue by announcing that he would link the community to Ward's Island. The bridge opened in 1951.

Moses' vast sports complex, however, was never fully completed, because the island was never entirely his domain. In 1937, a sewage treatment plant opened on the one section of Ward's Island not owned by the parks department. More significantly, the Manhattan State Hospital refused to leave. Although its buildings were decrepit and conditions depressingly reminiscent of 1887, the state law mandating its shutdown by 1943 was ignored due to overcrowding elsewhere. Moses continued his battle, but in 1954 voters approved a $350 million bond issue to build new mental health facilities on the island.

Historical Detour: Training for the Devil

There is one place in New York where starting fires is legal, and, in fact, essential: the Fire Department Training Academy on Randall's Island. (The academy moved to Randall's from Roosevelt Island in 1975.)

The academy is used for "probies" (new, probationary firefighters) when there's an incoming class, but it is also used each day for training more experienced members of FDNY. The program skillfully re-creates the challenges of firefighting, with firefighters rappelling down buildings, groping blindly through a maze in a race against time, and, of course, facing the flames.

The academy's stodgy brick buildings and junkyard autos have all the ambience of an abandoned factory town. This is where firefighters learn to work the hoses as a team, to cope with everything from a high-rise building to the confined space of the subways, from overturned cars to smoke-filled apartments. In the burn building, where everything is steel—even the kitchen sink—computers control the duration and intensity of propane blazes that can reach twelve hundred degrees.

Movie and video directors often visit the academy and use the props or set up their own buildings to burn under the firefighters' watchful eyes. Within this controlled environment, however, are reminders of fire's real dangers; the streets are named for firefighters who died in a 1966 conflagration.

The vote of confidence and three new buildings didn't end the hospital's troubles, however. In the late 1960s and early 1970s, after decentralization had split the institution into three distinct hospitals, fear invaded the complex. Patients and staffers were robbed and raped on several occasions, usually by outsiders who had slipped past lax security. In 1974, the *Times* reported that sixty-three retarded patients transferred from Staten Island's notorious Willowbrook mental hospital sat idly in empty rooms while expensive equipment—designed to teach them balance, dexterity, and other skills—stood unused nearby due to understaffing and mismanagement. Three years later, Congressman Ed Koch, a mayoral candidate, slammed the hospital's unsanitary conditions, poor recordkeeping, and careless dispensing of drugs.

As mayor, Koch opened what the city referred to as a temporary emergency shelter on Ward's Island for two hundred homeless men. But temporary is a relative term in politics, and today the Charles H. Gay Homeless Shelter remains in operation. The East Harlem community felt the shelter was too near the pedestrian bridge linking the island to their neighborhood, while the mental hospital sued to keep these unmonitored newcomers from settling down virtually next door to their children's complex. Newspapers like the *Daily News* editorialized that while group homes were politically unpopular, they were a good alternative to these large, impersonal shelters. Hoping to produce a more compassionate refuge, the city later turned shelter operations over to the Volunteers of America (VOA), making it the city's first privately run shelter. By 1981, the shelter had five hundred male residents, many of whom essentially made it their permanent home.

In the early 1990s, the shelter had been a continual source of controversy—the adjacent hospital accused the residents of stealing, trespassing, and exposing themselves to children, while East Harlem saw its Ward's Island bridge deteriorate into a frightening lair for crack dealers and addicts. The atmosphere around the shelter improved after the creation of the Randall's Island Sports Foundation, which worked with an army-run, inner-city youth program to clear overgrowth that was choking century-old trees and providing cover for illicit activities. The foundation and parks department also cleared overgrowth near the footbridge to East Harlem and pressured the VOA into installing guards and fences at the shelter's border. Relations between the shelter and its neighbors steadily improved. Today there are nearly six hundred men living at the VOA shelter, which has split into different programs, one focusing on the chronic homeless and one on people whose lives are in transition. Another nonprofit, Help USA, also runs a two-hundred-person program for homeless people who are employed or employable. The programs are considered well run, clean, and generally safe, with a wide array of services. A sure sign of the island's shifting identity is that the footbridge to Harlem, once closed at night to reduce unsavory traffic, now remains open around the clock.

The Randall's Island Sports Foundation hopes to eventually gain the land now devoted to the shrinking population at the Manhattan Psychiatric Center (in the distance), and it has already revitalized much of the island, including the wetlands (in the foreground), which are now used in educational programs.

Meanwhile, the hospital—reconsolidated in 1979 into the Manhattan Psychiatric Center—is also vastly different than the Dickensian institutions of old. Today, MPC bills itself as a rehabilitative institute, "A Bridge to Recovery." It offers a wide array of innovative programs, some of which are patient run or involve patients doing work or art. More than half the patients work, and all spend time learning community skills. The population has shrunk dramatically from its high of seven thousand in 1926—by 1995 there were only nine hundred patients, five years later, it was down to four hundred, and by 2010 there were just 260 patients living at MPC. But the deinstitutionalization process is done with more care and support these days, getting patients more than just a chit for an SRO. In fact, MPC has ninety patients living in transitional housing on the island and six hundred patients still coming back to the island for outpatient treatment.

Boden meets regularly with officials from these institutions (as well as the Department of Environmental Protection and the Fire Department) and they have cooperated with RISF's development plans. One "major breakthrough" came when the state Office of Mental Health agreed to pull back their Manhattan Psychiatric campus from the water's edge. "It reduced the

size of their footprint and gave us access to the water," Boden says. "It used
to be like the night of the living dead in that corridor, but now you see people biking and pushing baby strollers."

Another clear sign that a new day has arrived on the island are the
Sunken Garden Fields that the foundation built right in front of the homeless shelter on the former site of a dilapidated old building that had once
been taken over by crack addicts. The fields are pristine, and there have
been no problems with the homeless.

In the 1990s, the sanitation department and police detectives unit left
the island, and the foundation persuaded the fire department to give back
seven acres for recreational use. They went back to the FDNY again when
working on redeveloping the tennis courts. A company named SportimeNY
was investing $19 million for a splashy new Randall's Island Tennis Cen-
ter—160,000 square feet with a mix of hard and clay courts and an upscale
new clubhouse—and they wanted to site the facility properly.

So the foundation persuaded the FDNY give up another sliver of land
and move their driving practice area to a spot behind the homeless shelter.
The tennis center's headliner is tennis legend and native New Yorker John
McEnroe, who is overseeing an elite academy meant to compete with the

*One of the biggest new additions to the island is the $19 million tennis facility, which fea-
tures a tennis academy headed by John McEnroe.*

nation's most prestigious programs in Florida. When it opened in 2010, McEnroe's public feud with his brother Patrick—who heads the United States Tennis Association's player development program—over their differing approaches to training young talent, brought the media spotlight to Randall's Island. There is also a team called the New York Sportimes in the World TeamTennis professional league that plays matches here. (Each WTT features major stars, past or present, who play when they are available. The Sportimes franchise was founded and is co-owned by Patrick McEnroe but features John McEnroe.)

The tennis center joins the Icahn Stadium, a track and field arena that opened in 2005, as a shiny symbol of the island's new image. Moses' Downing Stadium was ugly and uncomfortable. The $45 million Icahn Stadium (businessman Carl Icahn donated $10 million of the money) is more intimate and appealing. The stadium hosts a steady stream of track events for New York City school and college athletes, but it also has begun attracting the field's elite, hosting the annual Grand Prix event.

At the 2008 meet, before a crowd of 6,500 people, sprinter Usain Bolt set a 100-meter world record of 9.72 seconds. (Bolt has since bested his own mark.) In 2010 Icahn Stadium became just one of two American sites on the International Association of Athletics Federations (IAAF) Diamond League circuit.

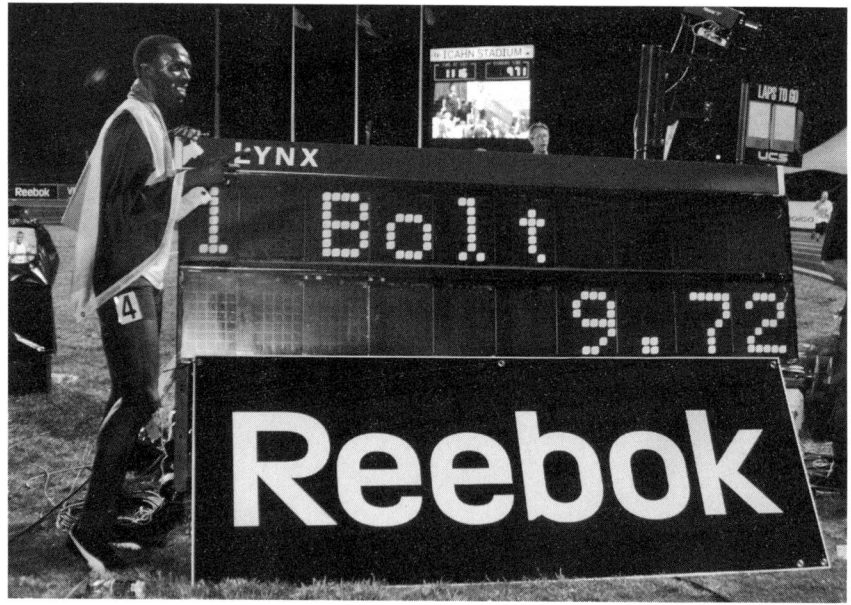

Usain Bolt after setting a 100-meter world record on Randall's Island in 2008.

Historical Detour: A View from the Cheap Seats

After six decades of providing uncomfortable seating for memorable events, Downing Stadium was demolished in 2001, joining
the Polo Grounds and Ebbets Field as a part of New York's past.
And while this old arena—which hosted everything from semipro
soccer leagues to jazz concerts—lacked the lustrous history of the
old ballparks, there are some wonderful and some bizarre
moments worth recalling.

When the twenty-one-thousand-seat stadium opened with
Olympic tryouts on July 11, 1936, the occasion was overshadowed
by the Triborough Bridge dedication and undermined by a mal-
functioning public-address system that created chaos among athletes. No one knew when to report for events, and spectators often
couldn't tell who was competing.

In the sweltering heat, only a "pitifully small crowd of 8,000"
showed up to sit on the rows of concrete benches for what the
Daily News called "the most poorly conducted major meet in the
history of American track." But they got to see Ohio State star
Jesse Owens earn two Olympic slots, with victories in the hundred-meter dash and broad jump. The next day, he won the two-
hundred-meter dash in twenty-one seconds, a new world record.
Owens later won four Olympic gold medals in Berlin.

Two years later, the stadium played home to what is considered the first outdoor jazz festival ever, the 1938 Carnival of
Swing, a five-hour, forty-five-minute memorial for George
Gershwin starring Woody Herman, Gene Krupa, Duke Ellington,
and Count Basie. Audio for this legendary event was only recently discovered and is now at the National Jazz Museum in Harlem.
(The island would host jazz festivals again in the 1950s and
1960s, with performers including Sarah Vaughan, Dave Brubeck,
Dizzy Gillespie, Thelonious Monk, and Ray Charles.)

In 1944, at the Outdoor Track and Field Championships, six
runners lined up for the finals of the hundred-meter dash, but
nobody reached the finish line. Race official Jack Lavelle disquali-
fied the six sprinters on false starts and recalls, then declared,
"There will be no hundred-meter champion this year." Meet directors protested, but Lavelle, a popular local sports figure, would only

stage the new race as an exhibition. Officials, however, later added the winner, Buddy Young, into the record books.

Even more controversial was the disastrous New York Pop Festival held the weekend of July 19, 1970. This Woodstock wannabe (minus camping) was sabotaged when an assemblage of mostly white radical groups tried using the concert for their own purposes. They demanded that concert producers provide bail money for political prisoners and microphone access for speeches, while staging local bands of their choosing. When the producers and radicals reached a compromise, the Young Lords (the Puerto Rican equivalent of the Black Panthers) stepped in with their own wish list. Since this was East Harlem's local park, they said, some of the profit should go toward community TB testing and free breakfasts for kids.

The concert's opening night was delayed two hours when white radicals instigated gate-crashing and manhandled concert-goers under the guise of crowd control. *Rolling Stone* reported that "the mood of the audience was strange—like a strangled scream." Nonetheless, Grand Funk Railroad and Steppenwolf performed. But it was the electrifying presence of Jimi Hendrix, in one of his last American appearances before his death a few months later, that mesmerized the crowd and helped prevent a riot.

The atmosphere worsened Saturday afternoon when the white radicals tore open fences and admitted people for less than the price of a ticket, pocketing the donations themselves. The overflow crowd of fifty thousand restlessly awaited big-name acts that never materialized; without ticket revenue the producers had no money, so all the scheduled bands except Ten Years After backed out. The performers for the Saturday and Sunday shows were supposed have included a band combining Miles Davis, Eric Clapton, Joe Cocker, Delaney & Bonnie, and Ravi Shankar. None played.

Radio disc jockey and emcee Dave Herman was sent out to calm the audience. "It was a very, very rowdy place," Herman remembers. "There was a sense of tension, that we were on the verge of disaster. This crowd was not a peace and love crowd. There were moments when I was wondering how I was going to get out of there."

After losing $300,000, the producers admitted defeat and invited everyone in free on Sunday to see Mountain, Dr. John, and

Little Richard. It would be nearly a quarter of a century before rock festivals returned to Downing Stadium.

Capacity crowds once again flooded Downing Stadium on June 16, 1975, this time for a soccer game. The New York Cosmos, featuring international star Pelé in his first home game, also attracted three hundred reporters and television crews from twenty nations. By 1977, the stadium's limited capacity and unbearable Triborough tie-ups on game days forced the Cosmos to move to the Meadowlands.

After a twenty-five-year hiatus, the Outdoor Track and Field Championships returned to Downing Stadium on June 13, 1991. Only a few hundred spectators—along with several large rats—were in the stands that day to see athletes competing on poorly prepared surfaces.

Attendance improved during the week, however, and the crowds were treated to several compelling dramas: Emerging star Dan O'Brien bested Dave Johnson in the decathlon, finishing with 8,844 points, three shy of the world record. In another tight contest, Carl Lewis barely preserved his ten-year, sixty-five-match winning streak in the long jump. On his sixth and final jump of this competition, Lewis leaped twenty-eight feet, four and a quarter inches, beating Mike Powell by a half inch. But Lewis could not keep pace with Leroy Burrell in the hundred-meter dash, finishing second as Burrell broke Lewis's world record with a 9.90-second run. Lewis reclaimed the record two months later, blazing to a 9.86 on the island of Japan.

In the mid-1990s, after the birth of the Randall's Island Sports Foundation, major events returned to Randall's Island for the first time in a generation. In 1994, the island hosted the alternative-rock tour Lollapalooza starring bands like Green Day and Smashing Pumpkins. On consecutive weekends in 1997, there was a Tibetan Freedom Concert featuring everyone from U2 to the Beastie Boys to Taj Mahal to Patti Smith and the Irish-inspired Fleadh Festival with Irish performers including Van Morrison, Sinead O'Connor, and Christy Moore and Americans such as Suzanne Vega and Wilco.

In 2002, the foundation demolished the stadium to make way for the vastly superior Icahn Stadium, but the island has continued hosting major cultural events, including regular visits from Cirque du Soleil and music festivals ranging from Rock the Bells (hip-hop) to Electric Zoo (electronica) to Farm Aid (featuring a range of artists that included Merle Haggard, Willie Nelson, Neil Young, John Mellencamp, and Dave Matthews) to Little Stevie's Underground Garage Festival (with Iggy Pop, the New York Dolls, the Romantics, and the Strokes).

Only two major artifacts from Downing Stadium were deemed worth preserving, a sign touting the Cosmos, and the lights, which are still in use. The irony is that the lights are considered a vital part of New York history because they'd been brought over from Ebbets Field when the home of the Brooklyn Dodgers was demolished.

The foundation also has completed more than sixty new playing fields, including some for lacrosse, rugby, softball, field hockey, and cricket (the only cricket pitch in Manhattan). Foundation deputy administrator Eric Peterson says the island has about 30–40 percent of all the baseball fields in Manhattan. RISF has also created a vast new complex for five soccer fields—these dedicated fields also mean that soccer games no longer cut across the outfield of Little League games. The soccer fields were placed near the footbridge for easy access because the artificial turf allows them to be used more months than the baseball fields.

The foundation's plans go beyond sports fields. Bicycle and pedestrian paths are being expanded, with benches, lighting, and plantings. Amtrak has contributed $15 million from federal stimulus money to do the work necessary for the paths to loop underneath the train tracks and connect both to the rest of the island and to the Bronx. "We really owe Amtrak a lot," Boden says. "They caught the spirit of what we're trying to do here."

Eight acres of wetlands—four acres of salt marsh and four of fresh water by the Hell Gate inlet—can now be used for educational programs. There are interpretive signs on a boardwalk and access for teachers to go down to the wetlands themselves. (The foundation now has a full-time wetland natural area manager.) In addition, there's an apple orchard and a small plot where tomatoes, kale, and other edibles are grown as part of educational programs.

Of course, even as the foundation has gained momentum, there have been snags and stumbles. Plans for a family-oriented water park drew criticism when it grew from twelve to twenty-six acres (at a projected cost of

$215 million), especially when the city did not allow new bids from other developers after the footprint grew. Worse, that original developer, Aquatic Development Group failed to meet one financing deadline after another and the city finally had to kill the project in 2007 even though the foundation was counting on money from the water park to cover maintenance of the island's other facilities.

A much bigger controversy arose over permits and payments for the new ball fields. A collection of private schools offered to pay $52.6 million toward the construction of the island's sports fields if they'd be guaranteed permits for two-thirds of them each school day afternoon in spring and fall. Since those private schools had previously controlled nearly 100 percent of the after-school permits for Randall's Island and they would legally be grandfathered in for the new fields, the foundation thought reducing their usage to 67 percent and getting money to cover the construction was a good deal.

But public school parents, community groups, and park advocates all saw this as "pay to play." With well-known activist attorney Norman Siegel representing them, they took the Bloomberg administration to court, where it was determined that the city had bypassed the proper land-use procedures. A second attempt, where the private schools paid $44 million for 50 percent of the fields while guaranteeing that public schools would get 40 percent, was also deemed unacceptable for failing to provide due process. "This was a handful of people who had no skin in the game and they prevailed on a tortured legal decision," says parks commissioner Adrian Benepe, who also condemns the media coverage for misrepresenting this as a land grab by rich families. "It was a bone-headed, ego-driven case. Our plan would have been a huge win for everyone."

So, the city ended up footing the entire bill, but because the private schools have their permits still and can better afford buses they end up using the fields the majority of the time anyway. In 2010, these independent private schools used the fields 56 percent of the time in those after-school time slots, public schools used them 13 percent, with other private schools—like Catholic schools—and local youth groups and community or Little League organizations getting the fields for the remaining 31 percent of the time. "The fields are spectacular—among the best in the nation— but this was a terrible tragedy," Benepe says. "It is a real blot on the legacy of Norman Siegel. The net effect is that the private schools now play without having to pay anything. We hope that eventually out of a civic sense of duty they might decide to contribute to the upkeep."

Boden and Peterson say other challenges remain. Fund-raising in a tight economy is difficult enough, but the foundation's top priorities these days are also less glamorous for donors. A major infrastructure overhaul is needed. "Everything—water, electric, sewer—is crossed into everything else," Peterson says. There had been no electrical upgrades since Robert Moses' day. "It's a mess."

Additionally, the foundation is shifting gears toward a stewardship and programming role, and raising money for maintenance is never easy. But they've found innovative ways to save money, including tens of millions by not trucking out the huge boulders dug up during construction and instead using them to decorate the paths. Still, all the tangible progress and the recent media attention has brought a younger generation to the foundation board looking to get involved and raise more money.

Ultimately, the island's revitalization is nothing short of astonishing. Before the foundation started, this land, with all the wasted space, unsafe areas, and rundown parkland, looked like an exercise in bad urban planning. Today, while there are still bridge abutments and institutions carving up the real estate, the island has a more definitive identity—it is a park, and a welcoming one, with the other distractions fading more into the background.

"It took much, much longer than I expected," Cohen says. But she still has her eyes on other prizes, too. "This is a dream come true, but I'm not done."

Some of her ideas are relatively feasible—a skate park, playgrounds with imaginative sprinklers—but some ideas, she admits, require a leap of imagination similar to the one she first took in 1992.

When the psychiatric hospital's lease expires in 2012, she hopes the foundation can persuade the state to move the remaining patients off the island and give RISF the land. "I'm a dreamer, but that's my goal," she says, "even if in my lifetime we don't even have the money to do more than tear the buildings down. There are forty-seven acres there, and we could put bubbles up for year-round access to sports like skating and bowling."

Cohen also would like for someone to give the golf center a makeover similar to the one the tennis facility just got. More important, she harbors hopes for a major science center to teach children ecology and farming. "I'm looking for $30 million," she says, knowing how far-fetched that sounds, although perhaps it is no more grandiose than the amphitheater for outdoor music—with a view looking down the river toward the skyline—she has long tried to get built. Of course, in 1992, sixty new ball fields, a wetlands, and a new track stadium seemed pretty hard to fathom.

"I know I'm a dreamer," she says. "But you have to always want more—that's how you get more."

Exploring the Island

For information about the ball fields, track center, public events, and other amenities related to the Randall's Island Sports Foundation, call 212-830-7719 or go to www.randallsisland.org.

For the **tennis courts**, call 212-427-6150 or go to www.sportimeNY.com/Manhattan. (Of the twenty courts, ten are available for use with New York City Parks Permits in season.)

For **Randall's Island Golf Center**, which has a driving range, batting range, and miniature golf, call 212-427-5689.

If you're interested in bridge architecture, you'll want to roam or cycle beneath the imposing towers and arches of the Robert F. Kennedy (formerly Triborough) and Hell Gate Bridges—Robert Moses liked boasting that the Triborough tower on Ward's was taller than the pyramids. Photographers will also be captivated by the juxtaposition of city infrastructure, parkland, waterways and the new plantings along the pedestrian and bike paths.

New plantings and paths have made the island more appealing for pedestrians, bicyclists, and photographers.

Island Hopping

🚌 *By bus:* From the East Side, take the M35 from 125th Street and Lexington Avenue. From the West Side, take the M60 from 116th Street and Broadway to the foot of the Triborough Bridge. Change to the M35 or walk over. You can also reach the M35 by subway. From the West Side, take the A, B, C, D, 2, or 3 to 125th Street for the bus. From the East Side, take the 4, 5, or 6 to 125th Street to the bus. Randall's Island Golf, 212-427-5689, offers limited shuttle bus service from the Upper East Side.

🥾 *By foot:* From Manhattan, walk across either the Robert F. Kennedy (formerly Triborough) Bridge or the Ward's Island footbridge at 103rd Street and the East River. You can also walk across the bridge from Queens or the Bronx.

🚗 *By car:* From Manhattan, drive north on FDR Drive, south on the Harlem River Drive, or east on 125th Street to the Robert F. Kennedy (formerly Triborough) Bridge. From the Bronx, drive south on either the Bruckner Expressway or the Major Deegan Expressway. From Queens, take the Brooklyn-Queens Expressway or the Grand Central Parkway.

13. Rikers Island

"Those who are laying this cornerstone today do so with mingled feelings of humility and hope; humility because of the realization of the multitude of threads of heredity, environment, education, association, and mental and physical and emotional equipment which go to form the fabric of the offender; and hope that the treatment which these unfortunates will receive in this institution will be the means of salvaging some lives which would otherwise have been wasted."

—Excerpt of text sealed into the cornerstone of the new Rikers Island Penitentiary, dedicated July 28, 1931

COURTESY OF NEW YORK CITY DEPARTMENT OF CORRECTION

Rikers Island

WHEN IT OPENED WITH much hoopla and hope in 1935, Rikers Island Penitentiary promised a dramatic break from the medieval cellblocks of the Blackwell's Island Penitentiary, where inmates idled the days away in cramped quarters. The city's new $10 million Rikers facility would provide modern accommodations and the latest in rehabilitative services, enabling prisoners to leave as "better citizens, with clear eyes, hard muscles and better mental and moral health as well," Commissioner of Correction Richard C. Patterson Jr. predicted in 1928.

Instead, by the 1970s, Rikers Island had evolved into a notoriously overcrowded and explosive community with young, hot-tempered inmates, including an increasing number of gang members, prone to outbursts of violence. As the population grew, the city created a hodgepodge of ten jails, often hastily built and scattered over a 415-acre complex. Today, somewhere between eleven and thirteen thousand inmates are held each day in one of the world's largest lockups. It is an infinitely calmer place than it was during its most crowded years in the late 1980s and early 1990s, yet strife and tension are still far too common.

Today, about three-quarters of Rikers' inmates have not been convicted of a crime but instead are detainees awaiting a trial. Many are held on Rikers because they are poor and can't make bail. Their future is uncertain—if found guilty of a felony, they will be sent up the river to a state penitentiary. Detainees are held on Rikers an average of fifty days and—along with the small number of inmates just convicted and awaiting transfer—are far more volatile than inmates sentenced to Rikers Island for nonviolent misdemeanors. Those inmates, who serve less than a year, make up only 17 percent of the Rikers population.

The cost of housing one inmate in 2010 was about $77,000 a year. That same year, the Department of Correction had a $1 billion budget, which covers the cost of operating Rikers' own fire department, power plant, infirmary and public school. (It also includes several small jails elsewhere in New York.) And while the city has finally begun revamping Rikers' infrastructure and replacing outmoded jails, budget cuts in the DOC and an uptick in crime have raised concerns that the cauldron of Rikers Island could again begin to bubble.

Native Americans sold Rikers Island—off the shore of Astoria, Queens, where the East River veers east toward Long Island Sound—in 1664 to William Hallett, sheriff of Flushing. When Peter Stuyvesant, the surly Dutch governor of New Netherland, learned of Hallett's unsanctioned purchase, he sought revenge. In his final official act before surrendering the colony to England, Stuyvesant fired Hallett and gave the island to Abraham Rycken, a respected farmer, whose family later changed its name to Riker. English governor Richard Nicolls reconfirmed the grant. In the eighteenth century, the family built at least one house on the island, where they lived into the nineteenth century.

New York's Department of Public Charities and Correction bought the island in 1884 for $180,000. (It is unclear whether the island still belonged to Riker descendants at the time.) While many New Yorkers believe that Rikers Island is in Queens—indeed, the jail has a Queens address and is linked to Queens by bridge—it is actually part of the Bronx. When New York City purchased Rikers, it was in Newtown, Queens, and was annexed to the city's 23rd Ward. After the city was consolidated, the ward and Rikers eventually landed in the Bronx.

The city planned a new prison on Rikers Island to replace the crumbling, overcrowded penitentiary built in 1832 on Blackwell's Island (now Roosevelt Island). The transfer also promised to improve the lives of the poor and the mentally and terminally ill living in Blackwell's myriad institutions in the shadow of the penitentiary. "It has long been a reproach to this city that the sick and unfortunate who are the legitimate objects of charity are sent to Blackwell's Island, which is generally associated in the public's mind with a penal institution," said Mayor Thomas Gilroy in 1893.

Despite the rhetoric, it took decades before the Rikers Island Penitentiary was built. In the meantime, the island became the municipal farm, an adjunct of the main penitentiary, where prisoners were sent to work on vegetable and pig farms. Rikers also became a municipal landfill, allowing New York to end the ocean dumping that had caused refuse to wash up on Coney Island and the New Jersey coast. The landfill also provided the material needed to transform Rikers Island into a larger, more valuable piece of real estate.

While only forty-three of the island's original eighty-seven acres were above the high-water mark, there were seventy-nine acres of shoal ground west of the island and 315 shallow acres to the east. Using prison labor, the

city planned to fill the sandbars with city refuse and dirt from the excava-
tion of the Lexington Avenue subway.

Although several prominent physicians advocated incinerating the
garbage, Health Commissioner Joseph D. Bryant assured residents that its
use would not endanger public health, explaining that once the refuse
reached the low-water mark it would be covered with ashes or fresh earth
or otherwise disinfected and sanitized. In 1893, the city began dumping on
Rikers a mishmash of trash including street sweepings, horse manure,
ashes, rubbish (inorganic material), and garbage (organic material). The
dump's untenable odors soon wafted over to northern Queens and the South
Bronx, inciting impassioned protests from residents.

Then, in 1895, Colonel George E. Waring Jr. was appointed street cleaning commissioner. Waring became known as the Apostle of Cleanliness for
successfully implementing reforms such as recycling and waste utilization.
In 1896, the city contracted with the New York Sanitary Utilization Company, a reduction plant on Barren Island that transformed garbage into fertilizer and soap, and until 1919, the Rikers Island landfill received less
objectionable debris—primarily ashes and street sweepings that didn't rot
and cause odors.

After the Barren Island plant closed and the recycling market collapsed
in the 1920s, every kind of refuse was again dumped on Rikers Island,
where it often smoldered for years under a blanket of ashes. "From the
shores of Queens and the Bronx any day the smoking island looks like a
volcano preparing for eruption," the *Times* reported in 1926. By this time,
more than 450 prisoners worked there, some of them housed in the island's
flimsy, wooden dormitories.

A year later, the state commission of correction advised the city that
Rikers Island—its trash mounds swarming with flies and thousands of
giant rats—was not an ideal place for a new prison. In 1930, the Department of Sanitation imported wild dogs to assist rifle-toting workers in their
attempts to pare the rat population, but when two hundred dogs "did not
find the rats all that they were recommended to be in the way of sport," they
killed several pigs from the municipal farm's piggery, the *New York World*
reported. This led to a bitter feud between the Department of Correction,
which wanted the dogs removed, and sanitation workers, who wouldn't go
near the dump without canine protection. Several renegade dogs were
killed, and the city turned to poison gas to combat the rats.

When the new jail finally opened in 1935, the state commission of correction implored the city to end dumping on Rikers. But it took a combina-

tion of citizen complaints, the 1939 New York World's Fair, and Robert Moses to finish off the Rikers Island landfill operation.

Parks Commissioner Moses was charged with helping to ensure that the World's Fair in nearby Flushing was a hit. Realizing he couldn't close the dump immediately, Moses—along with Sanitation Commissioner William Carey—screened the island with a small forest so the mounds of refuse, some one hundred feet tall, wouldn't be visible from the fair. By 1940, the island's 50-acre nursery contained seven thousand trees, used to supply city parks with foliage.

In the meantime, Moses battled with Carey over dumping on Rikers Island. Moses favored incineration and recycling, declaring that dumping was a policy "so stupid, costly and barbaric that neither my friend, Carey, nor any other public official can survive it." Carey argued that landfill created new land without offense to anyone. He also said families shouldn't have to recycle because it was inconvenient. In 1939, a compromise plan transferred dumping operations for several years from Rikers to the east Bronx to create a park in the neighborhood of Soundview. Tons of Rikers ash were also used as fill for what is now LaGuardia Airport. In 1948, the city began dumping garbage in Staten Island's Fresh Kills landfill.

While garbage was piling up on Rikers' southern side, the northern end, or original island, was being readied for the new prison, which had problems even before it opened. In 1934, with the facility 95 percent complete, the city's commissioner of accounts suspended payments to the architect and contractors until leaky walls and roofs and other inferior construction were corrected. The commissioner further alleged that Tammany Hall Democrats had squandered public funds during the jail's construction. (Mayor Jimmy Walker served from 1926 to 1932 before resigning under a cloud of corruption charges.)

Inmates from the penitentiary and workhouse on Welfare Island were transferred up the river to Rikers in 1935. Unlike the fortress-style prison on Welfare Island, Rikers Island Penitentiary had no outer walls, only a wire fence with guard towers. The turbulent waters surrounding the island, which hindered escape attempts, provided additional security. Considered innovative for its time, the prison included eight cellblocks, an auditorium, and exercise space.

The prison also boasted employment, education, medical and psychological services, and individualized treatment for its inmates. Not only would offenders—males arrested in the city and serving no more than three years—be incarcerated at the Rikers Island Penitentiary, city officials promised they would be reformed. The prison ran a sixty-acre farm and a piggery that in the early 1940s produced 110,000 pounds of pork annually, feeding residents in many city institutions. And in 1940, Rikers' seven-story, three-hundred-bed hospital became the nation's first prison hospital approved for internship training by the American Medical Association, which praised the hospital's dedication to restoring the health of sick inmates and preparing them for society.

"Such operations as the correction of crossed eyes, the removal of unsightly abnormalities, the correction of badly shaped noses and the elimination of scars are performed with the idea that the individual may be thus released from an embarrassment that might contribute to his anti-social behavior," reported the *Times*.

The prison's accommodations for twenty-two hundred inmates, however, quickly became overcrowded; the population climbed to twenty-five hundred by 1941. To house the extra inmates, shop buildings were used as dorms. And while the inmate population throughout the city system decreased significantly during World War II, between 1945 and 1954 the total number of prisoners at Rikers nearly doubled, leaving each inmate fewer opportunities for work, recreation, education, and psychological attention. By 1954, the city's overall inmate population exceeded capacity by 88 percent.

The island has grown increasingly crowded over the decades with many new jails added as crises arose.

Rather than build new prisons or confront the social issues causing the increase in the prison population, the government relied on Band-Aid solutions to "fix" this chronic problem. Rikers handled overflow from all the city's detention centers with makeshift cells and by doubling up prisoners; the city also shipped prisoners to the workhouse on Hart Island. A former inmate, who used the fictitious name Stanley Conrad in a 1953 *New York Post* article, called Rikers a "penitentiary laboring under a 1933 system . . . For modern operation, it still has 20 years to catch up."

In the 1960s, the city finally committed to expanding the prison system. New York hoped to save money and improve efficiency by centralizing its facilities on Rikers Island, which still had several hundred acres of isolated land available. This strategy shifted most of the city's detention jails to Rikers, which ultimately created overcrowding issues.

The late 1960s and early 1970s—a volatile time in American cities—signaled another turning point for Rikers Island. As in other jails, racial violence and inmate suicides grew along with the overcrowding. In 1969, black inmates were attacked after moving into an area of the correctional institution controlled by whites, who made up about 35 percent of its population. (With the city's changing racial makeup, the percentage of white inmates has declined since 1930, when the system was about 85 percent white. These days more than 90 percent are black or Latino.) Four months later, more than forty adolescent inmates and five correction officers were injured during another jail brawl. That year, 152 inmates attempted suicide in city jails.

By 1970, approximately fourteen thousand inmates were housed in a citywide system built to accommodate eight thousand. On March 14, 1970, fifteen hundred Rikers inmates staged a hunger strike and work stoppage protesting a 1967 state law reducing the amount of jail time that could be shaved from a sentence for good behavior. The inmates said the law contributed to overcrowding. A few days later, convicts clashed with officers during a violent mess-hall melee, and in May, correction officers protested conditions by picketing the city's jails.

"Once again . . . overcrowding is the single greatest crisis in the city prison system," stated the Department of Correction in its 1971 annual report. "To ignore this warning is to jeopardize the lives of correction officers, the possibility of intelligent prison administration, and the humane treatment of prisoners. . . ."

This era of social unrest affected prisons around the nation. In 1971, some twelve hundred inmates at Attica Correctional Facility in upstate

New York held thirty-seven guards and civilian employees hostage for several days while demanding better conditions. When negotiations failed, armed lawmen stormed the prison, leaving forty-one dead, including thirty-one inmates. At Rikers, the most hostile upheaval came in 1975, when sixteen hundred inmates in the House of Detention for Men (originally Rikers Island Penitentiary; later the maximum-security James A. Thomas Center) held five officers hostage for seventeen hours, threatening them with pipes torn from cellblock railings, toothbrush handles embedded with razors, and sharpened tiles ripped from bathroom walls. The inmates took over six cellblocks before a settlement was reached granting them amnesty and the promise of reduced overcrowding—a pledge the city found impossible to keep.

The first new jail built on Rikers Island after 1935 was the Correctional Institution for Men, which opened in 1964 and was expanded in 1973. Three additional jails were built between 1971 and 1978. (In 1966, a three-lane automobile bridge linking Rikers to Astoria, Queens, replaced the island's snail-like and expensive ferry service. Mayor John Lindsay dubbed it the Bridge of Hope, although by then idealism about the prison system was starting to sound perilously naive.)

By 1981, Rikers' six jails, with more than seven thousand inmates, were again above capacity. Throughout the 1980s, Rikers' environment remained turbulent. A city proposed state takeover failed. In 1981, Correction Commissioner Benjamin Ward installed security fences and posted armed officers around the island's three-mile periphery to thwart escapes. (Guns are not carried inside the prison for fear inmates will snatch them and turn them on officers. While Rikers Island was originally considered escape-proof, the bridge and a LaGuardia Airport runway built within five hundred feet of the island slowed the current of surrounding waters that had served as a barrier.)

To avoid trouble, officers increasingly forged "gentlemen's agreements" with inmates, turning away while inmates engaged in drug use, sex, and violence against other inmates. As Phil Seelig, then president of the Correction Officers Benevolent Association, put it in 1981, "Everyone is conspiring to keep the lid on, and we're paying the price."

But the lid always seemed to pop off at Rikers, especially during the crack epidemic. From 1984 (referred to by one inmate as "B.C." or "Before Crack") through 1994, inmate population increased by 300 percent, approaching twenty thousand daily inmates, with some inmates being held on barges set up next to the island as an emergency measure. There was even a 500 percent increase in women prisoners to a total of about fifteen hundred.

Historical Detour: Parting Gifts

Rikers Island parting gifts, circa 1953: "When a prisoner is released from Rikers," an ex-convict using the alias Stanley Conrad told the _New York Post_ in 1953, "he is given 50 cents and two baloney sandwiches on white or rye. And some clothes. If he was an inmate of the penitentiary, he gets a thin suit, and if it's sub-freezing, a topcoat. If he's released from the workhouse, he gets a blue-grey denim shirt, striped cotton pants, and if necessary, a light cotton sweater. If he's a parole violator, he gets a pair of blue pants and a lumber jacket. The doors open wide for him and he's on his own."

Rikers Island parting gifts, circa 2010: Prisoners are given a Metrocard good for two subway rides and a transfer. A policy of delivering them to Queens Plaza after midnight has been changed, and releases take place in the morning.

"It was absolute chaos," says Richard Koehler, who was correction commissioner in the 1980s. "The amount of violence was substantial." He says that with a federal court monitoring the overcrowding, the department was actually rotating different groups of inmates from beds to receiving rooms to court to prevent a massive release of prisoners.

In 1990, a correction officer was assaulted in a stairwell in one of the two new jails opened in the late 1980s. Six days later, officers blocked the bridge to Rikers to protest overcrowding. After thirty-five hours, inmates began rioting inside that jail. A total of 120 inmates and twenty-one correction employees were injured. A city investigation concluded that DOC brass mishandled the incident, correction officers used unnecessary or excessive force during the disturbance, and budget constraints had compromised employee security. Four years later, fifteen inmates and seventeen officers were injured within a week in two more serious disturbances. Other trials and lawsuits in the early 1990s revealed brutal violence perpetrated against inmates by correction officers, including the beating of shackled prisoners, with officers subsequently falsifying reports.

Meanwhile violence had become more organized, with gangs recruiting within the jails, with Hispanic gangs like the Latin Kings and the Netas vying for turf and privilege with black gangs like the Bloods and Crips. In

1995, a federal judge allowed New York to ban gang-identifying beads and bracelets that the city says contribute to violence.

Norman Seabrook, president of the Correction Officers Union, also warned that low morale, lack of training, and staffing cuts meant the city was on the verge of another Attica.

Soon after, the city made major investments on Rikers Island, boosting the number of correction officers from about eighty-two hundred to more than ten thousand, providing more training and adding a slew of new equipment and aggressive tactics that resulted in a startling decline in violence on the island.

The department added a unit to monitor gangs and a SWAT team to deal with violent outbreaks. Officers were given shields, pepper spray, mace, and the BOSS chair (a body orifice scanning system that uses magnetic sensors to find weapons stashed inside inmates' bodies). "They help us do our job and motivate us even more," Seabrook said then. "We're not as reluctant to do certain things the way they're supposed to be done." Officers began conducting far more searches than ever before, particularly at random hours, like 3 AM. "That used to be unheard of," Seabrook says.

As a result, inmates had fewer weapons and were deterred from violence or subdued more easily during cell and personal searches and during confrontations. Also, inmates were now handcuffed behind their back instead of in front, and those who slash other inmates have their hands clamped into "the mitts," foot-long protective tubes. Inmates charged with infractions like punching a guard or weapons possession found themselves rearrested and charged with new crimes rather than merely being disciplined. And more often the most dangerous inmates were separated out while fewer state prisoners were transferred to Rikers to await court dates.

The results were astonishing. From 1994 to 1999, the annual total of stabbings and slashings among inmates plummeted by over 90 percent, from more than a thousand incidents to less than a hundred. A decade later there were only about thirty per year.

The new approach prompted complaints from inmates and their advocates, but Seabrook made no apologies: "We patrol the toughest precinct in New York. We are often assaulted with urine and feces by inmates."

Inmates have long complained that officers dehumanize them, rarely acknowledging their names, but officers say remaining detached is necessary because eye contact and friendly banter open the floodgates to emotional involvement and inmate trickery. But the more critical complaints revolved around criminal behavior by correction officers.

One of the biggest headlines came in 2003 when three correction officers were arrested for stealing a Salvador Dalí painting out of a locked display case in the lobby of one jail, replacing it with a lackluster fake. Dalí had donated the painting in 1965 after having to cancel a scheduled talk about art with the Rikers inmates. Ironically, the painting had been moved out of the inmate dining room in 1981 for safekeeping. (The painting was not recovered.)

Other infractions were far more serious, and the first decade of the twenty-first century was riddled with accusations. In 2007, the *Village Voice* broke a story about gang beatings at Rikers Island. Sources—including former correction officers—alleged that some officers empowered certain inmates and gangs to act as enforcers. The *Voice* also disclosed court records detailing other violent incidents and excessive force used by the officers. Meanwhile, officers were also implicitly and even explicitly permitting adolescent inmates to be pitted in fights against each other—after one teenager was beaten to death, three officers and twelve inmates were charged with running a criminal extortion ring.

"I'm not going to portray correction officers as a group of saints who've come down from the mountains and can do no wrong," says Seabrook in response to these recent issues. (Seabrook himself has recently faced a spate of sexual harassment allegations.) "There's always going to be someone in any union who will screw up."

While the Department of Correction often denies systemic problems at Rikers Island, the city has paid out millions of dollars to numerous inmates injured on the island, and the DOC has changed its tactics, separating teenage inmates by age and potential for violence, installing video cameras, and creating a new use-of-force policy and guidelines for misconduct investigations.

Still, the city also paid tens of millions more because correction officers repeatedly violated a law on strip-searching people held on misdemeanor charges who couldn't afford bail and also because the administration lied about fixing the situation after a court order was issued.

Seabrook, meanwhile, warns that budget cuts, which have trimmed the number of correction officers from 10,500 to eight thousand in 2010 (the department claims the figure is closer to nine thousand), have again damaged morale and the officers' ability to safely run the jail. "We are short-staffed, and the city is being penny wise but pound foolish," he says. "What good is the equipment if we have no one to man it? What good is the gang intelligence office if we have no one to work it and rearrest the inmates?"

There is also dissent between the union and the department over new

Correction Commissioner Dora Schiro's efforts at rehabilitation for inmates, with the union claiming this is impossible given the short stays at city jails and should be left to the state prisons.

Koehler, the former correction commissioner who is now counsel for the officers union, emphasizes that life at Rikers is "much calmer" than in the 1990s. And while no one expects a return to the city's worst years in terms of crime—and concurrent turmoil on Rikers—he says reductions in the police force, the bad economy, the recent rise in homicides and other crime do not bode well. "Things are going to get bad, and the second place to feel it, after the streets, is in Correction," he says.

Still, there is some hope that life on Rikers will soon become safer and more efficient for both inmates and officers. The city has begun investing in new operations and buildings. DOC also says processing will be revised with a centralized admission and discharge center and a modern inmate classification system that will utilize more sophisticated risk and needs assessment. The city is also reducing the island's capacity by about three thousand beds (although at about fourteen thousand, there will still be room to accommodate a surge in inmates.) It has added one new eight-hundred-bed unit and is planning a new energy-efficient and streamlined fifteen-hundred-bed facility to be completed in 2017. These will replace four thousand aging and substandard beds in fifty run-down temporary structures scattered throughout the island. The original House of Detention, which was built in 1935 and now sits empty, will no longer be used as a jail. Its future is undecided.

14. North and South Brother Islands

"It was one hell of an experience. We made up the laws and rules. It was a pathological zoo."

—FRANK LIMA, FORMER PATIENT AT NORTH BROTHER ISLAND'S RIVERSIDE HOSPITAL, A NARCOTICS REHABILITATION FACILITY FOR TEENAGERS FROM 1952 TO 1963

North and South Brother Islands

IT IS A TALE OF TWO SIBLINGS, islands with lives so drastically dissimilar that no one would ever guess they were related. One has remained small and silent, a wholly private entity. The other, larger island has lived an exceedingly public life defined by tragedy and failed schemes, an inspiration for writers and artists. It is only in recent years, with a flock of new residents, that North and South Brother Islands have finally achieved solidarity.

North Brother Island lies approximately two thousand feet east of the Port Morris section of the Bronx and twenty-five hundred feet west of Rikers Island. Its twenty acres of overgrown vines and deciduous woods threaten to swallow the skeletons of more than a dozen abandoned buildings. South Brother Island, approximately seven acres of undeveloped brush, is about five hundred feet southeast of its big brother, and about twenty-five hundred feet north of Astoria, Queens. The waters here—where the East River makes a sharp turn before flowing into Long Island Sound—are not as treacherous as those of Hell Gate to the south, but are nevertheless powerful and dangerous.

Captain Adriaen Block claimed the islands for the Dutch West India Company in 1614. Block christened the duo De Gesellen, which translates to "the companions." In 1695, the British government granted the two Brother Islands to a James Graham. Then officially part of Queens, the islands remained undeveloped for nearly two centuries, chiefly because of the surrounding currents. North Brother was sold in 1871 to the town of Morrisania (in the Bronx). South Brother remained part of Queens until 1964, and is the only major island in New York City never publicly owned.

Although many newspaper articles claim that nothing has ever been built on South Brother, in 1894 Colonel Jacob Ruppert, a beer magnate and owner of the New York Yankees during the Babe Ruth era, built a summer home there. He used the retreat until 1907; it burned down in 1909. The land remained untouched until 1944, when Ruppert's estate sold the property to John Gerosa, president of Metropolitan Roofing Supplies. Gerosa generously announced a plan to establish a summer resort for his employees there, but the cottages were never built. Gerosa sold South Brother

Island in 1958; it later changed hands several times until a company called Hampton Scows bought it—reportedly for $10. (The company, which apparently was in the sand and gravel business, was always purposefully vague about its business and its plans for the island when questioned.) Meanwhile, the city felt compelled in 1964 to unite the two brother islands by moving the borough boundary to include South Brother in the Bronx. (The island is held in such low esteem that Bronx officials vehemently insist they sent it back to Queens in the 1980s; Queens officials dismiss this claim and deny any affiliation with South Brother.) North Brother probably welcomed the company, having recently been abandoned after eight tumultuous decades of use.

North Brother was utilized like many other city islands in the late nineteenth century—society's castaways were warehoused there in hospitals. But how North Brother joined this league of quarantine islands is shrouded in mystery.

The traditional story presented in most articles and books recalls an island unused except by the lighthouse keeper until 1880, when the local Sisters of Charity or Sisters of St. Stephen built a hospital there. In 1885, the city assumed control of the island, transferring Riverside Hospital there from Blackwell's Island to expand the existing clinic.

In describing the city's construction plans, the *New York Times* reported in 1881 that the lighthouse keeper and his family were the only residents. They cultivated a farm with laborers who resided in what was once the Westchester County pesthouse for smallpox.

But a 1913 city department of health history offers a more dramatic tale. It reports that until 1880 residents of small towns in Westchester, which then included the Bronx, would chase smallpox victims into the city, forcing New York to care for them on Blackwell's Island. New York finally forced the suburbs to build their own hospital—a small shack along the East River. When residents discovered that the one patient there was black, they burned the shack and forced the caretaker and patient into a boat. Set adrift, the duo found refuge in an unoccupied house on North Brother Island. (Who had built the house is unexplained.) Thus, a hospital was born.

The city took over the island in 1885, rushing to complete Riverside Hospital at the height of a typhus epidemic. The Sisters of Charity maintained a tent colony for suspected typhus patients there for six months before the facility was completed.

Whatever its genesis, Riverside Hospital opened on North Brother Island in 1885 to care for victims of infectious diseases like typhus, cholera, yellow fever, and smallpox. Through the end of the century, River-side also received immigrants with smallpox from the state quarantine at Hoffman and Swinburne Islands. After New York consolidated in 1898, Riverside was largely used for Bronx residents, except in emergencies.

The hospital complex included a two-story brick building for eighty patients, with plans for three additional frame structures, each with forty beds, for patient overflow during epidemics. It turned out much more was needed. Massive immigration and rapid industrial and urban development provided fertile breeding ground for infectious diseases. The city's public hospitals were flooded with cases. In 1886, five wooden pavilions were added to ease overcrowding at Riverside. Then, in 1892, two structures were built specifically for smallpox patients. A typhus plague a year later forced the hospital to import three portable houses.

By the turn of the twentieth century, the city was awash with another grave peril: tuberculosis. The highly infectious lung disease killed thou-sands of New Yorkers—more than one in ten deaths were attributed to TB. In 1903, several vacant pavilions were used to forcibly detain infected patients whose willful carelessness posed a danger to their community. When those forty-eight beds quickly filled up, a renewed building frenzy began. During the next decade, the city enlarged North Brother Island with four acres of landfill and constructed many buildings, including four con-crete pavilions for 320 new TB patients. While the wealthy sought treat-ment in sanatoriums, derelicts and the indigent were sent to North Brother's Riverside Hospital. Their care was an extension of government efforts to use science to resolve issues dealing with the poor and immi-grants, says Dr. Barron Lerner, historian of medicine at Columbia Univer-sity. "This solved both a medical and a social problem."

But a more urgent crisis was still to come. Before 1916, poliomyelitis was a relatively rare disease: From 1912 through June 1916, it had killed only 171 New Yorkers. But from July 1 through September 9, 1916, polio fatalities averaged 209 per week. The disease was especially grim because 90 percent of its victims were under the age of ten. The city transformed contagious disease hospitals into polio centers. (The Swinburne Island quarantine served Staten Island.) Riverside Hospital treated 1,211 patients in those turbulent weeks. (Interestingly, children living on islands, and insulated from the greater society, were not affected by the epidemic. There were no polio cases among the eighty youngsters of Governors Island. Even the 350 children on Brooklyn's Barren Island—a poor community plagued by flies, mosquitoes, and rats, with no sewage or public water—were not infected.)

In 1938, with 350 TB patients and seven typhoid carriers on North Brother Island, the city began building the final and grandest of Riverside's buildings—a $1.2 million tuberculosis pavilion. Construction of the 150-bed facility was frequently stalled during World War II as the government shifted priorities and redirected supplies. The facility was completed in 1943 but was never used as a tuberculosis hospital, because the Riverside complex had deteriorated and fallen into disuse.

In 1946, North Brother Island was resuscitated with an influx of healthy boarders. The GI Bill had caused a rush at colleges as well as dormitory shortages at City College, Columbia, and Fordham Universities. So New York State leased the island from the city and turned the new pavilion and several other buildings into veteran-student housing, from which it ferried the students to school each day. One pupil, Evan Hunter, later wrote the novel *Blackboard Jungle*, the screenplay for Alfred Hitchcock's *The Birds*, and a short story called "Happy New Year, Herbie" set on North Brother Island.

Historical Detour: Island Exile

Mary Mallon was an unknown, hardworking immigrant, and the picture of health: robust, agile, and powerful. She was also a walking plague feared by every citizen in New York. Confined to North Brother Island for nearly three decades until her death in 1938, Mallon achieved eternal notoriety as Typhoid Mary.

Typhoid fever, an acute, highly infectious disease, was a grave and perplexing problem in New York at the turn of the twentieth century. Many experts believed it spread through polluted water or milk or through the sewers, but could neither establish a source nor halt its deadly march. In 1906, there were 3,467 cases and 639 deaths from typhoid.

That August, an epidemiologist named George Soper investigated an outbreak of typhoid in a family whose cook, Mary Mallon, had just moved on to another job. Soper, who believed the disease was transmitted by people, not pollutants, traced Mallon's career back to 1900 and discovered that seven other typhoid epidemics—resulting in at least twenty-five illnesses and one death—had originated in households where she had cooked.

In early 1907, Soper contacted Mallon to tell her she was

spreading typhoid when she handled food. Mallon rejected Soper's request for an examination by attacking him with a carving knife. Soper went to New York's health department and arranged for police protection. When Soper visited Mallon again, she escaped through the back of her house, climbed a fence, and led the cops on a lengthy chase that ended with Mallon barricading herself behind several barrels. Finally trapped and apprehended, Typhoid Mary was sent to Riverside Hospital on North Brother Island.

Soper described Mallon, age thirty-seven, as having blond hair, blue eyes, healthy color, a masculine gait, and "a determined mouth and jaw." The five-foot-six-inch Mallon was fairly heavy but was in good health; she carried typhoid yet was wholly unaffected by it.

On North Brother Island, Mallon was given a small bungalow set on the riverbank. Although not in prison, Mallon loathed the forced isolation. A native of Ireland, she had no visitors and no family in the area. Nurses left food at the door and hurried off. Except for a dog, Mallon was utterly alone.

Mallon stubbornly dismissed the diagnosis, pointing to her hardy condition as proof of her well-being. Instead, she filed a writ of habeas corpus in 1909, suing the city for detaining her without due process. Several doctors and Soper—who had become a local hero after Mallon's capture—persuaded a judge that she was a danger to the community.

Mallon was released a year later on the conditions that she refrain from cooking or handling other people's food and that she check in regularly with city officials. When Mallon couldn't find work, the city got her a job as a laundress. Mallon, who felt unjustly persecuted, was not satisfied. In 1911, she threatened to sue the city and health department for $50,000. Then she abruptly changed her mind, and rather than pursue the suit before a critical public, simply disappeared.

For more than two years, Mallon eluded city investigators by working in hotels and restaurants under aliases like Marie Breshof and Mrs. Brown. Then twenty-five people—mostly doctors and nurses at Sloane Maternity Hospital where "Mrs. Brown" was working—contracted typhoid; two died. Officials discovered that Mrs. Brown was actually Mallon and traced her whereabouts to Corona, Queens. There they had to climb through a second-story window to appre-

After being sent to North Brother Island, Mary Mallon, a.k.a. Typhoid Mary, lived alone in this cottage.

hend her. In March 1915, the board of health declared Mallon a public menace to be held indefinitely on North Brother Island.

Mallon never tried to flee, although occasional rumors of her escape often put the city on edge. She kept to herself, but this time the Riverside Hospital staff reached out to Mallon, providing her with a job in the hospital's laboratory and a cottage. Eventually, officials even allowed her to take day trips to the mainland. In 1932, Mallon suffered a stroke. She never walked again, spending her last years in the hospital.

Mallon wasn't the only typhoid carrier in New York, just the most infamous. While some modern writers argue that Mallon was singled out unfairly because she was a lower-class, immigrant woman, when she died at age sixty-nine on November 11, 1938, there were six other carriers in isolation, and 350 more registered with the city's department of health who were checked on regularly. Mallon's case inspired compulsory health exams for, and licensing of, all food handlers in the city, and Mallon was studied by high school health classes and medical schools. Mallon even found her way into the English language. Anyone called a Typhoid Mary is "a person from whom something undesirable or deadly spreads to those nearby," according to the dictionary. Even in death, Mallon couldn't shake the stigma. Only nine people attended her funeral, and they would not identify themselves to a local reporter who covered the service.

The city reclaimed the island in 1952, returning Riverside Hospital to its historic purpose of isolating undesirables. A 152-bed rehabilitation center for adolescent drug addicts opened in the old tuberculosis pavilion and several other buildings. Financed jointly by the city and state, the ambitious project was the first of its kind. It had a full-time staff of 306, including psychiatrists, teachers, and social workers who provided vocational guidance, schooling, family therapy, and follow-up care. Some patients were referred by hospitals, but most were arrested on drug charges and sentenced to the island as an alternative to jail.

At the time Governor Thomas Dewey and Mayor Vincent Impellitteri predicted the facility would eliminate teenage drug addiction as a serious local problem in five years. Six months later, Hospitals Commissioner Dr. Marcus Kogel told the *New York Times* he had "serious doubts" about the program.

Riverside had expected well-behaved and malleable adolescents but mainly received hard-core heroin addicts, two-thirds of whom were between nineteen and twenty-one. The program was haunted by both a high recidivism rate (one patient returned seventeen times) and constant escapes. Some patients drowned during their exodus, but most deserters were picked up by police waiting onshore.

In 1956, the city considered moving the program to City Hospital at the southern end of Welfare Island (now Roosevelt Island) and relocating the Women's House of Detention in Greenwich Village to North Brother Island. The idea was kicked around for years as Riverside's program became widely viewed as a failure by the city and the media.

"It was just too corrupt," says Frank Lima, a former addict treated on the island several times following arrests in the late 1950s and early 1960s. While the facilities were clean and the food was decent, prostitution and bribery kept the island awash with drugs, says Lima, now a published poet and a teacher at the New York Restaurant School. "We did anything we wanted, whenever we wanted."

Herbert Walcoe, a social worker there, recalls a prison culture in which white, black, and Puerto Rican patients segregated themselves, infusing the island with the racial tension of the streets. Guards and aides were "ripe for making an extra buck" while professionals averted their gaze, he says. A civil service mentality pervaded even the psychiatric staff. "They were going through the motions," says Walcoe.

"It was a depressing island," he adds. "There wasn't really much of an effort to cheer it up. The grounds were weedy and unkempt. The subtext was that this was a hopeless situation."

Riverside Hospital finally closed in 1963, putting an end to North Brother's institutional history (women's detention went to Rikers instead). But the island had one moment of notoriety remaining—it stepped into the Broadway footlights and helped launch actor Al Pacino's career. *Does the Tiger Wear a Necktie?* starring Hal Holbrook and the twenty-eight-year-old Pacino opened in 1969 at the Belasco Theater. Written by former Riverside teacher Don Petersen, the play examined the relationship between one educator and his troubled students. It was a commercial flop, closing after thirty-nine performances; *Newsweek* panned it as "woefully weak in structure" with "all the standard blackboard jungle types." But Pacino's Broadway debut as a young tough on the edge won rave reviews and the Tony for Best Supporting Actor, bringing him bigger offers that soon took him beyond his decrepit fifth-floor walk-up on East Fourteenth Street.

North Brother Island inspired dreamers again in 1970, when the city offered the abandoned island and its dilapidated buildings for sale, asking for an opening bid of $1.1 million. Entrepreneurs came out of the woodwork. Proposals included an amusement park, power plant, movie studio, casino with convention center and hotel (dubbed the Las Vegas of the East), and an integrated urban village connected to the city by monorail.

The cost of construction, transportation to the island, and installing a sewage system—not to mention the airplane noise from nearby LaGuardia Airport—discouraged investors. And finally, the notion of selling North Brother Island was swallowed by red tape when Bronx Borough President Robert Abrams decided the city shouldn't relinquish this "irreplaceable resource" to commercial developers. Abrams, who envisioned an environmental-monitoring facility and park there, repeatedly rallied the board of estimate to block any sale. In 1976, the board approved a plan to lease the island, but there were no bids.

The city continued trying to get North Brother Island onto the tax rolls, but the only serious offer came from the state, when Governor Mario Cuomo considered building a prison for a thousand inmates there in the 1980s. What was touted as an $82 million project in September 1983 became a $125 million undertaking by March 1984, when Cuomo approved the plan. (Riverside's TB pavilion was the only building that wouldn't be razed.) The plan was abandoned in 1985 after Cuomo, conceding that meeting environmental requirements and repairing the island's seawall would drive the price tag above $200 million, decided to build the prison in upstate New York.

Throughout the decade, plans for the island surfaced and sank quickly. Mayor Ed Koch's 1988 notion of shipping the homeless to Hart and North

Brother Islands was met with vehement objections in editorials and by
advocates for the homeless. Robert Hayes, counsel for the Coalition for the
Homeless, called Koch's plan "the gulag mentality of social welfare."

The ferry slip on North Brother Island lies in ruins as do the buildings on the island.

Meanwhile, a rookery was discovered amid the overgrowth on South
Brother Island in 1978 with cattle egrets, snowy egrets, and black-crowned
night herons. By 1983, double-crested cormorants had joined the colony.
And as the plans for jails and shelters were being bandied about for North
Brother Island, it was quietly evolving into a true companion to its sib-
ling—by 1989, some of the birds from South Brother had discovered North
Brother Island next door.

Both Brother Islands eventually became part of the Harbor Herons Project, which started on Prall's Island, Shooter's Island, and Isle of Meadow off
Staten Island. The project is dedicated to protecting the birds' habitats.
And in 2007, the Trust for Public Land (on behalf of the Wildlife Conservation Society and other groups) brokered a deal, buying the island from
Hampton Scows for $2 million. Much of the money came from the federal gov-
ernment and was secured by Congressman José Serrano. The Trust then donated
the land to the city's parks department to protect the wading birds that nest there.

South Brother Island was, for many years, the harbor's first- or second-most- popular nesting spot. While Hoffman Island and Canarsie Pol have surpassed it, its numbers in 2010 were healthy, showing 230 black-crowned night herons, 132 great egrets, and seventy-four snowy egrets. However, these waders have to contend with a growing number of double-crested cormorants nesting on the island. The cormorants compete for nest sites with the waders, and their acidic feces can destroy habitat for other birds. (Some environmentalists not associated with New York City Audubon have taken the controversial view that the cormorants should be kept in check and possibly even hunted.) Another pressing issue for the waders of South Brother is that one of their favorite types of tree on this island, the Box Elder, is also a target of the invasive Asian Longhorned Beetles. Given that the city's current plan for dealing with any beetle sightings involves cutting down all potential arboreal hosts in the area, New York City Audubon is concerned that this policy could wipe out South Brother as a nesting colony.

Experts say wading birds often nest in one general area but move the colony's center from island to island. But habitat destruction, invasive plant species, mammalian predation, human disturbance, and pollution can all affect the birds' ability to nest. For example, in 2000, North Brother was home to nearly two hundred nesting pairs of waders (mostly black-crowned night herons), nearly one-third more than it had in 1994. But in the next decade the island faced a steady decline in population. To reverse the trend, the Parks Department removed stands of Norway maples and battled the invasive kudzu, planting in its place native trees and shrubs the wading birds prefer. It was to no avail. "Sometimes we think we know what's best but the birds make their own decisions," says Parks commissioner Adrian Benepe. "We got rid of the invasive species and the vines and the birds still moved to South Brother Island."

By 2010 North Brother Island was essentially empty of wading birds, perhaps also in part because of a new problem—raccoon tracks were recently found on the island. A recent Harbor Herons Project report raised questions about steps to deal with raccoons there and on other islands. But Benepe says city policy states that the raccoons are left alone if they're not rabid or near humans. He says nature will take its course because without bird eggs here, the raccoons may leave, opening the door for the birds to return. It's not like North Brother is an avian ghost town. There are plenty of species beyond those found in most New York backyards, including American oystercatchers, various ducks, swans, ospreys, and owls.

These birds live among the remains of North Brother Island's human past, from Riverside Hospital's brick morgue to the ruins of the old pavilions and staff residences. They have been ravaged by time and choked by vines and forests, yet a few buildings remain visible, a faithful reminder of North Brother's history.

EXPLORING THE ISLAND

Visitors can get fairly close to the islands without disturbing nesting birds by joining a New York City Audubon naturalist-led **Sunset Eco-Cruise** aboard the New York Water Taxi. The 90-minute trip (fee required) starts at South Street Seaport then continues up the East River to North Brother Island. Each trip is limited to 100 participants and is offered June through August. To reserve a seat, contact New York Water Taxi at 212-742-1969 or go to www.nycaudubon.org.

Historical Detour: The Darkest Hour

It never should have happened. "Limp, charred bodies were laid out in long rows on the grass," *Munsey's Magazine* wrote in 1904. "This was not murder, it was massacre. By midnight, six hundred and eleven lay on the lawn and four hundred more were still in the river."

The families aboard the ill-fated *General Slocum* excursion steamer should have been picnicking on Long Island, not laid out in groups of corpses on North Brother Island: six Gresses, eleven Rheinfranks . . . The island, long a place for healing the ill, had become a gruesome, makeshift morgue for tallying the dead.

Few tragedies seem as reprehensible, as criminal, as the burning of the *General Slocum* on June 15, 1904. The second worst maritime fire in history, it is a saga of negligence aggravated by incompetence, and a tale of an unsuspecting community that chartered a ship and was annihilated in a single afternoon.

On a sunny Wednesday morning, 1,358 members of St. Mark's Lutheran Evangelical Church in Little Germany on the Lower East Side clambered aboard the *General Slocum* for their seventeenth annual picnic in bucolic Huntington, Long Island. The passengers were primarily German immigrants who could neither speak English nor swim, and most of those on this weekday sojourn were women and children—fewer than one hundred men were on board.

On the surface, the *Slocum* looked superb. The 264-foot vessel, named for Civil War general and Brooklyn congressman Henry Warner Slocum, was constructed of locust, white oak, and yellow pine. She featured mahogany interiors, ornate carvings, and wicker furniture with red velvet. The three decks had recently been repainted white. The ship's flags whipped in the wind, bands played, and revelers enjoyed ice cream and fried clams.

While the *Slocum* had been extraordinarily popular when it first took to the water in 1891, a slew of accidents, breakdowns, and groundings—all with Captain William Van Schaick at the helm—eroded its appeal. By 1904, the ship was having trouble getting business. The tightfisted Knickerbocker Steamboat Company left Van Schaick, sixty-seven, in charge of an unseasoned crew who worked cheap. The hired hands were unemployed ironworkers and dockmen with minimal experience running a rig.

After departing from the Third Street Pier that fateful day, the *Slocum* headed up the East River. Shortly before the boat passed Ward's Island, children on board started complaining about a smoky smell, but their warnings went unheeded. When Lillie Mannheimer declared the boat was on fire, her aunt shushed her, and a neighbor said it was clam chowder burning. One boy rushed to the pilothouse, yelling, "Hey mister, the boat's on fire." Van Schaick, not wanting to be distracted by what he thought was a prank at Hell Gate—the journey's most arduous stretch—snapped, "You shut your trap. Get out of here." Finally, another boy dragged deckhand John Coakley away from his free beer and toward the smoldering storeroom.

The previous night a deckhand had helped church members unpack glasses in the bar. He had stuffed hay from the crates in the storeroom, despite fire regulations prohibiting its presence on board. The danger was heightened since the hay was jammed in with inflammables like wooden furniture, hemp line, and three barrels of oil.

Upon seeing black fumes seeping out from under the door, Coakley foolishly yanked the door open. Then he grabbed whatever was nearby to smother the fire, which happened to be a bag of charcoal. "That did no good," Coakley admitted at the inquest in a masterful display of understatement.

Just past Sunken Meadow Island (now connected to Randall's Island), the smoldering hay exploded into flames. When Van Schaick received word of the emergency, he ordered full speed ahead for North Brother Island, about one mile north. Afterward, most people condemned Van Schaick's decision to bypass piers just three hundred feet away in Queens and the Bronx. But Claude Rust, who wrote *The Burning of the General Slocum* and whose grandmother had died in the disaster, felt that with lumberyards and oil tanks dotting the shoreline, Van Schaick had made the only move possible. And move he did: The ship's acceleration combined with strong winds to fan the flames; tugs coming to its rescue couldn't keep up with the blazing inferno.

En route to North Brother Island, the crisis quickly evolved into a full-fledged catastrophe, revealing an insidious chain of negligence. Rotten fire hoses quickly burst when used; lifeboats were nailed or lashed to the boat. Despite a law requiring weekly fire drills, the crew had never executed one, and crew members helped out only haphazardly; most abandoned ship. After passengers finally got a lifeboat in the water, a frenzied crew member leaped in, capsizing it.

Additionally, 90 percent of the ship's life preservers were thirteen years old, five years over their normal life span. The cork inside them had dried, and many preservers disintegrated upon hitting the water. (Subsequent investigations revealed that Knickerbocker executives had altered invoices to make it seem as if they'd ordered new ones.) To meet weight specifications, some preservers were even stuffed with cast iron instead of buoyant cork because iron was cheaper per pound at the time. A man named John Kircher later testified that after he put his seven-year-old daughter Elsie into a Kahnweiler Neversink preserver, she "sunk as though a stone were tied to her."

Panic tore into the passengers. As the *Slocum* voyaged north, women who couldn't swim clutched their babies and jumped overboard to escape the flames. One boy was sucked into the boat's paddle wheel.

At the last minute, Van Schaick considered the Bronx, before making a sharp turn toward the North Brother ferry slip. The maneuver proved deadly, sending passengers on the upper deck hurtling into the rail, which collapsed, toppling everyone into the now boiling river. The current was rapid and powerful; five hundred people were swept into the river's deeper midchannel. Nonswimmers clutched onto swimmers, dragging them under.

By the time fireboats and police arrived, the *Slocum* was already beached, but the nightmare had just begun. As in any disaster, the fire brought out the best and worst in human behavior.

Ghoulish scavengers rowed out to the wreck and robbed corpses. Others dove for pocketbooks and shoved survivors away from boats if they had no money. One unconscious floater came to and found a man leaning out of a tug, calmly removing her locket and chain. She had to plead before he'd take her ashore.

But one Good Samaritan, a Brooklynite named Samuel Berg, rowed out from 144th Street in the Bronx and saved two women and a child. Reserve policeman Thomas Cooney saved eleven people, then drowned going for a twelfth. Tug captain John Wade risked his livelihood, guiding his rig *Wade* up against the flaming *Slocum* and rescuing more than one hundred passengers.

On North Brother Island, doctors and nurses from the island's Riverside Hospital set up first-aid stations. Patients and kitchen staff pitched in. A convalescent patient named Mary McCann rescued twenty children before collapsing. Even inmates from nearby Rikers escaped their prison briefly to help out.

As the burning ship collapsed, she was towed away to prevent the island's buildings from catching fire. Left behind were many grisly reminders of what had transpired—rescue workers found four dead women with their hands desperately clamped to a railing.

"My mother was burned up and down her left side," says ninety-seven-year-old Adella Wotherspoon, who was only six months old when she, her parents, and two sisters boarded the *Slocum*. "She carried those scars her whole life." Adella's father also survived, but her sisters Anna and Helen did not; Helen's body was never recovered. It is believed that she is buried among the unidentified dead in the Lutheran All Faith's Cemetery in Middle Village, Queens.

The public and the press were outraged. The New York *American* called it "the usual story of such events in this country, where . . . love of money deadens the conscience."

Van Schaick, partly blinded and with a fractured leg, was hidden by police to prevent his lynching. He, the unlicensed first mate, Knickerbocker Steamboat Company officials, and inspector Henry Lundberg, who had certified the boat during inspection the previous month, were found guilty during an inquest and faced criminal charges in federal court.

When no action had been taken by December, the public outcry escalated. In *Munsey's Magazine*, a writer named Herbert Casson warned that disdain for ethical behavior would continue unless "irresponsible directors are taken from their corporate pedestals and treated like ordinary breakers of the law. In short, this aristocracy of crime must be destroyed."

Several inspectors were dismissed, and ships subsequently came under stricter scrutiny. In 1906, Van Schaick received a ten-year sentence for manslaughter. The others went free, including four employees from Nonpareil Cork Works charged with having put iron in the preservers. Some observers felt Van Schaick was made the scapegoat, but most believed he was justly punished and were only angry the others had not been convicted, too.

Van Schaick served less than four years before 250,000 sympathizers petitioned President William Howard Taft for his release. Despite protests, Taft pardoned Van Schaick, who bought a farm upstate with funds donated by supporters and lived there until the age of ninety.

While the legal farce played itself out, the East Sixth Street congregation and the Little Germany community mourned and, ultimately, fell apart. Of the 1,358 people on the *Slocum* (some accounts say 1,331), 1,021 died. Six hundred families lost a loved one, and one hundred people committed suicide in the fire's aftermath.

"My father walked the streets for days and visited every morgue and every possible place looking for my sister Helen," says Wotherspoon. "I think the disaster had a great deal to do with his declining health." He died six years later, at age thirty-six, of tuberculosis.

The toll was felt most acutely in the schools. Thirty-nine of the fifty-one children in the church's kindergarten program had died. P.S. 25 lost 100 students, then 150 more when bereaved families fled the neighborhood in an effort to put the horror behind them.

The *Slocum* crashed on North Brother Island, but the impact of the disaster was felt for generations throughout the city—especially in areas like Yorkville and Astoria, where new, smaller German communities were suddenly founded, and on the Lower East Side, where a society disappeared. Today, the *Slocum*'s victims are memorialized by two monuments. One, in Lutheran All Faith's Cemetery in Middle Village, Queens, remembers the sixty-one unidentified dead. The monument was unveiled in 1905 by Wotherspoon, who was the youngest *Slocum* survivor. (She and another woman are the only known survivors alive today.) Each year, to mark the tragedy's anniversary, the Organization of the *General Slocum* Survivors—made up mostly of *Slocum* descendants and historians—keeps the memory of the *Slocum* alive by holding a graveside memorial service. The other monument is on the Lower East Side in Tompkins Square Park. It is dedicated to the children who died aboard the *Slocum* and simply states: THEY WERE THE EARTH'S PUREST CHILDREN, YOUNG AND FAIR.

15. Forgotten Islands of the East River

U Thant Island • Mill Rock Island • Furman's Island

Tiny U Thant Island is a popular spot for cormorants.

DON RIEPE

Forgotten Islands of the East River

U Thant Island

The East River's smallest island has perhaps the grandest aspirations. A mere one hundred by two hundred feet, this island was built on Man-o'-War Reef in the 1890s, using rocks and soil excavated from a tunnel being built by William Steinway. The piano manufacturer wanted to bring trolleys from Queens into Manhattan. Steinway died in 1896, leaving his Steinway Tunnel unfinished, but financier August Belmont completed it for his then privately owned Interborough Rapid Transit subway line. Excavated material again augmented the tiny isle.

For the next seventy years, the island was called Belmont Island, but in 1976 it took on a new life. The island sits opposite the United Nations and caught the attention of some UN employees who meditated with Indian spiritual leader Sri Chinmoy, who lived in Queens. Sri Chinmoy preached love, religious tolerance, peace, and service to the larger world. Hoping to promote the themes that Sri Chinmoy espoused, his followers leased the island from New York State and planted flowers, bushes, and trees on it. They also unofficially renamed the island in honor of Sri Chinmoy's good friend, U Thant, a Burmese diplomat, who was United Nations secretary-general from 1961 through 1971 and who ascribed to the same beliefs regarding peace and spirituality advocated by Chinmoy.

The group, which pays $20 a year as a lease, has occasionally held functions on U Thant Island. They erected a thirty-foot-high peace arch made from silver steel tubing. A time capsule buried there includes some of U Thant's speeches, photos, and personal effects, such as his favorite tie clasp.

The island was never formally renamed; many maps still call it Belmont Island. These days, however, it could just as easily be named Cormorant Island, as about thirty double-crested cormorants make their home here each year, building nests in the trees and on the peace arch.

Mill Rock Island

The largest intentional manmade explosion prior to the atomic bomb took place in the most unlikely of places and for the most unlikely of reasons. On October 10, 1885, some three hundred thousand pounds of explosives produced on Great Mill Rock and Little Mill Rock Islands were detonated in the East River. But this wasn't war, this was business—the army was violently eliminating Flood Rock, the river's most hellish obstacle, to make the waters safe for ship traffic.

The shipping industry had suffered for years from the reefs and rock islands in this part of the river, which had caused hundreds of wrecks and prevented larger vessels from venturing through. The Dutch called the area Hellegat, meaning "bright passage" or "beautiful pass." (They may have been referring to the entire East River). The English corrupted the name to Hell Gate, which perfectly described this treacherous portion of the East River.

The War Department first took on Mother Nature in 1851 and, over the next seventy years, blasted some of the most colorfully named islets in the city out of the water: Hen and Chickens; Hog's Back; Frying Pan; Bread and Cheese; and Bald Headed Billy.

Toward the end of the century, the army set up a base for mixing explosives on Great Mill Rock and Little Mill Rock Islands, located a thousand feet off Ninety-sixth Street in Manhattan. Here, the army developed its newest invention, "rackarock," an explosive stew that was poured over chlorate of potash and mixed with wooden hoes.

On that fateful day in 1885 when nine-acre Flood Rock was annihilated, the *New York Times* wrote of the Mill Rocks: "People looked at these rugged brown spots with feelings that were deeper than respect."

The hyperbole was understandable considering the buildup. Planning began in 1875, but unsteady financial support from Congress caused endless delays. Finally, engineers constructed a temporary island around Flood Rock's perimeter, from which workmen prepared for its explosion. A week before the 1885 detonation, newspapers were filled with reports of the gradual dismantling of the peripheral island's machinery and houses. Articles also recommended vantage points from which to view the imminent spectacle.

On October 10, approximately a hundred thousand spectators planted themselves on the East River's banks, scaled trees and lampposts, and boarded tugs and rowboats circling the Mill Rocks and Flood Rock. Even patients housed in asylums on Blackwell's and Ward's Islands poured out to watch.

At 11:14 AM, the moment of truth arrived. According to the *Times*, there was "a deep rumble then a dull boom. Up, up and still up into the frightened air soared a great ghastly writhing wall of white and silver and gray." The blast created some fifty geysers, with three fountains spewing water two hundred feet high, then plummeting down "with a wild hissing as if 10,000 huge steam valves had been opened." The river transformed into a boiling mass of white foam covered by a gaseous cloud that turned yellow, green, and blue before dissipating.

Shocks from the blast were felt as far away as Princeton, New Jersey. The *Times*, which devoted its entire front page to the event, declared the blast "another triumph of human skill over the resistance of nature."

Fragments of Flood Rock were used to fill in the area between Great Mill Rock and Little Mill Rock, and by 1890, a new 8.6-acre, key-shaped island—Mill Rock Island—was formed. The army continued using Mill Rock Island until 1949 as a base for surveying and blasting operations and for repairing boats and buoys.

Great Mill Rock and Little Mill Rock were sold in 1664 by Native Americans to Dutchman William Hallett, who snapped up much of the land in the area. Great Mill Rock was first developed between 1701 and 1707, when John Marsh built the tidal mill there that gave both the islands their names. During the War of 1812, the army built a blockhouse with cannons on the island to deter the British from making their way from Long Island Sound. The blockhouse burned down in 1821. In 1850, John Clark claimed squatter's rights to Great Mill Rock and began selling food and booze to passing boats. A decade later, he sold the island for $40 to Sandy Gibson, who moved his entire household there, right down to the cows and chickens. Three years later, Gibson sold the land to a Charles Leland for $300, but stayed on for several more years as a tenant, catching eels and flounder for food.

Good mythmakers and bad fact checkers have often distorted Gibson's story. A 1938 *New Yorker* article said Gibson lived on Great Mill Rock from 1840 until 1898, when he was evicted by soldiers who were "just starting the job of clearing the reefs out of Hell Gate. . . . Nobody knows where he went with his cow and his chickens after fifty-eight years." This fabrication errs at both ends of the timeline, since Gibson arrived in 1860 and had to be gone well before the 1885 explosion. Yet it was repeated in a 1951 *New York Herald Tribune* article and other publications through the years, giving it the aura of fact.

Once the army retired Mill Rock, Parks Commissioner Robert Moses—claiming that commercial interests might develop the abandoned island—had the federal government deed Mill Rock to his department in 1953. When money finally became available in 1967, Moses razed all the buildings on Mill Rock, planting willow and poplar trees in their place. The island wasn't used as a park until the 1980s, when Asphalt Green, an Upper East Side not-for-profit group, offered leadership training for young teens there. The group even tried camping out once, but after dark the island swarmed with rats. "The kids loved it," says art coordinator Dave Mosher. "They got to stay up all night with flashlights and brickbats beating bushes and making noise. But it was not an experience we cared to repeat."

After nor'easters demolished the Asphalt Green dock in the early 1990s, the organization stopped journeying to Mill Rock Island. As is always the case in New York, someone else stepped in to grab this opportunity for open space. In recent years, the Harbor Herons Project has counted a growing number of wader birds nesting on the island. In 2010, there were seventy-five nesting pairs of black-crowned night herons and smaller numbers of great egrets and snowy egrets. It is a much quieter existence for Mill Rock than the day the earth shook here.

Furman's Island

Once surrounded by beautiful freshwater wetlands, the island known as Furman's Island experienced a crude transformation early in the twentieth century when progress stitched it to the mainland. Today warehouses, like the enormous New York City Transit Authority storage facility, blight this once-green haven with gray.

The island in Newtown Creek, which flows from the East River and divides Queens and Brooklyn, was called Arnhem in 1638 when it became one of the first settlements in Queens. Located just west of Maspeth and separated from the mainland on its eastern side by the slim, marshy Shanty Creek, this Dutch hamlet of quaint gabled cottages and a church coexisted for a time with Native American wigwams. In 1643, Native Americans destroyed the village in retaliation for Dutch hostilities elsewhere, and colonists fled to Fort Amsterdam in what is now Manhattan.

In 1815, Judge Garrit Furman bought the land south of Newtown Creek, including Furman's Island, and on these fifty-four acres built a mansion where he entertained many New York City millionaires. The pastoral set-ting also offered Furman great fishing and hunting and inspiration for poetry. One collection, *The Maspeth Poems*, published in 1837, includes a selection titled "Petition of the Shell-Fish, on Maspeth Island, for Protec-tion Against the Turnpike-Makers, That Are Working the Williamsburg Turnpike." In it, the shellfish of Newtown Creek solicit Jove to take pity on their fate—one, ironically, orchestrated by Furman.

For, despite his love of nature, Furman entered into a partnership with the builders of a toll road and bridge (The Maspeth Avenue and Toll Bridge Company) that crossed his island and provided a direct route from

Williamsburg and Bushwick to Maspeth, Newtown, and Flushing. The road, which appears on some maps as Maspeth Avenue, was no more than twenty feet wide and operated until 1866. It then lay abandoned for ten years, and the toll bridge built over marshy Newtown Creek gradually became dangerous for traveling. In 1876, the town of Newtown replaced the old road with Grand Avenue, a new thoroughfare a quarter mile south of the old turnpike.

In 1855, four bone-boiling plants occupied Furman Island. These facilities made boneblack—roasted bones that were used in ink production and sugar refining—and used fat from animal bones to make soap. Eventually, manure and horse-rendering plants also opened on the island, an ideal spot for foul-smelling businesses since there were no residential neighbors.

By 1870, formerly pristine Newtown Creek had become polluted by raw sewage and refinery oil. (In 2010, the still-tainted waterway was declared a Superfund cleanup site by the Environmental Protection Agency.) The Furman estate was sold in 1899 to a Manhattan business syndicate that planned to build an industrial park in the area. While the project never materialized, it's likely that the entrepreneurs began filling in Shanty Creek to join the island to the rest of their property, the late Queens historian Vincent F. Seyfried once said, adding that no one knows exactly when Furman's Island ceased to be an island. "'Who cares?' was probably the sentiment."

Part V

Jamaica Bay

BROAD CHANNEL • FORGOTTEN ISLANDS OF
JAMAICA BAY AND THE ROCKAWAYS

*Secluded from the Atlantic Ocean by the slender Rockaway Peninsula,
Jamaica Bay has lost much of its area to landfill. The bay, about eighteen
square miles in Brooklyn and Queens, is dotted with more than a dozen
islands, some as large as three square miles, others tiny marshy flats that
disappear with the tide.*

16. Broad Channel

"Broad Channel is an enclave in the middle of a federal wildlife refuge. It is akin to a small town fishing village, with many people who were born there . . . and never left."

—DON RIEPE, RESIDENT AND DIRECTOR OF THE AMERICAN
LITTORAL SOCIETY, NORTHEAST CHAPTER

Broad Channel

SOME OF THE HOUSES are built along canals and on stilts in the water. Boats are parked on narrow streets like cars. No gas station, no pharmacy, no movie theater in this town. And if you need to pick up a package at the post office or file an accident report at the police precinct, you'll need to pay a toll and cross a bridge.

Broad Channel, the only inhabited island in Jamaica Bay, is a peculiar outpost within the confines of New York City. At first glance, this tiny neighborhood—a mile long and four blocks wide—seems nothing more than a whistle-stop between mainland Queens and the Rockaway Peninsula. But to many who live here, Broad Channel is a tight-knit community whose unique and welcomed isolation has fostered both a vivid history and an enduring sense of place.

Nobody in town owns a gondola, but many of Broad Channel's 2,630 residents have modest boats and spend hours fishing, crabbing, or lazing on Jamaica Bay. And when the tide is high and temperatures warm up, kids partake in a perennial ritual—jumping from a diving board straight into a sluiceway that goes under Cross Bay Boulevard. "That has been going on for seventy to eighty years," says Dan Mundy, who has lived all his seventy-two years on Broad Channel. "That's something that hasn't changed."

Change is coming to Broad Channel, moving in slowly but inexorably like the tide. There are some new faces in town, new, larger homes on the streets, and even a new bagel shop near the bridge. Local kids no longer attend the local Catholic school, which recently shuttered its doors, and the bridge toll is no longer free for island residents. And sea level rise is also affecting the community, worsening the impact that high tides have on their homes and streets. "The rise increases one inch every ten years," says Mundy, Chairman of the Environmental Committee at Community Board 14, and who with his son, Dan Jr., founded the Jamaica Bay Ecowatchers. "And while that may not seem like a lot, it is. It's not unusual for low-lying areas to get several inches of rain in their homes at high tide."

When evening seduces the sun beneath the distant Manhattan skyline,

Broad Channel appears worlds away from the city to which it belongs. But belying the island's peaceful exterior is a rough-and-tumble history—from its days as a primitive fishing village to Prohibition-era rumrunning—and a philosophy that you can fight city hall.

Broad Channel is both part of New York City and a world away from it.

Broad Channel is situated just west of the channel from which it derives its name. The community inhabits the southern half of the island, while the Jamaica Bay Wildlife Refuge—a federal park—occupies the northern portion. The entire island mass—approximately twelve hundred acres in size—was once a group of small islands (including Big Egg Marsh, The Raunt, Goose Creek, Black Bank Marsh, and Ruler's Bar Hassock) when the Jameco and Canarsie tribes and, later, Dutch colonists hunted and fished the bay region.

The bay's fishing tradition prospered after the Civil War, when ferries carried vacationers from Canarsie, Brooklyn, to beaches on the nearby Rockaway Peninsula. A handful of oystermen, clam diggers, and fishermen like Joe, Ben, and Bill Shaw lived in shacks on Big Egg Marsh during summer, providing boats and bait to visitors for $3 a day.

The bay islands remained sparsely populated until 1880, when the New York, Woodhaven, and Rockaway Railroad erected a 4.8-mile-long wooden trestle across Jamaica Bay. The line, which connected mainland Queens to Rockaway, made four stops—Goose Creek, The Raunt, Broad Channel, and Beach Channel—and accommodated far more passengers than the ferries.

Within four years, as many as eighty-seven crowded trains chugged through the Jamaica Bay islands each summer day. The route was sold in 1887 to the Long Island Railroad, and by 1895 the trains carried a million and a half passengers. In 1902, three and a half million fun-seekers rode the line. Transportation put Jamaica Bay on the map. Tiny fishing shacks, boathouses, fishing clubs, and small hotels—many built on stilts—rose near the railroad trestle. Goose Creek became known for its weakfishing and had a fleet's worth of boats ready for hire. The Raunt became popular for its rod-and-gun clubs, and Broad Channel had elegant hotels that attracted wealthy fishermen and visitors.

The bay developed a reputation for its shellfishing, with the Rockaway oyster being especially popular. In 1906, an estimated 450,000 tons of oysters and clams, valued at $2 million, were harvested from the bay.

The Jamaica Bay islands were a homesteader's paradise during the late nineteenth century. The town of Jamaica had jurisdiction, but did not exercise title or collect taxes, encouraging squatters to settle there. That changed in the 1890s, when an enterprising and corrupt town supervisor, Frederick Dunton, arranged for the land to be leased for the next hundred years to his business cronies. Dunton and a developer named Patrick Flynn had ambitious plans for the remote area. Dunton leased some of the land he then controlled to Flynn and supported Flynn's plan to build a trolley line across Jamaica Bay to compete with the railroad. The project, which included a bicycle path and lane for carriage drivers, angered executives of the Long Island Railroad, which held a monopoly in the region.

While costly lawsuits were waged by the Long Island Railroad, New York City (which Queens joined in 1898), and others against the Flynn-Dunton interests, a route was designed, land dredged, trestle spiles erected, trolley cars ordered, and tenants thrown out of their homes. The project was halted in 1902 after New York had the Dunton leases invalidated in court. Title to the land and water eventually reverted to the city.

Flynn lost about $1 million and abandoned several miles of newly constructed roadway and embankments. Twenty years later, the city used them to build Jamaica Bay Boulevard, later renamed Cross Bay Boulevard, the 5.5-mile thoroughfare that begins in Ozone Park, Queens, and ends in Broad Channel, bisecting the island.

The city then issued permits to anyone who wanted to live in, or develop, the bay area. Broad Channel, unlike the patchwork communities on The Raunt or Goose Creek, grew into a thriving community. By 1908, there were stores, a church, a volunteer fire department with 185 firemen, and four hundred houses, each paying an average of $25 rent to the city's dock department.

In 1915, the city leased a five-hundred-acre parcel of Broad Channel to real-estate developer Pierre Noel with the condition that the land be improved. Noel sublet the lease to the Broad Channel Corporation, which built roads, provided running water and electric light, and subdivided about 150 acres into lots one hundred feet by twenty-five feet. The corporation rented each parcel for about $116 a year to anyone wanting to build a summer home. Broad Channel prospered as a summer resort, offering bungalows and boating to weary city folk in search of respite. People were soon receiving postcards from friends celebrating the lazy life in fashionable Broad Channel.

Grandiose plans were also afloat to transform Jamaica Bay into a commercial port unrivaled by any in the world. Beginning in 1906, an array of private developers and government planners took to the task. The state endorsed the plan three years later, with Congress authorizing $7.4 million for the project if New York City built the docks and basins. The city kicked in $1 million, and in 1913 the bay was partially dredged by the federal government. The project picked up steam during the next decade, when a massive dredging and landfill undertaking thoroughly altered the bay. Channels were deepened in anticipation of the arrival of large boats, and landfill connected some of the islands and eliminated marshes and creeks. Lack of rail freight service and poor coordination at various levels of government doomed the project in the 1920s.

The bay nonetheless felt the negative effects of growing industrialization and New York's burgeoning population. In 1912, seafood caught in Jamaica Bay was blamed for a typhoid scare in Brooklyn and Queens. The U.S. Department of Agriculture temporarily banned commercial fishing in the bay—jeopardizing five thousand jobs—rather than investigate the deluge of untreated sewage pouring into the bay. By 1917, plants in Queens and Brooklyn were discharging fifty million gallons of inadequately treated waste into the bay daily, poisoning clams, oysters, and ultimately people. The water became so polluted that in 1921 the department of health abolished shellfishing in Jamaica Bay altogether, destroying both a major industry and a way of life.

Despite the demise of the long-established fishing industry and the collapse of plans for the harbor, Broad Channel flourished, albeit illegally. During Prohibition, the island, too remote for police raids, proved the perfect venue for rumrunning. This sleepy island getaway suddenly became a notorious nightspot. Yacht clubs, speakeasies, and lodgings like the Enterprise Hotel sprang up on what became known as Little Cuba, a homegrown Havana tucked away in New York City.

"The yacht clubs would put on regattas," said Joe Carey, a retired subway motorman whose grandparents moved to Broad Channel in 1897. "You would be in your glory—you could watch the races and get drunk."

Broad Channel's popularity increased when Cross Bay Boulevard was finished in 1923. Motorists in dandy new cars now zipped to the island at whim, free from train-schedule constraints. The road also paved the way for Broad Channel's growth as a year-round community, a change ushered in by the Great Depression and the need for cheap housing. Bungalows were winterized, and many summer residents moved in permanently.

Eventually hard times befell the Broad Channel Corporation, and it went bankrupt in 1939. Suddenly, New York City found itself landlord to a thousand tenants. Residents negotiated with the city to purchase the land under their homes, but were rejected. The citizens of Broad Channel were stuck as permanent renters, a situation that pitted residents against city government for more than forty years.

While Broad Channel continued developing as a community, the islands and marshlands to the north—a wilderness virtually ignored up until the 1930s—were eyed for another purpose. In 1938, Parks Commissioner Robert Moses maneuvered to have Jamaica Bay placed under his jurisdiction, protecting it both from Department of Sanitation attempts to dump refuse there and from new developers, whom he dismissed as "crackpot industrial theorists."

Jamaica Bay was to be Moses' crown jewel, providing him with a legacy rivaling that of Frederick Law Olmsted and his Prospect and Central Parks. Moses dreamed of a tremendous recreational area along the bay's shore and a wildlife refuge on the islands. Like city officials for decades to come, Moses was indifferent to the plight of Broad Channel, calling the community "a slum" whose four thousand residents should be removed.

After World War II, Moses enlisted wildlife management specialists to help design a bird sanctuary for the Jamaica Bay region, but the project, which included construction of two freshwater ponds, was too expensive. The plan remained unimplemented until 1950, when a fire destroyed much of the wooden Long Island Railroad trestle spanning the bay. When the company abandoned operations, the Metropolitan Transportation Authority (MTA) asked the city for permission to build a subway line in its place. The MTA needed Moses' approval to dredge within the parks system; Moses consented, provided that the MTA build the two ponds.

During construction, the MTA filled in the waters between Broad Channel, The Raunt, Goose Creek, and Ruler's Bar Hassock. The MTA displaced an informal community living without gas or fresh water on The Raunt, and created the single twelve-hundred-acre island, which lies between the North Channel and Cross Bay Veterans Memorial Bridges. Today, the A train and the Rockaway Park shuttle run along the MTA line, and the hundred-acre East and forty-five-acre West Ponds are the cornerstones of the Jamaica Bay Wildlife Refuge. No one, however, bothered giving the merged landmass a formal name. Most residents, city officials, and cartographers refer to the entire island as Broad Channel, although some nautical maps and refuge officials still call the northern half Ruler's Bar Hassock.

Despite its urban environs, the Jamaica Bay Wildlife Refuge has flourished as a vital habitat for birds since it was started in 1953.

The city's Department of Parks opened the 9,155-acre refuge in 1953, with Herbert Johnson, the department's turfgrass specialist, in charge. While Johnson was not a wildlife expert, his background in botany and his creative planning were instrumental in planting the proper vegetation to attract birds to the ponds. Within five years, 208 species of birds were identified, and today more than 330 species have been recorded.

Johnson retired in 1972, the same year the city, which had never had the money to fully staff or fund projects there, turned the refuge over to the U.S. Department of the Interior and the newly created Gateway National Recreation Area. Since then, it has gained international renown as one of the country's most important urban wildlife refuges.

"It's the favorite place for a lot of people who want to get out of the city and still be in the city," said Kathy Krause, Chief of Interpretation for the Jamaica Bay Unit of Gateway. "Most of our visitors are from the New York metropolitan area, but we do get visitors from out-of-town, outside the state, and internationally."

While the northern end of the island flowered, the town of Broad Channel became ensnared in bureaucratic red tape that incessantly threatened its very right to exist. Throughout its history, islanders have had to battle the government for acknowledgment, respect, and standard city services. In 1948, the Board of Estimate proposed canceling all homesite leases, which would have fulfilled Moses' desire to clear out the area, but after eight hundred residents marched on city hall, the idea was dropped.

Channelites were again threatened with eviction in 1967, when Mayor John Lindsay called the community a health hazard. He cited the overflow of raw sewage from residents' septic tanks into Jamaica Bay as a source of infectious hepatitis in Queens. Again, the solution was to remove the community, rather than to install a sewer system—a basic amenity in modern cities. In typical Broad Channel fashion, the community retained its own health expert, disputed the city's contention, and forced Lindsay to retreat. The city finally installed a sewer system in 1988, but residents were required to install their own sewer pumps and pay to hook up to the main line (a cost of about $2,000).

Islanders were almost uprooted again in 1968, when the Port Authority of New York and New Jersey proposed extending two runways at John F. Kennedy International Airport—already only one mile away—into Jamaica Bay and toward island residences. The mayor's office said it would be impossible to maintain the community if the project was granted. Although the city's planning commission had long supported phasing out

Broad Channel, the project was rejected because it would damage the quality of life for birds at the refuge. (Unfortunately, new plans recently arose to expand Kennedy Airport by filling in parts of the bay crucial to the flora and fauna; if the proposal moves forward, environmentalists are girding for a major battle.)

Lindsay also tried casting the community adrift in the early 1970s by subsuming Broad Channel under Gateway National Park legislation, which would have meant clearing the island of all residents and buildings. Thousands of residents marched in protest, and again the city backed down. The threat of eviction finally ended in 1982, when Mayor Ed Koch passed special legislation enabling residents to purchase their lots "as is," at a cost of $500 for land underwater and up to $2,500 for land on a canal. (When the city's board of estimate, which was selling the land, was abolished in 1990, more than a hundred homeowners were forced to resume their battle. The remaining land did not become available until 1995.)

Property ownership hasn't dampened the feistiness of the people of Broad Channel. Unlike in many communities, where apathy reigns, Channelites remain passionately involved in issues close to home. In 1991, the island's civic association successfully sued the city, blocking its inexplicable attempt to shift 162 of the 2,500 residents from Congressional District 32 to District 31 as part of a citywide redistricting plan. For a community as cohesive as Broad Channel, losing some of its family was unfathomable. The city gave in, redrawing the district line on the opposite side of the train tracks, where no one was living. The following year, the state Department of Environmental Conservation shocked residents when inspectors issued dozens of fines—up to $10,000 each—citing a slew of decks, docks, and bulkheads in violation of the 1974 Tidal Wetlands Act. Residents sued, complaining that the fines were outrageously high, especially since the government hadn't told them permits were required. In fact, it had taken the state eighteen years to notice the illegal improvements. The state eventually lifted or reduced most of the fines, allowing all but the most flagrant violations to remain intact. Island activism, spearheaded by Mundy's Jamaica Bay Eco Watchers, also pressured the government to do something about the marshland that was disappearing at a rate of forty-four acres each year in Jamaica Bay. Marshland provides the basis for the entire Jamaica Bay ecosystem. Money has since been allocated to improve nearby water treatment plants that dump nitrogen in the bay, effectively killing marshland. A marsh restoration program initiated in 2003 has so far netted fifteen new acres of marshland in the bay. For years, islanders were at loggerheads with the city over the toll on the Cross Bay Veterans Memorial Bridge, the island's gangplank to the Rockaways, where vital city services are stationed. In 1998, EZ Pass customers in both the Rockaways and Broad Channel were permitted to use the bridge for free. That was rescinded, however, in July 2010 when the financially strapped Metropolitan Transportation Authority began charging local residents a discounted rate for their first two trips of the day with E-Z Pass, with all subsequent trips that day free. In typical Broad Channel fashion, more than two hundred people marched across the bridge to protest the toll.

Though the tiny community often appears vulnerable, most Broad Channel residents zealously safeguard their small-town way of life and would do almost anything to keep outside influences at bay. "All we have to do is go up and down the blocks in the fire truck and call people to action," says Frank Harnisher, past president of the Broad Channel Civic Association. "We're not afraid to fight. We'd blow up both bridges if we had to."

Broad Channel is the black sheep in a city where image and formality are often preoccupations. The only things stilted about the Channel are some of its houses. It's a casual place where islanders turn to their neighbors for help. "If I get caught in the rain, I know I can knock on any door and wait there until the rain stops," says Jessica Guittieri, twenty-seven, who was born and raised on Broad Channel, before moving to Florida and then returning to the island to raise her son. Her parents, former marina owners, have spent their entire lives on the island.

"We don't think in terms of years or decades," says Dan Tubridy. "We think in generations." His family counts four generations on the island.

That sense of community cohesion is perhaps personified by the all-volunteer Broad Channel Fire Department, headquartered in a frame house at 15 Noel Road. Established in 1900, the department has about forty-five active members—some of whom have been involved for decades—and is only one of a handful of volunteer companies remaining in the city. There is no paid rescue service on the island.

Even the police have a minor presence—the 100th Precinct is stationed across the bridge in Rockaway. Crime is low, however, and misdeeds are often handled the old-fashioned way, with residents straightening things out on their own.

In fact, when Channelites speak of their community, they don't call it a neighborhood as do others in New York City; they refer to it as a town and one that is often misunderstood by outsiders. "I think there are a lot of misconceptions about this town," says Guttieri. "It is all white, and people take that. . . . differently."

Indeed, all but 147 of Broad Channel's 2,630 residents were white in the 2000 Census, figures that had barely changed from ten years earlier. Most residents are Catholics of Irish and German descent and are working-class—only 11.7 percent of residents are college graduates. But while 9 percent of the households live below the poverty line, the median income is a prosperous $51,818 per household with a stunning 77 percent of homes owner occupied.

The community lost some of its stability when, in 2006, St. Virgilius Catholic School closed after decades in the community. (The island has a K–5 public school, and middle-school and high-school students go off-island for their education.) Two years later, St. Virgilius's parish merged with St. Camillus in Rockaway Park, so the community no longer has a full-time priest. The only other church on the island, Christ Presbyterian Church-by-the-Sea, has a very small congregation, served by a visiting pastor.

Resentment has simmered toward neighborhood millionaire Charles Howard, a fourth-generation islander with a successful portable toilet business, Call-A-Head. He built a megamansion of imported mahogany and marble on Channel Road and bought up twenty properties on the island, hoping to transform the retail area. His attempts to spruce up the boulevard largely failed, however, with his fancy Wharton Apothecary closing after a few years; his plans for a hotel and a year-round Christmas store never materialized.

Most of Broad Channel's infrastructure still consists of small, weathered bungalows built before the 1950s, although many have gotten new leases on life since Mayor Koch began the process of allowing residents to own their own land. "Now older homes are being knocked down, and new homes are being built," Mundy says. "One-story bungalows are being expanded to two floors." The picturesque "pole homes" at the entrance to Broad Channel, just after the refuge, have been restored, yet retain their old look.

While most residents savor the Mayberry R.F.D. spirit of their town, the climate can also breed conformity and insularity. In this neighborhood, gossip is a serious pastime. "Everyone is in everyone's business," says Guttieri. "It has its positives and its negatives."

The island's homogeneity revealed an ugly side in 1998, when its annual Labor Day parade featured a racist float, with white men dressed in black-face throwing watermelon slices and fried chicken while bouncing basketballs. Even worse, one man was dragged along behind the truck in a sick "parody" of a Texas lynching of a black man that had occurred earlier in the summer.

Local newscasts showed video footage, and newspapers reported that in past years Channelites had voted floats like "Hasidic Park" and "Gooks of Hazzard" as the year's "funniest." Some residents were angry at outsiders for judging them—particularly when Mayor Rudolph Giuliani fired the city police officer and two firefighters involved in the float, and then revoked money from the volunteer fire department that had sponsored the parade. Other residents, however, made a public act of contrition. When the Reverend Al Sharpton marched with protesters into Broad Channel, some citizens—including Tubridy and his brother—greeted them with lemonade, crumb cake, and a warm welcome—a far cry from the response Sharpton has received in other predominantly white neighborhoods like Bensonhurst, Brooklyn.

Still, the reputation has lingered. In 2006, a Halloween incident turned ugly when an undercover police car was egged by local teens. When the detective on hand, who was black, began questioning people, a confrontation quickly developed. A crowd of about one hundred locals gathered as some attacked the officer physically and others shouted racial slurs.

Rob McCarthy who runs a kayak rental with his wife, Trish, at the Sunset Marina, says the island is gradually opening up. It used to be said that Broad Channel boys married Broad Channel girls and just moved down the block.

"It was almost unheard of selling a house outside the family," McCarthy says. But word of mouth is no longer the only way homes change hands anymore—houses, selling between $300,000 and $500,000, now are regularly posted on the Internet. "There was a time when I knew every single person on 14th Road, but that's not the same," says Mundy.

"There are a lot of new faces here," adds McCarthy. "It has changed, and hopefully for the better."

Also gone are the days when residents would just build an addition or a deck without notifying the city. "Now we are under strict guidelines," says McCarthy. "We weren't used to that here. We just did it."

Lower-lying streets in the community are also getting regraded to combat the effects of high tides on their homes and streets. "I remember the high tides," says Michael Tudda, who lived on Channel Road from 1980 through 1991. "I remember putting on boots and rolling up my pant legs and then getting to the corner and putting my shoes on to go to school."

Even with some new streets and new faces, Broad Channel is unlikely to reclaim its heyday, when it flaunted a bar on every block, seven gas stations, barbershops, butchers, and fourteen restaurants. Yet some of the empty storefronts along Cross Bay Boulevard have been filled, mostly with everyday businesses like a Laundromat, bagel shop, and pizzeria. But don't expect a Gap on every corner or a mall in the marina. Broad Channel's limited size and out-of-the-way location deter invasion by retail giants like Walmart, Home Depot, and modern-day Pierre Noels. And most islanders like it that way.

Broad Channel may be an urban outpost, an inconvenient place to live within the grand scheme of New York City, but its residents are rooted here by tradition and love of the bay. Each day the sunrise and sunset stretch out unobstructed across the horizon. The subway chugs along like a rinky-dink railroad through brown reeds and russet meadows and past tiny box houses that fly Old Glory every day—not just on Flag Day. Everything changes slowly on Broad Channel, or not at all. It's a city neighborhood clinging to its small-town soul.

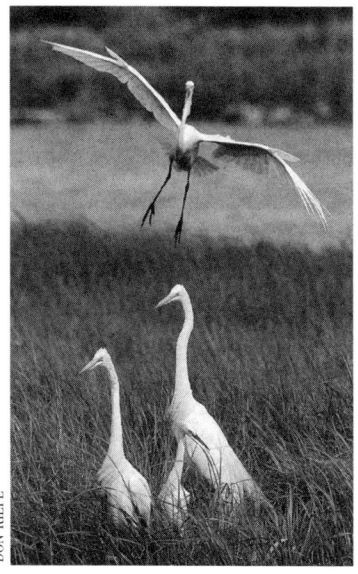

DON RIEPE

During summer, egrets are numerous at the Jamaica Bay Wildlife Refuge.

EXPLORING THE ISLAND

The **Jamaica Bay Wildlife Refuge**, 718-318-4340 (www.nps.gov/gate) is truly a respite from the push and shove of urban life. More than 330 species have been spotted in this ornithological melting pot along the Atlantic Flyway. Within this gorgeous avian mosaic are black-bellied plovers, American oystercatchers, marbled godwits, white-rumped sandpipers, short-billed dowitchers, Wilson's phalaropes, egrets, black-crowned night herons, osprey, and others.

The refuge is not just for birds, however, even though it was created with their flight paths in mind. Rangers have introduced plants that attract butterflies like the tiger swallowtail, painted lady, and question mark—sixty butterfly species have been recorded there. Reptiles like the diamondback terrapin regularly nest here, and amphibians, like the spring peeper and gray tree frog, are here as well. So pack your binoculars.

Before heading out on one of the refuge's two trails—the **East Pond** or the **West Pond** trails—check in at the new, "green," $3.3 million **Visitors Center**, which opened in June 2007.

The main exhibit tells the history and ecology of the Jamaica Bay area and has a huge life-size model of an osprey nest (real osprey can be seen on their nests from the West Pond Trail). In a side meeting room, be sure to check out the labeled, live plant specimens on display (this will help you identify what you'll see along the trails) and the natural artifacts, such as bird feathers, shells, and horseshoe crab remains.

Glossy ibis are among the 330 species of birds seen at the Jamaica Bay Wildlife Refuge.

Pick up a free visitor's card, trail maps, and a Junior Ranger's program guide for the kids. Check the schedule of events; rangers offer dozens of free programs and tours throughout the year, from everything you ever wanted to know about horseshoe crabs to harvest moon and terrapin nesting walks. Popular programs may require advance reservations. The center also has a nice selection of nature-inspired souvenirs, toys, and books, including field guides. Admission to the refuge is free. While the visitors' center closes at 5 PM, the trails are open from sunrise to sunset.

The 1.75-mile West Pond Trail begins behind the visitors' center, wraps around the forty-five-acre pond, and offers little shade from the sun much of the way. The more popular trail, it is accessible year-round and offers views of the city juxtaposed against the marshland of Jamaica Bay with its ducks, geese, and the occasional beached boat.

An auxiliary terrapin trail along this walk is closed in June and July, when diamondback terrapins lay their eggs. At West Pond, there are benches where you can quietly observe the everyday routines of the sanctuary's waders and waterfowl or maybe even see a peregrine falcon swoop down on a flock of gulls. The refuge's osprey nests are a popular draw, with eight nesting pairs at the refuge in 2010. Called fish hawks, these predators are known for grabbing their prey and then positioning the fish headfirst so as to be more aerodynamic in flight. The final stretch, or Upland Trail, heading away from the pond and back toward the visitors' center, is markedly different in ambiance. The North and South Gardens are populated by a wide array of trees and shrubs: autumn olive, gray birch, red maple, willow oak, and Japanese black pine trees, along with salt-spray rose shrubs, yucca, and even prickly pear cactus. You'll hear an ensemble of chirps, caws, and whistles as the birds whoosh past you from one thicket to another.

The Jamaica Bay Wildlife Refuge is a hot spot for shorebirds during spring and fall migrations.

Those inclined toward an even more secluded experience may prefer the primitive East Pond Trail across the street from the visitors' center. It's well worth the dash across six lanes of traffic on Cross Bay Boulevard—just wait for a break in the flow of cars. To create mudflats for migrating shorebirds, the water level is lowered in summer. Because much of the three-mile trail rings the hundred-acre pond, it's frequently a mucky trek, so wear duck shoes or boots. The rewards to those who proceed undaunted are solitude and lots of wildlife. (On especially muddy days—mostly in spring and winter—portions of the trail are closed.) One highlight is the four-person blind looking out onto a window of life at half-acre **Big John's Pond**. Named for a bulldozer operator who helped create the pool in 1983, the pond offers plenty of action: Painted turtles bask in the sun; glossy ibis pluck insects from the water's surface with their long, slender beaks; and dragonflies move about as if their darts and dives were choreographed. By the time you reach East Pond, the din of Cross Bay Boulevard has faded. All is quiet except for the occasional wing beats of majestic swans or flutter of small ducks sailing on the pond and the periodic whoosh of a nearby subway train.

The ideal seasons to visit the sanctuary are spring and fall, although more and more people are braving the cold to view the increased number of wintering birds here. Spring features the greening of the salt marsh, the blooming of wildflowers, and the arrival of songbirds. In summer, the refuge is a hot spot for waders like egrets and herons. (Unfortunately, flies, poison ivy, and ticks also summer here, so bring insect repellent and dress appropriately.) Autumn finds the area populated by shorebirds and hawks, while saw-whet, long-eared, and snowy owls, along with snow geese and bufflehead ducks, all drop by in winter.

About a half mile farther down Cross Bay Boulevard from the sanctuary is the community of **Broad Channel**. While there are no historic sites or museums, you can get a feel for this unique neighborhood by strolling the side streets. Many old bungalows and pole houses (check out East 5th Road for the best) are still around, although home ownership has inspired some modernization. You can drop a fishing line off the Cross Bay Veterans Memorial Bridge and catch weakfish, porgies, and fluke.

Smitty's, 301 East Ninth Road, 718-945-2642, was founded in 1938 and rents sixteen-foot skiffs with outboard motors and carries a full line of bait and tackle from spring through fall.

Sunset Marina, 64 West 10th Road, 718-474-3256, rents kayaks by the hour, in season, and has reasonable rates. The fleet includes six singles and one tandem. The best hours for kayaking are between 10 AM and 12 PM and 4 PM and 6 PM, says operator Rob McCarthy. "It's like a puddle out there, like a lake." A trip around Jamaica Bay offers nice views of the city skyline and refuge and has a few surprises like a secluded beach island in the middle of the bay that locals call "The Sandbar."

Broad Channel is also bicycle friendly, with designated routes along Cross Bay Boulevard. (Pick up a map at your local bicycle store or go to www.nycbikemaps.com.) Either take your bike on the "A" train, get off at Broad Channel and tool around the island, or park at the refuge and explore from there. There is no cycling permitted inside the refuge.

Where to Eat

While Broad Channel has little to offer the hungry visitor, there is a new bagel shop and a place for lunch, dinner, and/or drinks near the toll bridge.

Rock-n-Roll Bagels, 20–10 Cross Bay Blvd., 718-945-2233, opened in 2010 and offers just about anything to quell your hunger pangs: bagels, paninis, sixteen kinds of burgers, breakfast sandwiches, a deli counter, hot food, soft-serve frozen yogurt, and smoothies. You can even watch the bagels being individually hand-rolled, boiled, and baked via a viewing window.

Bayview Restaurant and Lounge, 25 Van Brunt Road, 718-634-4554, offers seafood, burgers, sandwiches, and Italian dishes. Best of all, however, is that you can sit outside and enjoy views of Jamaica Bay in all kinds of weather; the restaurant has a retractable glass atrium.

Island Hopping

By car: Take the Belt Parkway east to exit 17, make a right onto Cross Bay Boulevard, through Howard Beach and over the North Channel Bridge. Continue about one mile to the Jamaica Bay Wildlife Refuge—the visitors' center is on the right side—or continue straight into the community of Broad Channel.

By subway: The A train stops right in Broad Channel. To get to the refuge, walk west to Cross Bay Boulevard, then make a right and continue a half-mile. The visitors' center is on your left.

By bus: The Q53 express bus from Roosevelt Avenue, Jackson Heights; the Q21 from Woodhaven and Queens Boulevards, or Liberty Avenue and Cross Bay Boulevard; and the Q21A from the New Lots Avenue subway station all stop in Broad Channel. Walk a half mile back along Cross Bay Boulevard to the refuge visitors' center.

17. Forgotten Islands of Jamaica Bay and the Rockaways

Ruffle Bar - Canarsie Pol - Subway Island - Barren Island
Bergen and Mill Islands - Hog Island

Forgotten Islands of Jamaica Bay and the Rockaways

Ruffle Bar

While many islets in Jamaica Bay were home to squatters' fishing huts in the late nineteenth and early twentieth centuries, Ruffle Bar came the closest to rivaling Broad Channel as a full-fledged community. Located just over the Brooklyn border in the bay, Ruffle Bar gained popularity after the Civil War as a ferry stop for tourists traveling from Canarsie to Rockaway. By the 1880s, a group known as the Windward Club sponsored boat races at Ruffle Bar; in the 1890s, the town of Flatlands leased lots on the 150-acre island, and the Skidmore House hotel opened.

Ruffle Bar got another boost around 1914, when Pierre Noel founded the Ruffle Bar Association and began developing the island. By 1926, landfill helped the marshy island accommodate forty buildings including one housing the Certified Oyster Company. Children rowed to the Rockaways for school. But the Depression decimated the community, and by the 1940s only a handful of squatters remained. The island is abandoned today, with broken dishes, coal stoves, and building foundations the only vestiges of a lost community.

Canarsie Pol

This 220-acre island, built up with soil and sand from past dredging projects, is flourishing as a home to wading birds—with 497 nests in 2010, it was the second most populated island in the city, surpassing South Brother Island.

The black-crowned night heron numbers have surged here, and there are healthy numbers of great egrets and snowy egrets, but it was also home to 129 glossy ibis nests, almost as many as the combined total found on Hoffman, Subway and South Brother Islands, the only other places the ibis currently nest. This was also the only island in the city on which tricolored heron and cattle egret nests were observed in 2009 and 2010. However, there are also a growing number of cormorants in the vicinity—most likely because of work done by the Army Corps of Engineers on nearby Elder's Point Marsh, where the cormorants used to nest—which could ultimately harm the waders' habitat.

Subway Island

The name explains it all: this is the island in Jamaica Bay over which the A train runs its track. Yet despite the presence of the subway, there were, in 2010, more than one hundred waders nesting there, including the city's third-largest collection of glossy ibis.

Barren Island

For centuries, Barren Island maintained a low-profile, pastoral serenity. But as New York struggled with industrial-age growing pains, the island emerged as a site so crucial to urban life that it could no longer be ignored. In fact, after its factories arrived, nearby residents denounced Barren Island as the most noxious and noisome of neighbors.

Today, Barren Island is no longer an island. It's part of the Gateway National Recreation Area's Floyd Bennett Field at the southern end of Brooklyn's Flatbush Avenue. Until landfill connected it to the mainland in 1926, Barren Island was a triangular-shaped isle at the western edge of Jamaica Bay. One of the area's largest landmasses, it contained seventy acres of salt marsh that were submerged in spring and thirty acres of uplands that featured forests of cedar trees fringed by white sand beaches. Barren Island lay among dozens of islets large and small, though only a few, like Riches Meadow, Plum Island, and Big Slop Marsh, were individually named. Native Americans called the area Equindito, or "broken lands."

Europeans arrived around 1625, starting with the Dutch West India Company. The Dutch called it Beeren Eylant, prompting the English variants Bear Island, Barn Island, and Barren Island. At low tide, the water was shallow enough for livestock and men to wade from the mainland to the island, where rich salt-hay pastures were grazed and harvested. But nobody settled on Barren Island until the early nineteenth century.

The first resident was a man named Dooley, who built a house on the eastern end and operated an inn for sportsmen and fishermen. John Johnson took over Dooley's business in 1830 (see Historical Detour: Fools and Gold), by which time three or four families lived on the island.

Still, the island remained essentially barren until the late 1850s, when entrepreneurs found its location—isolated, yet easily accessible by boat through the Rockaway inlet—ideal for industry. From 1859 through 1933, more than two dozen companies set up shop at different times, virtually all of them in the fertilizer, fish-oil, or garbage disposal businesses.

The first two businesses were fertilizer plants that focused on horse rendering. William B. Reynolds, who had a municipal contract to remove dead animals, butcher's blood, and other refuse from the streets of New York, owned one. In one month, Reynolds collected five hundred horses and cows, one hundred to 220 dogs, cats, other small animals, and quantities of blood, offal, and bones, all for the handsome sum of $1,500. The island's western bay soon changed from Dooley's Bay to Dead Horse Bay.

The plants, including Reynolds's, transformed this goulash into glue, bone dust, and fertilizer, which was sold throughout the world, even to grape growers in Europe's Rhine Valley. The two original fertilizer companies didn't last long, but horse rendering remained an important ingredient in Barren Island industry until 1921.

Fish-oil plants were the next arrivals, opening in the late 1860s, after large schools of menhaden were discovered in the nearby Long Island waters. Menhaden oil was used for tanning leather and mixing paints; the fish scraps were used in fertilizer. By 1883, the fish-oil plants employed ten steamships and 350 men. The laborers, most of them single, were southern blacks and European immigrants. They lived in segregated dorms and usually worked separately, too.

The island earned an unsavory reputation as a site of filth, squalor, and nasty odors. And with nearby Coney Island, the Rockaways, and Jamaica Bay developing into havens for tourists, residents, and fishermen, a conflict was inevitable. In 1890, when several government investigations castigated the Barren Island businesses for leaving thousands of dead fish on the docks, company officials pledged to clean up their act. It was a promise Barren Island businesses would make, and fail to keep, continually for the next thirty years.

Historical Detour: Fools and Gold

In November 1830, Captain William Thornby brought two new workers—seaman Charles Gibbs and steward Thomas Walmsley—aboard the *Vineyard* for a run from New Orleans to Philadelphia. What should have been a routine venture for a brig laden with staples of the South evolved into a sordid tale of murder, greed, and misfortune on the islands of New York.

The *Vineyard*'s cargo consisted of cotton, molasses, sugar . . . and $54,000 in Mexican currency. Unbeknownst to Thornby, Gibbs and Walmsley had just fled Cuba and nasty reputations as ruthless pirates. When they discovered the cash, they hatched a mutinous plot, enlisting seamen Aaron Church and Henry Atwell and cabin boy Robert Dawes. Gibbs and Walmsley bludgeoned the captain to death and threw his corpse overboard. Church and Atwell badly wounded mate William Roberts and, when he begged for mercy, tossed him into the deep.

Then the pirates made their own fatal misjudgment: They let the remaining seamen James Talbot and John Brownrigg live, promising each of them a cut of the cash if they'd keep their mouths shut.

Instead of steering toward the City of Brotherly Love, the *Vineyard* headed for Long Island. With land in sight, the crew burned and sank the ship, split the booty, and escaped in two small boats. Their glorious plans quickly went awry when they were overwhelmed by fierce gale winds near Rockaway Bar: Church, Talbot, Atwell, and $23,000 were lost at sea; Gibbs, Walmsley, Brownrigg, and Dawes dumped all but $5,000 to lighten their load.

The survivors pushed on to Barren Island's Pelican Beach, where they buried the remaining treasure. They told a tragic tale of shipwreck to resident Nicholas Williams (in some accounts William Johnson), who sent them to his brother-in-law, John Johnson, proprietor of Dooley's, the local inn.

That night, while the others slept, Brownrigg confessed the misdeed to Johnson. Rather than confront the criminals, Johnson took them to Sheepshead Bay to arrange for transport to Manhattan. Then he and Williams raced to the spot Brownrigg had mentioned, dug up the loot, and rehid it. Meanwhile, as Gibbs negotiated for a ride to the city, Brownrigg confessed to the authorities. This time they all ended up in jail.

Brownrigg and Dawes turned state's evidence, and the pirates were scheduled for execution. Gibbs admitted to killing over a hundred men and women in his brutal career, and the hanging became a major event. On April 23, 1831, hundreds of boats filled with spectators turned out to see Gibbs and Walmsley hanged at Ellis Island.

On Barren Island, the tale was far from finished. Johnson went behind his brother-in-law's back and stashed the booty in two places

along the beach. When Williams learned he'd been duped, he tattled
to the ship's insurers, who sued Johnson. No evidence was found, and
Johnson was acquitted of theft. He retrieved one bag, but the other,
containing $1,600 in silver, had been swept away by the tides. Local
lore has it that a decade later, in 1842, a storm washed Johnson's lost
loot onto the shore, but the water pulled most of the coins away before
residents could snatch them up.

Part of the problem was resolved after a national depression and menhaden shortage, between 1890 and 1894, wiped out most of the fish-oil factories. But a new generation of fertilizer and horse-rendering factories
flourished—in one blistering five-day stretch in August 1896, one company hauled in 1,256 dead horses.

The smells got worse that year when New York, after ending its policy of
dumping garbage in the ocean, awarded a lucrative garbage disposal contract to Barren Island's newest tenant, the New York Sanitary Utilization
Company. The city had tried burying garbage on Rikers Island, but the
odors were discernible in Manhattan and Queens. Barren Island was considered ideal, because it was so remote that "few New Yorkers would know
how to find it," wrote the *New York Times*.

For the first time, existing laws about separating trash into different cat-
egories were enforced; garbage went to Barren Island, while old rags and
paper were separately collected and sold by the city. Ashes were still sent
to Rikers Island. The Sanitary Utilization Company transformed garbage
into fertilizer as well as grease for soap and candles. (During World War I,
the raw product was sold to the government for making glycerine for
bombs.) The company's vice president was Thomas White; he and his
brother Andrew were the barons of Barren Island. They owned most of the
island, including a rendering company, and were already collecting
garbage from New York hotels.

The New York Sanitary Utilization Company, along with the other refuse
disposal and fertilizer factories on the island, was a major headache for politicians. In 1897, Brooklynites as far as four miles away testified before the
board of health that they had to close their windows when the wind was blowing. Once again, the companies were merely warned to abate the nuisances.

Tired of holding their noses, the Anti–Barren Island League extracted
election-year promises in 1898 from state legislators of both parties to shut

down the Sanitary Utilization Company. After a heated battle with plant proponents Mayor Robert Van Wyck and Governor Theodore Roosevelt, the legislature overrode the governor's veto and abolished the garbage reduction process in Brooklyn.

In an era ruled by big-business interests, the courts declared the bill unconstitutional, saying the legislature had overstepped its authority by disregarding the city's autonomy and the private property of the Sanitary Utilization Company. So the company kept churning along, with a thousand tons of garbage arriving daily on Barren Island.

The prosperous rendering and processing industries gave birth to a true community of barbers, butchers, hotels, and saloons along Main Street, the island's only thoroughfare. A small boat, *Fannie McKane*, ferried residents to and from Canarsie twice daily. The population, which had grown to eight hundred by the mid-1890s, peaked at fifteen hundred, with Poles and Italians adding to the ethnic mix. In 1900, a second church, St. Andrew's Catholic Church, opened. Families now outnumbered single male inhabitants. In 1901, P.S. 120, with six classrooms and a playground, replaced the old one-room school.

When the bay froze and stranded residents, they lived off their livestock and homemade German bologna. Other hardships were less bearable—besides being scorned by their Brooklyn neighbors, these lower-class residents were shortchanged by the government and battered by Mother Nature. They had no public water supply and no sewage system, there was no fire department, and medical care was limited. It took three hours to reach a hospital in bad weather.

Worst of all, Barren Island itself was literally falling apart. During thirteen terrifying minutes in November 1905, a four-hundred-by-two-hundred-foot chunk of the island's southeast corner was sucked into the bay, taking a two-story warehouse with it. Only six months later, a fire wiped out sixteen Sanitary Utilization buildings, causing more than $1 million in damage and forcing the evacuation of six hundred families. Then, in April 1907, two of the company's new buildings and a pier were swept away as the island ruptured again.

The company survived the disasters, only to encounter more dangerous foes in the next decade: budget-conscious politicians and outraged citizens. The escalating controversies eventually doomed the community.

In 1912, city officials proposed selling the rights to collect New York's garbage, rather than to continue paying the Sanitary Utilization Company an average of $200,000 a year for the chore, since the company was reaping nearly $1 million annually from its postreduction products. Nothing changed, but the issue would come back to haunt politicians.

Despite improvements made to minimize the smell, complaints from nearby homeowners' associations inspired investigations by the city's health department over the next three years. The plants were forced to close occasionally in the summer due to the stench. Then, in 1916, Mayor John Mitchel's administration announced that a modern processing facility would be built on Staten Island, with a new by-products company paying for its construction and the right to collect the city's garbage.

Staten Island, which had its own disposal plant, angrily opposed hosting the rest of the city's garbage. Swinburne Island was considered, but was dismissed as too small, while others suggested building an island on Romer Shoals in the Lower Bay. Despite the fury of Staten Islanders, construction began in the now notorious Fresh Kills area.

Garbage disposal became a major issue in the vicious campaigns of 1917. By this time, the new Metropolitan By-Products Company on Staten Island was functioning at 50 percent. Complaints poured into city hall, but the Mitchel administration defended the plant, blaming the offending stink on nearby New Jersey factories. Ironically, Tammany Hall Democrats cried corruption, claiming that Mitchel, a Republican, was in cahoots with real-estate developers seeking to protect ventures in the Rockaways by investing in Metropolitan By-Products. They also accused Mitchel of promising the company a payoff if Staten Islanders blocked the project. Democratic mayoral challenger John Hylan promised Staten Islanders he'd repeal the contract, although he avoided detailing alternative sites for the garbage.

After defeating Mitchel, Hylan investigated the Metropolitan By-Products Company and threatened to revoke its contract if health issues weren't resolved. Hylan then had fifteen barges of city garbage dumped in the ocean rather than use the facility. The refuse washed up on Coney Island, and at the same time, the Metropolitan By-Products Company defaulted on its contract. After long denying rumors about reviving Barren Island as the city's wastebasket, Hylan acknowledged he had nowhere else to turn.

Brooklynites protested the return of the New York Sanitary Utilization Company, and Hylan took political heat for his financial fiasco—the city was to pay the company $1,000 a day to process the garbage. But in 1919 the mayor "solved" the dilemma by reverting to the city's unsanitary but politically palatable policy of dumping garbage at sea. The Sanitary Utilization Company dismantled its facilities in 1921, with one small processing company staying on until 1933.

In the meantime, the advent of cars killed off the horse-rendering industry. By 1918, Barren Island was bringing in only six hundred carcasses a year, the number previously averaged in twelve days. The last plant closed in 1921, and the island became an economic has-been.

While industry and opportunity faded, a newcomer to Barren Island inspired hope in the community. Jane Shaw, a teacher transferred to the island's P.S. 120 in 1919, became known as the Angel of Barren Island. Devoted to her students and their families, Shaw taught English to immigrant parents in the evenings, and on Sundays showed movies in the school. When the island's doctor left after the factories closed and population declined, residents turned to Shaw for treatment of minor ailments.

Shaw eventually became principal of the school and successfully lobbied Senator Robert Wagner to assign official names to the island's anonymous streets and change the community's name to South Flatlands to lessen residents' isolation from the rest of Brooklyn. In 1930, Shaw took on the Census Bureau after it omitted this urban outback, and forced the bureau to send an inspector to the community to count the remaining 416 residents.

By this time, however, Barren Island had lost its island status. In the 1920s, Brooklyn was extended by landfill into Riches Meadow and finally out to Barren Island to accommodate the rapidly developing borough. A young Brooklyn pilot named Paul Rizzo then established Barren Island Airport, which caught the eye of city planners looking for a municipal airport site. But to accommodate New York's first airport, the city needed more room than tiny Barren Island could supply. New York added nearly eight hundred acres of landfill and renamed the area Floyd Bennett Field (for Admiral Richard Byrd's copilot on his Arctic flights).

More than twenty-five thousand visitors witnessed a defense display by an aerial armada of 597 planes (one flown by Charles Lindbergh) when the airport was dedicated on May 23, 1931. Two years later, Wiley Post took off from there on the first solo flight around the world. While Floyd Bennett Field failed commercially, it was an important military airfield during World War II.

During these developments some residents held steadfast to their homeland, living as tenants on city-owned property. In 1935, Robert Moses decided to expand Brooklyn's nearby Marine Park and ordered the residents to leave by the following year. A few diehards, who still called themselves islanders, were unwilling to relinquish their world, and moved onto a fifty-one-acre tract still owned by the White family. In 1942, the federal government bought the White tract to expand the air base. The tenacious

community, which had lived amid the stench of garbage and horse carcasses, and had survived decades of hostile attacks by nature and neighbors, faded into oblivion.

Exploring the Island

Barren Island is all but forgotten these days, subsumed beneath the area's
identity as Floyd Bennett Field.

The new public face of **Floyd Bennett Field** is **Aviator Sports &
Events Center**, 3159 Flatbush Avenue, 718-757-7500, www.aviatorsports
.com, a Chelsea Piers–style playground in Brooklyn. The twenty-five-acre
complex, which operates as a concessionaire of the National Parks Service,
opened in 2006 with the main 170,000-square-foot space created within
four of Floyd Bennett Field's historic hangers. Indoor and outdoor facilities
include ice-skating, gymnastics, basketball, volleyball, soccer, lacrosse,
rock climbing, and a membership-only fitness center. It even hosts a minor-
league hockey team, the New York Aviators.

Aviator also stages outdoor concerts and in recent years has showcased
everything from teen pop stars Burnham and Josh Golden to Blue Öyster
Cult and Eddie Money.

Although located within Gateway National Recreation Area, the fourth
most visited unit of the National Parks System, Floyd Bennett Field is
extremely underfunded. Even so, Floyd Bennett Field has plenty of natural
resources to offer its visitors.

Start by stopping in at the visitors' center, temporarily located in a small
building just inside the entrance to Floyd Bennett Field, 718-338-3799. At
the visitors' center, you can purchase park use permits for camping,
archery, fishing, launching boats, and community gardening. There's also a
small on-site bookstore. Kids can ask for the Junior Ranger activity book-
let and earn a patch from the National Parks Service.

(This will close when restoration of the Ryan Visitor Center, which once
served as the airport's passenger terminal building and still houses its first
air-control tower, is complete. That larger building will also be home to
exhibits related to Floyd Bennett Field's history and other programming.)

Floyd Bennett Field hosts cultural and ethnic festivals and offers ranger-
led programs that focus on the area's flora and fauna and aviation history
rather than on its pungent Barren Island days. The schedule is available
online at www.nps.gov/gate. Programs include seining the bay, bird and
butterfly walks, tours of Dead Horse Bay and hangar row, where you'll see
historic planes like a 1940s Indiana National Guard relic, as well as canoe-

ing, kayaking, and sailing instruction, from beginner to advanced.

If you have your own kayak, you can launch it from the seaplane ramp near Hanger B, but you must purchase an annual use permit, which is good for launching two kayaks or boats. It is only from the water "that you will feel the drift of the tide, the push of the wind, the shimmer of the silversides breaking the surface inches from your boat, or the spray of the water off your bow," says Ranger John Daskalakis, who runs the park's free kayak and canoe programs.

Floyd Bennett Field has the only public campsites in New York City.

Perhaps the old airfield's best asset is its public camping area, the only one in New York City. Use permits must be purchased in advance (718-338-3799). Four sites are available—two are best for single tents, a third can accommodate several tents, and the last can comfortably host fifteen tents and fifty people. The sites are relatively tame, like a huge backyard with picnic tables—except that you might spot raccoons, possums, rabbits, herons, and even falcons. There's also a cooking pit for campfires and barbeques. Camping has become so popular that the National Park Service is planning to add more sites.

You can fish in Jamaica Bay, which is only two hundred yards away, visit the park's huge community garden with its six hundred volunteer-maintained plots (www.fbga.net), or walk the nearby North 40 Nature Trail with its two miles of winding trails and a bird blind. Cyclists can pedal Floyd Bennett Field's historic runways.

Campsites are available April through November, and reservations are recommended—long unknown, these campsites have received a fair splash of press in recent years and now get booked weeks or months in advance. (There is also a second campsite—Ecology Village—reserved for groups, which features six wheelchair-accessible platform tents.)

Aviation enthusiasts can check out the **Historic Aircraft Restoration Project** in Hangar B, where volunteers repair and restore vintage aircraft. The hanger is open Tuesdays, Thursdays, and Saturdays. Or head over to the old airstrip to watch hobbyists fly radio-controlled model airplanes. There's bleacher seating from which to view these sophisticated craft loop, roll, and hum through the sky.

Island Hopping

🚗 **By car:** Take Flatbush Avenue south to the end, or the Belt Parkway to exit 11-S, then take Flatbush Avenue south to Gateway.

🚌 **By bus:** Take the Q35 from Flatbush and Nostrand Avenues to Gateway.

🚆 **By train:** Catch the 2 or 5 to Flatbush Avenue, and transfer to the Q35 bus.

Bergen and Mill Islands

Long before Wall Street became America's financial capital, moneymakers of the land converged on Bergen and Mill Islands in the northwest corner of Jamaica Bay. The currency wasn't coins or dollars, it was clams—and their abundance made the islands integral to the Native American wampum industry of the day.

Other nearby sites were also wampum producers, but these Brooklyn isles offered one major advantage—their geography discouraged intruders. For enemy Mohawks to attack Bergen Island, they had to cross a creek and open meadows, while the Canarsies who lived there fired at them from the shelter of the forest.

When white pioneers arrived, Mill was two small bits of arable upland and Bergen was sixty acres of uplands and meadows. During peaceful times, many tribes and European settlers, who acknowledged the currency's legitimacy, visited the islands for white wampum and dark or blue wampum—called Indian's gold by settlers. Once New Amsterdam was well established, Bergen and Mill lost their strategic value for the Native inhabitants; soon after, the whites took over the islands.

Aside from nearby Barren Island, these were the only two islands in the region inhabited by Europeans during the colonial period. Mill Island derives its name from a gristmill built there around 1666, which operated until the 1880s. In 1675, Jan Martense Schenck bought the island; his descendants owned it for a century and a half. In the late nineteenth century, Robert Crooke transformed the pastoral island into an industrial site, building a lead-smelting plant. He later sold the island to oil refineries and smelting companies.

Bergen Island was the subject of bitter feuds from the seventeenth through the nineteenth centuries, as litigious descendants of the original settlers squabbled over deeds and titles. The fracas spawned an identity crisis for the island, which donned a variety of names, including Meutelaers, Bestevaers, and Omities Island. By the 1850s, it had begun appearing on maps as Bergen Island, named for Cornelius Bergen, who lived there with his wife and son.

Little changed until the 1890s, when chewing gum manufacturer Thomas Adams bought the land and, together with Percy Williams (who later became a vaudeville theater magnate), established the Percy Williams Amusement Park. It featured musical extravaganzas in the casino and a castle-shaped roller-skating rink, as well as free vaudeville acts on the pier near the Grand Esplanade.

On opening day of the 1905 season, thirty thousand fun-seekers reveled in the attractions, which also included a Ferris wheel, a 150-foot slide called the Slippery Slip, and stuntman Professor Jakob, who set himself afire before diving 90 feet into a pool of water.

Over the next decade, the masses came by trolley and ferry to play at what was called Bergen Beach. Two more amusement parks opened, and entertainers built homes on the island, making it a fashionable place to live. The sensation, however, was short-lived. By 1920, pollution in Jamaica Bay, declining trolley service, and the overwhelming popularity of nearby Coney Island put an end to the merrymaking.

Bergen and Mill Islands were incorporated into Brooklyn as part of a plan to create a commercial harbor in Jamaica Bay. Landfill restructured Mill Island into Mill Basin by 1922; today it's a middle-class neighborhood. According to some maps, Bergen Island was connected to the mainland as early as 1911; others record it as autonomous until 1918. Bergen Island once extended northwest as far as Avenue T and Island Avenue, which is now Veteran Avenue. Today the community of Bergen Beach and the Gateway National Recreation Area shares the former island.

Island Bonus

The two-room clapboard house Jan Martense Schenck built in 1675 stood on Mill Island/Mill Basin until 1952, when it was moved to the Brooklyn Museum, 200 Eastern Parkway, 718-638-5000, for preservation. The one-and-a-half-story house—with a loft for sleeping and grain storage—appears as it might have in 1730. Dutch touches include an open hearth and a large, ornate bureau called a *kas*.

Hog Island

A tiny island. A brief existence. For nearly a century, Hog Island was the missing island in the story of New York's archipelago.

This barrier island rose from the waters just south of the Rockaways during the 1860s, growing by the next decade to be one mile long. Like many of the small Jamaica Bay isles nearby, Hog Island attracted summertime visitors and entrepreneurs, who built bathing houses and restaurants. But in August 1893, one of the most devastating hurricanes to ever hit New York demolished the island, causing $80,000 worth of damage, wiping out pavilions, restaurants, and cabins. Although the island resurfaced several times in the next decade, another round of storms finished it off in 1902.

Hog Island vanished from memory, too, until coastal geologist and Queens College professor Nicholas Coch and his students—looking into erosion of the Rockaways—discovered artifacts that tipped them off to the existence of a long-gone island. Archival research turned up further details, leading to a 1997 *New York Times* feature on Hog Island, which once again found itself in the spotlight for but a moment.

Part VI

South Brooklyn Waters

CONEY ISLAND • FORGOTTEN ISLANDS OF SOUTH BROOKLYN

*Coney Island Creek is now just an inlet off Gravesend Bay and is separated
from Sheepshead Bay by landfill. The creek once ran the length of Coney
Island, dividing the island from the Brooklyn mainland.*

18. Coney Island

*"Like the mad Russian monk Rasputin, Coney Island has been stabbed,
shot, poisoned, clubbed, and has still survived."*
— Mario Puzo, *New York Magazine*, September 3, 1979

SHARON SEITZ

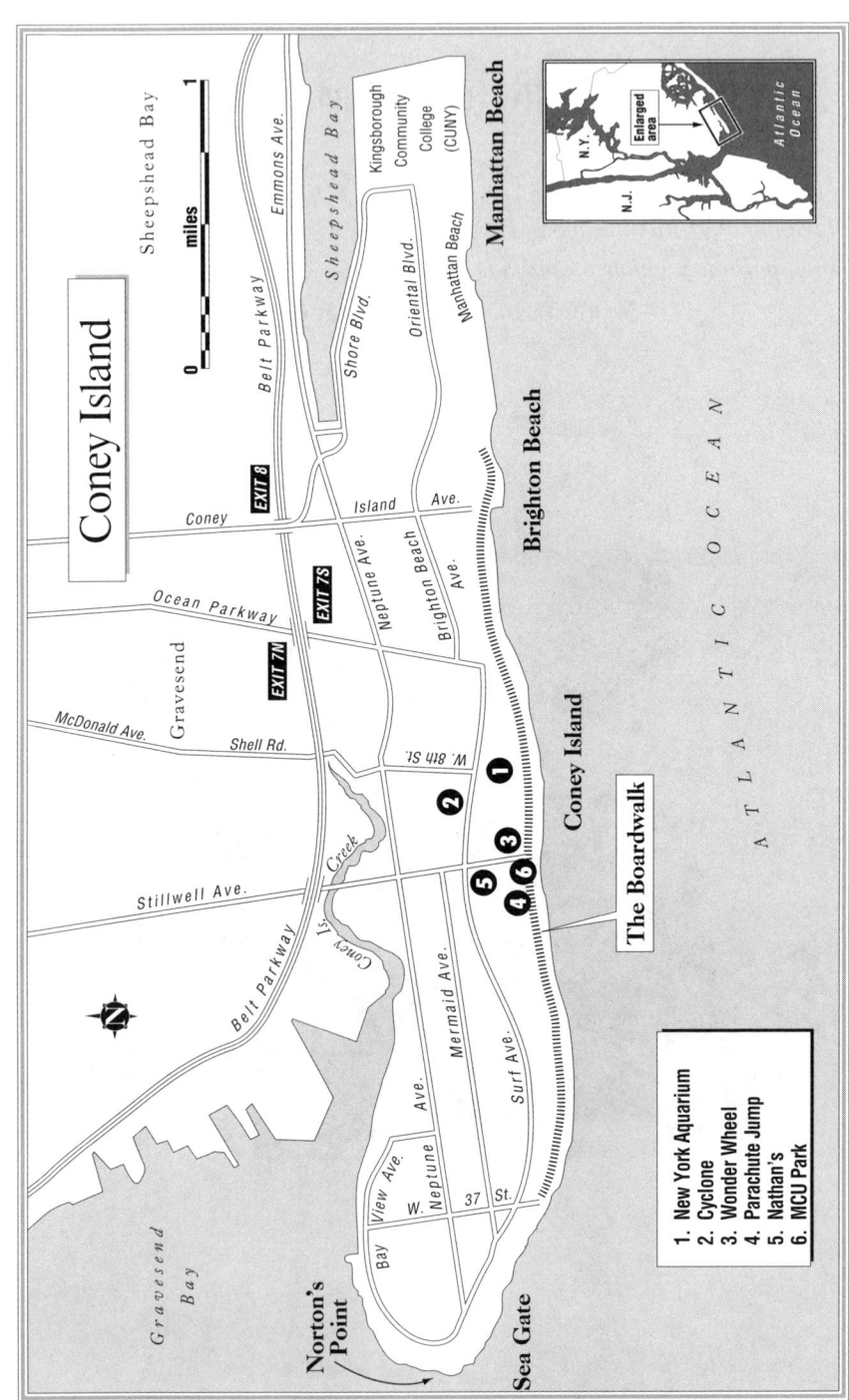

Coney Island

Sheepshead Bay

miles
0   1

Manhattan Beach

Kingsborough
Community
College
(CUNY)

Emmons Ave.

S h e e p s h e a d   B a y

Shore Blvd.

Oriental Blvd.

Manhattan Beach

Belt Parkway

EXIT 8

Coney   Island   Ave.

Neptune Ave.

Brighton Beach Ave.

Brighton Beach

Ocean Parkway

EXIT 7S

Gravesend

McDonald Ave.

Shell Rd.

EXIT 7M

W. 8th St.

❷

❶

Coney Island

The Boardwalk

❸

❺ ❻
❹

Stillwell Ave.

Coney Is. Creek

Belt Parkway

Mermaid Ave.

Surf Ave.

Neptune   Ave.

Bay View Ave.

W.   37   St.

Sea Gate

**Norton's
Point**

*G r a v e s e n d
B a y*

N

A T L A N T I C   O C E A N

1. New York Aquarium
2. Cyclone
3. Wonder Wheel
4. Parachute Jump
5. Nathan's
6. MCU Park

**Enlarged
area**

N.Y.

N.J.

*Atlantic
Ocean*

Paul Woodward, © The Countryman Press

Coney Island

STEP RIGHT UP, CHECK IT OUT—it's the ultimate sideshow, ladies and gentleman, take a peek! We've got death-defying rides and bearded ladies, tall tales of political hooliganism and ripping yarns about entrepreneurial flimflammery, all guaranteed to be 100 percent tru . . . ly amazing!

This is Coney Island. It's an eternally evolving fable in which Erich Weiss polished his act in the 1890s before achieving international fame as Harry Houdini. A decade later, Israel Baline (Irving Berlin) performed at the local cabarets, while the next generation saw Archibald Leach (Cary Grant) work as a stilt walker at Steeplechase Park.

This is Coney Island. It's the home of hype and hucksterism, where every story must be taken with a grain of salt. Through the years the owners of Steeplechase Park advertised its size as fifteen, then twenty-one, then twenty-five acres, although it hadn't grown an inch—the numbers just increased with their ambition. And the hot dog's origins are so distorted that Coney Islanders held a fiftieth anniversary for it in 1939 and a one hundredth anniversary in 1967.

Even basic geography gets taken for a ride at New York City's playground. Once three islands collectively called Coney Island, they were later fused together by storms into a single five-mile strip. Around 1918, however, the island itself was physically joined to southern Brooklyn. When New Yorkers speak of Coney Island today, they refer only to the amusement area, formerly known as West Brighton. Actually the island-turned-peninsula also encompasses the communities of Manhattan Beach, Brighton Beach, and Sea Gate.

While the appellation Coney Island is internationally renowned, its origins are a conundrum. European colonists, who found coneys (rabbits) running wild on the islands most likely conceived the name, which first appeared on a map in 1670. But Coney may also be a corruption of John Coleman, an officer on Henry Hudson's Half Moon, who was killed on the island by Canarsie Indians in 1609. A more improbable tale involves an early resident named Cooney, who went insane after his wife, child, and crude hut were swept away by a tidal wave.

Coney Island's documented history starts in the 1640s, and from the beginning it was an unconventional place. In 1644, the Dutch government granted an eighty-eight-acre island—the middle island of Coney's triad— to settler Guysbert Op Dyck. Yet the following year, the government also granted the town of Gravesend—which included all three islands—to Lady Deborah Moody, a wealthy, liberal Englishwoman fleeing religious persecution in Massachusetts. This was the only grant ever made to a woman, and Gravesend was the only part of Brooklyn settled first by the English.

Guysbert's Island was sandwiched between Piney Island to the east and Sedge Bank to the west. The islands were separated from Gravesend (now part of Brooklyn) by what is today called Coney Island Creek, a tidal creek that ran from Gravesend and Sheepshead Bays.

In about 1661, Op Dyck transferred the title for Guysbert's Island to Dirck de Wolfe, a Dutchman who established a salt production plant there. De Wolfe's business lasted until he tried to stop English Gravesend farmers from grazing cattle on his island, and the confrontation turned ugly. The Gravesenders retaliated by destroying de Wolfe's garden and burning his fences, beginning what was to become a tradition of Coney conflagrations. They even threatened to throw de Wolfe into the fire, which nearly sparked an armed confrontation between the Dutch government and the English settlers. In 1662, the court awarded the English the rights to the island.

For the next 160 years, the islands remained uninhabited and were used primarily for hunting and grazing. Lumber was harvested from their cedar groves. The lone entrepreneurial development came from Thomas Stillwell, a descendant of Nicholas Stillwell, one of Gravesend's original settlers. In 1734, Stillwell deepened Coney Island Creek and turned it into a canal he hoped would provide a shorter, safer route for boats traveling from Jamaica Bay to New York Harbor. But the idea never caught on. Big changes came to the islands in the second half of the eighteenth century, when storms leveled the islands' high sand ridges, filling in the narrow inlet between Sedge Bank and Guysbert's Island. Coney Island remained two islands until January 1839, when a tremendous gale filled the remaining inlet, leaving one long island in its wake.

Enterprising Gravesenders, who formed the Coney Island Road and Bridge Company, first developed Coney Island in the 1820s. They constructed a toll road surfaced with shells leading from Gravesend to Coney Island, where they built an inn called the Coney Island House. Traffic on Shell Road was initially limited to a handful of wealthy New Yorkers headed for this remote resort, which because of its isolation grew in fits and starts.

One early venture was the Coney Island Pavilion, opened in 1844 by two New Yorkers named Eddy and Hart, who sold tasty clams and rented bathing suits to beachgoers. Churches throughout Brooklyn tried to dissuade people from frolicking at Coney's shore on the Sabbath, but had little luck, especially as the beach gradually became more accessible. Steamboat service from Manhattan began in 1847, and three years later, Coney Island Plank Road (now Coney Island Avenue) was laid. The guest list at the Coney Island House by then included Washington Irving, Herman Melville, Henry Clay, Daniel Webster, P. T. Barnum, and Jenny Lind.

Still, according to Walt Whitman, who swam naked there, Coney Island remained a "long, bare unfrequented shore, which I had all to myself, and where I loved after bathing, to race up and down the hard sand, and declaim Homer and Shakespeare to the surf and seagulls by the hour."

While Coney Island's growth was tempered by inconvenient and unreliable transportation—boats ran infrequently, and carriage rides were even more arduous than trains with their many connections—the surf and sun were too seductive to ignore. By 1865, Coney Island had numerous chowder stands, bathhouses, a dozen hotels, and a growing reputation. "We know a sand-bank where a wild time may be had for a very small outlay of money," the *New York Times* wrote in 1868.

In the early 1870s, weekend crowds soared to thirty thousand people, even though many establishments served mediocre food in ramshackle shanties, and often rented towels and bathing suits still wet from the previous customer.

Meanwhile, as Democratic boss William Marcy Tweed's men ruled and plundered New York, an air of lawlessness invaded Coney Island. The most notorious section was the West End, soon called Norton's Point after Mike Norton, a Tweed crony who opened the Point Comfort Hotel with loot he'd earned doing political favors for the Boss. Three-card-monte players brazenly set up shop along the beach, while pickpockets initiated weight-guessing games with gullible tourists who were patted down and subsequently liberated of their wallets. Norton went bankrupt in the 1880s, and the den of thieves shifted toward West Brighton, where superior transportation was delivering a daily supply of potential victims.

Indeed, transportation had significantly improved in 1875, when Andrew Culver united several small rail lines into the Prospect Park and Coney Island Railroad. That first year, the line transported one million visitors to West Brighton's beaches and Charles Feltman's new Ocean Pavilion, which fast became the area's most popular and influential institution, where the hot dog was invented . . . or so the story goes (*see* Historical Detour: A Dog's Tale).

The new rail was an astonishing success—two million people rode it the following year. To attract more tourists, Culver purchased the country's tallest structure—the three-hundred-foot-high Observation Tower—and brought it to Coney Island from the Centennial Exhibition in Philadelphia. The year 1876 also marked the completion of elegant Ocean Parkway, which stretched across Brooklyn to Coney Island.

The development of Coney Island then pushed eastward again, with Austin Corbin paving the way in 1877 with his magnificent Manhattan Beach Hotel. Corbin had stayed at the Coney Island House with his family in 1874 after doctors prescribed ocean air for his ailing son. A restless businessman, Corbin roamed the island and decided to build a luxury resort on the vacant eastern portion.

He bribed William Stillwell, Gravesend's surveyor, to help him illegally purchase the parcels needed. (Stillwell similarly abetted a man named William Engeman, who developed Brighton Beach.)

President Ulysses S. Grant presided at the opening of Corbin's resort, which catered to New York's moneyed society. One of the world's largest hotels, it staged plays and operas in its theater, reenacted historic battles under a fireworks-filled sky in its two-thousand-seat amphitheater, and each day served twenty thousand elegant meals in its lavish dining rooms. John Philip Sousa and his band performed there often; Sousa even penned a tune called "Manhattan Beach March."

Corbin provided convenient transportation via his New York and Manhattan Beach Railway, which made the trip from city to hotel in only an hour. Exclusivity ruled at Manhattan Beach, where Corbin, a ruthless aristocrat, had the private beach fenced in and patrolled by detectives. In 1879, the New Hampshire–born banker banned Jews from Manhattan Beach, stating, "We do not like the Jews as a class. As a rule, they make themselves offensive to the kind of people who patronize our road and hotel."

Suddenly, everyone wanted a piece of the action at Coney Island. Corbin's elitist hotel was soon followed by two other colossal resorts: the Oriental Hotel, which featured circular towers surmounted by minarets, and the Brighton Beach Hotel—described in 1899 by *Appleton's Dictionary of Greater New York* as "a resort for Brooklyn people. It differs from Manhattan Beach much as Brooklyn does from Manhattan borough . . . there is a little less of elegance . . . and more of a family and comfort-taking aspect." (The hotel did, however, serve draft champagne.)

The Manhattan Beach Hotel—along with its rivals, the Brighton Beach Hotel and the Oriental Hotel—was one of Coney Island's first major attractions, offering rides, historical reenactments, and other enticements for guests.

In 1878, the Iron Steamboat Company began delivering visitors to its new Iron Pier in West Brighton, which was lined with saloons and ballrooms. A year later, the Brighton Beach Racetrack opened, joining nearby racetracks in Sheepshead Bay and Gravesend and turning the region into America's racing capital. By 1884, six railroads stopped at Coney Island, and three additional lines ran shuttles from end to end.

The action, however, also had a sinister side. West of Ocean Parkway, a thriving brothel business and a dangerous slum called the Gut flourished under the intentionally averted gaze of nefarious Police Chief John Y. McKane, who once testified that, "houses of prostitution are a necessity on Coney Island." (*See* Historical Detour: The Chief.) The Gut's most infamous destination was the Elephant Hotel. Built in 1884, this unusual pachyderm-shaped building was 122 feet high, with tin "skin" and four-foot-tall glass eyes that glittered at night. By the time the hotel burned down in 1896, the phrase "going to *see* the elephant" in Coney Island parlance meant "being up to no good."

But it was another creature, which also arrived in 1884, that revolutionized Coney Island. Thirty-six-year-old Ohioan L. A. Thompson erected the world's first roller coaster, the Switchback Railway, on West Tenth Street.

The gravity-based ride traveled a mere six miles per hour (compared with today's eighty-mile-per-hour coasters) and was so primitive that passengers had to get out while workers pushed the cars up to the second peak. When two competitors advanced the technology, Thompson shot back with two new coasters, the Scenic Railway and Pike's Peak, each of which combined exotic scenery with a thrilling ride.

As America careened into the technological age, Thompson's invention inspired several generations of Coney coasters and scenic railways, among them Dragon's Gorge, Mile High Sky Chaser, Drop the Dip, Over the Great Divide, and Roosevelt's Rough Riders (the site of Coney's worst coaster accident in 1910, when seventeen people were thrown from a height of thirty feet, and three died). Thunderbolt, built in 1926, had a small house attached to the ride's frame where the owners lived; the ride was immortalized as Alvy Singer's childhood home in the Woody Allen film *Annie Hall*. The coaster closed in 1983 and deteriorated until it was demolished, amid mild protests, in 2000. However, the most beloved roller coaster of all, the Cyclone, is still active and is even an official New York City landmark.

The roller coaster wasn't Coney Island's only invention. William Mangels, a German immigrant who owned a carousel manufacturing company, designed several rides, including the Whip, a kiddie favorite featuring small cars that whipped around the bends of an oval track.

Coney's next major innovation, however, was not a technical feat. It was a marketing ploy. Captain Paul Boyton, who had gained international fame in 1875 when he crossed the English Channel in a thirty-five-pound rubber suit he had invented, pioneered the enclosed amusement park, which debuted in 1895. Dressed in his creation, Boyton later kicked his way down the Rhine, Seine, Danube, and Missouri Rivers.

The aquatically inclined Boyton opened Sea Lion Park between Surf and Neptune Avenues, offering attractions like juggling sea lions and a new water ride called Shoot-the-Chutes. However, Boyton failed with Flip-Flap, the first roller coaster to loop the loop; imperfectly engineered, it left riders with aching necks.

Boyton's amusement park concept sparked the imagination of George C. Tilyou, who had already proved himself one of the shrewdest entrepreneurs in West Brighton. Tilyou was three years old in 1865 when his father, Peter, opened Tilyou's Surf House restaurant and hotel on Coney Island. By fourteen, George was showing signs of Barnumesque salesmanship: He took bottles and cigar boxes from his dad, filled the bottles with salt water and the boxes with sand, and sold them to souvenir-hungry tourists. In 1882, he

George Tilyou's Steeplechase Park was Coney Island's centerpiece for decades. The park's Funny Face logo remains the area's unofficial emblem

opened Tilyou's Surf Theater, but five years later he and his father were forced out of business after the younger Tilyou testified in a state investigation against Chief McKane.

It wasn't until he witnessed the awesome debut, in 1893, of the Ferris wheel while honeymooning at the World Columbian Exposition in Chicago that Tilyou entertained visions of a Coney comeback. Unable to purchase the original Ferris wheel, Tilyou built a smaller version at Coney Island, which he audaciously touted as "the world's largest Ferris wheel." Four years later, he mimicked Boyton's park idea by building Steeplechase Park, which set bold new standards in amusement park size and style. Tilyou also introduced the combination ticket, which allowed customers to enjoy a mélange of amusements for one price, and later built Steeplechase Pier to funnel people straight from boats into his park.

Historical Detour: A Dog's Tale

In 1867, or 1871, 1874, or 1889—depending on the story—
Charles Feltman, hoping to supplement his business of selling
pies from a wagon, supposedly slapped a sausage in a bun and
invented the frankfurter. While Coney Islanders relish this myth,
neither an 1884 Feltman profile nor his 1910 obituaries mustered
a single mention of the hot dog's tale, celebrating instead
Feltman's rags-to-riches life and his pioneering role in establishing Coney Island as a seaside resort.

Born in Hanover, Germany, in 1841, Charles Feltman came to
Brooklyn alone at age fourteen and, after surviving the winter of
1857 on stale bread and water, worked in bakeries for a decade
before opening his own business.

In 1871, Feltman's bakery began selling bread and pastries to
Coney Island restaurants. Three years later, he opened Feltman's
Ocean Pavilion and, while others chortled, persuaded Andrew
Culver to include evening trains on Culver's new railroad line,
enabling beachgoers to stay for dinner. In his beer gardens at Surf
Avenue and West Tenth Street, Feltman served seafood dinners,
while the hot dogs at his stand soon replaced the clam as Coney
Island's most famous food. Feltman's also became Coney's first
restaurant with music—courtesy of Wannemacher's Seventy-first
Regiment Band—and, so his obits proclaimed, the first to have
Tyrolean yodelers. He hired orchestras and costumed Bavarian
folksingers, built a lavishly decorated three-story ballroom (supposedly the world's largest), installed Coney Island's first merry-
go-round, and later added roller coasters and movies.

Feltman's, which survived until 1954, drew two hundred
thousand customers annually in the 1880s, and peaked in 1923
with 5.2 million patrons. Whether Charles Feltman invented the
hot dog is debatable, but he certainly served a lot of them.

Tilyou capitalized on the popularity of Brooklyn racetracks by making a
mechanical horse race the centerpiece of Steeplechase. People jeered,
cheered, and even bet on the "horses," which were double-saddled with
paying customers who accelerated and braked their way around the entire

park via an iron rail, from Surf Avenue to the beach and from West Sixteenth to West Eighteenth Street. Although the ride cost $37,000 to build (a $600,000 value today), it held true to the simple themes that enabled Steeplechase to outlast its competitors, Luna Park and Dreamland. Both parks, built in the next decade, relied heavily on lavish spectacle, whereas at Steeplechase the customers themselves were the entertainment; giggling couples particularly enjoyed clutching onto and tumbling into one another on Tilyou's circuit of thrills.

Steeplechase classics included the Barrel of Love, the Human Roulette Wheel, and the Down and Out—a dark, steep, screw-shaped chute that dumped participants onto the spinning disks of the Human Pool Table. Visitors were also thrust onto the park's public stage, complete with falling scenery, moving floors, and skirt-blowing air, providing laughs for a seated audience. (By the time Steeplechase had run its course in 1964, modern social mores had rendered these semi-illicit thrills archaic.) Steeplechase's unforgettable logo was a garish face with leering grin and an improbable forty-four teeth. Hired hands marched around the Funny Place, as the park was known, in animal costumes, an idea Walt Disney later copied.

Tilyou's marketing know-how even enabled him to make disaster profitable. In 1907, while leaving church, Tilyou learned his beloved park had been destroyed by fire. Unfazed, he calmly instructed his men to wait until the fire cooled, then erect a fence and put up a sign advertising "Admission to the burning ruins 10 cents." Tilyou earned enough money to rebuild Steeplechase Park, a large section of which he enclosed to offer entertainment in any weather. Tilyou died in 1914, but his three sons kept drawing customers for another half century, adding attractions like the 1939 World's Fair Parachute Jump.

In his lifetime, Tilyou was not only savvy but also greedy. Steeplechase charged an entry fee to the beach behind the park; the practice was deemed illegal several years after his death. What's more, it was Tilyou's avarice that provoked the establishment of Steeplechase's greatest rival—Luna Park. At the 1901 Pan-American Exposition in Buffalo, Tilyou had persuaded Fred Thompson and Elmer Dundy to bring their new ride, Trip to the Moon, to Steeplechase. The ride was a smash in 1902, yet Tilyou wanted to cut the duo's share from 60 to 40 percent. Thompson and Dundy quit Steeplechase and took their ride down the block. The following summer, they opened Luna Park.

Dundy handled business matters and named the park for his sister Luna back in Des Moines. Thompson, a Tennessean who had studied architec-

ture, was the park's creative force, juxtaposing incongruous styles and toss-
ing tradition aside. One must "dare to decorate a minaret with renaissance
detail or to jumble romanesque with l'art nouveau," he wrote.

*Luna Park was Coney Island's fantasyland, a visual feast of towers, domes, and spires, lit by
250,000 bulbs when most people didn't have electricity in their homes*

What they concocted was an "electric Eden," a fantasyland of candy-
colored towers, trellises, domes, and spires illuminated by 250,000 electric
lights—a spectacular sight in an era before electricity was a basic amenity.

(Decades after the park was gone, budget-conscious New Yorkers reprimanded children who left lights on by saying, "What do you think this is, Luna Park?")

Built on the former site of Sea Lion Park, Luna Park drew forty thousand people on opening night and cleared $600,000 in profits its rookie year. Dundy and Thompson built a scenic railway called Trip to the North Pole and a romantic water ride called Canals of Venice, adding them to Boyton's Shoot-the-Chutes, which remained there. Other new attractions included Hagenbeck's Wild Animals, the Monkey Theater, a candy deli that sold confections shaped like hot dogs and fried oysters, and reenactment spectacles like Fire and Sword, which promised "realistic massacre together with many other features of real warfare at close quarters."

Anyone who believes that daytime talk shows and tragedy-of-the-week movies have reduced Americans to tasteless and morbid voyeurs has forgotten Coney's steady stream of macabre and popular exhibits, like the reenactment of the 1889 Johnstown Flood. Run independently of the big parks, its advertisements boasted, "Where the morning before had stood a noble town filled with prosperous and happy people, now all was desolation and death. . . . The Johnstown Flood appeals to all young and old and should be seen by every visitor to the island."

For sheer voyeurism, nothing topped Luna's Infant Incubators, where twenty-five cents bought a glimpse of premature babies. The infants received expert medical care, and mothers willingly offered them up to receive the free treatment. Dreamland lured the incubator exhibit away in 1904, but it returned to Luna Park for good in 1911.

In 1912, however, five years after Dundy's untimely death, the hard-drinking Thompson lost Luna Park in bankruptcy. The new owner, Baron Collier, kept Thompson on as manager until he died in 1919. But Collier wasn't innovative, and new technologies like talkies and radio eventually rendered Luna's wonders passé. The Heart of Coney Island slowly declined, and in 1946, after two fires in three years, the lights went out on Luna Park.

Former senator William H. Reynolds, whose Tammany Hall friends provided a sweet deal for property at Surf Avenue and West Eighth Street, opened Coney Island's last big park, Dreamland, in 1904. Based on the Luna model, the grander, more elaborate Dreamland promised to be the greatest amusement park of all. Its imperial design cost $3.5 million and included one million lights (four times as many as Luna's), a 375-foot-tall main tower with a beacon that shone fifty miles out to sea, and baroque-style columns, arches, gargoyles, and griffins so sophisticated they were analyzed by architecture critics.

But Dreamland's extravagant facade couldn't mask its obvious similarity to Luna Park. Dreamland's attractions were either derivative (scenic railways like Coasting Through Switzerland, spectacle shows like Fall of Pompeii and Fighting the Flames) or outright copies (Shoot-the-Chutes and Canals of Venice). Although dazzling, Dreamland lacked the boisterousness and whimsy of Luna Park, and never gripped the public's imagination the same way . . . until the day it burned to the ground seven years later.

At 1:30 AM on May 27, 1911—the season's opening day—a fire started in the wiring of Dreamland's turbulent water ride, Hell Gate. While Coney Island had experienced ten multialarm fires in eighteen years, this was by far the worst. As forty-four hundred firemen struggled against the inferno, Manhattanites could see the flames licking the night sky. Dreamland was left in ashes, and nearby restaurants, bathhouses, and attractions like Thompson's Scenic Railway and the Observation Tower were destroyed. Nobody died, but a lion named Black Prince from the wild-animal show staggered, bleeding and burning, onto Surf Avenue, before climbing the tracks of the Rocky Road to Dublin roller coaster, where he was shot. Scavengers armed with pliers yanked out Black Prince's teeth for souvenirs, and the next day, crowds paid ten cents to view his corpse.

Samuel Gumpertz, who had risen from managing Dreamland's Lilliputian Village—occupied by three hundred midgets—to managing the entire park, quickly built his own Dreamland Circus Sideshow on the old park's ruins. But with Dreamland's destruction coming on the heels of a reform that had closed the Brighton Beach Racetrack, many observers predicted the demise of Coney Island. Indeed, an era of elegance was ending—in the next decade, the Manhattan Beach, Brighton Beach, and Oriental Hotels were razed, making way for urban residential housing. The experts were wrong. Coney Island wasn't dying, it was simply taking on a new flavor . . . and it was about to become more popular than ever before.

Between 1915 and 1920, three subway lines arrived at Coney Island, and suddenly every New Yorker could reach the beach for only a nickel. With Nathan's, which had opened in 1916, asking only another nickel for a hot dog or a milk shake, Coney Island became the Nickel Empire—truly a summer resort for the masses, who would often sleep on the beach on Saturday nights rather than return to their sweltering tenements.

A million revelers, or 18 percent of the city's populace, visited Coney Island on a typical summer Sunday in 1920, a vast increase over 1900, when a hundred thousand people, or 3 percent of the city residents, made the same pilgrimage. To accommodate the throngs, Coney Island opened an eighty-foot-wide boardwalk along the beach in 1923, officially named Riegelman's Walk after former Brooklyn borough president Harold Riegelman. The 1920s also gave birth to Thunderbolt, the Cyclone, and Wonder Wheel. By 1938, Coney Island boasted thirteen carousels, eleven roller coasters, twenty shooting galleries, three freak shows, and two hundred eateries. In Coney Island's peak years just after World War II, the Coney Island Chamber of Commerce seems to have gleefully exaggerated attendance figures—newspaper reports of thirty-six million visitors in 1946 and 2.5 million on a single Sunday in 1947 sound mathematically improbable—but on hot summer days, the workingman's resort appeared packed with every man, woman, and child in the city.

In subsequent decades, the record crowds gradually dissipated as home air conditioners and car travel gave New Yorkers other summer options, amusement areas elsewhere became more sophisticated, and the misguided deeds of Robert Moses and the government transformed Coney Island's identity. In 1949, the fun-hating parks commissioner—who had previously banned everything from fishing to flying kites at Coney Island—stunned local merchants by denouncing Coney Island as "an over-commercialized mistake." He then began rezoning the amusement area for passive recreation. The influential *New York Times* supported Moses' endeavor, parroting his pronouncements that people preferred retreats like Jones Beach (a Moses creation) to "gadget resorts" like Coney.

Moses later changed course, however, and in his dual role as city construction coordinator and parks commissioner announced at the 1958 groundbreaking for the Luna Park high-rise apartments that Coney Island should instead be rebuilt as a residential community. Between 1960 and 1973, fifteen large housing projects and apartment buildings were erected on Coney Island. After Steeplechase Park closed in the 1960s, Fred Trump (Donald Trump's father) demolished it, planning to build four thirty-story towers there that were never realized. Instead, he later sold back the empty land to the city for a profit. Neighborhood shops and houses were also razed in anticipation of federal financing for more buildings, but President Richard Nixon cut off the funds, leaving this once dynamic area pockmarked with rubble-filled lots and forbidding housing projects. Jobs and commerce vanished as banks, small businesses, and movie theaters closed—all a chilling tribute to the destructive powers of poor urban planning. Although no longer an island, the government's neglect of Coney Island left it as isolated as if it were out at sea.

Historical Detour: The Chief

In 1869, John Y. McKane, an unknown, uneducated builder from Sheepshead Bay, was elected one of Gravesend's three town commissioners and authorized to lease the town's common land, which included parts of Coney Island. By the 1880s, McKane had metamorphosed from this low-profile administrator into the grand poohbah of Coney Island, a ruthless and dictatorial political boss whose powers stretched from the Elephant Hotel to the White House.

Born in 1841 in Ireland's County Antrim, McKane came to Brooklyn as an infant. In his teens, he worked as a carpenter's apprentice, later opening his own business and shrewdly capitalizing on the rapid development of Coney Island by building its bathhouses and beer halls. This thickset, ruddy-faced man didn't drink, smoke, or gamble and soon became superintendent of his local Sunday school.

A scrupulous and highly productive town commissioner, McKane more than doubled the town's leasing revenue in his first two years. But power seduced McKane, who soon subverted his principles in an effort to garner the post of Gravesend supervisor. Toward that end, McKane built support and made powerful friends by leasing land to them at a fraction of its worth. Austin Corbin, the developer of Manhattan Beach, paid $1,500 for land valued at one hundred times that amount. A similar bargain was afforded Paul Bauer, with McKane building Bauer's West Brighton Hotel and Casino. Developers often returned the favor by hiring McKane's company to do construction work.

McKane's shady deals paid off. In the late 1870s, he was the first working-class man elected to Gravesend supervisor. He convinced the state legislature to allow him to replace Brooklyn police with his own Coney Island force, and made himself police commissioner. As head of the town board, board of health, and water board, he wrote local laws and audited contracts. He also began giving land away to influential cronies. The Chief, as McKane was called, ran Coney Island as he saw fit, creating what the *New York Times* later called "Sodom-by-the Sea." He employed pickpockets for "detective" work, licensed the era's leading bank robbers to run saloons, allowed the notorious Gut district to prosper down the road from police headquarters, and crushed anyone who opposed him.

McKane's netherworld prompted an investigation by the state assembly in 1887. The Times wrote that his see-no-evil policy "largely turned Coney into a nest of dives, disreputable houses, gambling hells and cheap and nasty shows." McKane's brazen defense was "I do not make inquiries." In other words, unless he stumbled upon an illegal activity, he would not investigate.

The assembly committee called for McKane's indictment, but his comrades in Albany buried the report. McKane promptly retaliated against George Tilyou—the only islander to name names during the hearings—by forcing Tilyou and his father out of business. That summer, a thousand McKane disciples held a gala for the Chief at Bauer's Casino, where a massive portrait of McKane draped with the Stars and Stripes hung above the entrance. McKane was given a gold shield featuring a diamond star—surrounded by emeralds and more diamonds—worth $1,500 (more than $22,000 today).

McKane effected his greatest abuse of power on Election Day. In the 1884 presidential election, when New York State went Democrat by 1,047 votes, McKane's control of local voting booths was widely credited with helping put the reform-minded Grover Cleveland over the top in a crucial state. After a quarrel with Brooklyn's Democratic boss, Hugh McLaughlin, however, McKane switched parties. In 1888, McKane fixed the Gravesend vote, helping Republican Benjamin Harrison defeat Cleveland.

McKane's arrogance and unfettered authority ultimately proved his undoing. In 1893, reform candidates in Brooklyn tired of McKane's election shenanigans, and called for a fair count in Gravesend. While the town had only 1,700 legal voters, McKane had tallied 2,547 votes in 1891 and claimed 6,218 registrants in 1893. Reformers who confronted McKane were beaten up and jailed, and when a second group arrived with an injunction on Election Day, McKane had them roughed up, boasting, "Injunctions don't go here."

McKane's despotic declaration was played up in the local press, prompting a trial that brought national attention. He was found guilty of election fraud and misuse of public funds, and served four years upstate in Sing Sing. McKane returned to Brooklyn in 1898 and, after a series of strokes, died in September 1899.

The entirety of the former island was not written off, however. Manhattan Beach, with its stable upper-middle-class neighborhood and Kingsborough Community College, has remained unchanged for decades, and an influx of immigrants from the Soviet Union remade Brighton Beach into a Little Odessa. On the west end is the walled-in and increasingly pricey Sea Gate community, which has a large Russian segment and a major ultra-Orthodox Jewish population. (Ironically, Sea Gate was enclosed in the 1890s partially to keep out Jews.)

Cries about the amusement area's demise grew louder after the Thunderbolt closed in the early 1980s, and then in the late 1980s and early 1990s, amid violent teenage crime and medical waste washing up on the beaches. Shouts of Coney's imminent self-destruction, however, date back to the nineteenth century. In the 1880s, people complained about muggers who drizzled knockout drops into the drinks of unsuspecting saloon patrons; in the early 1900s, child prostitution was epidemic; and in the 1930s and 1940s, sewage stained the beaches.

In the latest go-round, Coney Island gradually began an arduous climb back toward prosperity, thanks in part to the government's reversal on anti-recreation zoning, the perseverance of community groups and entrepreneurial individuals, and the enduring appeal of the beach, boardwalk, and remaining rides. Dick Zigun, sometimes called the Mayor of Coney Island, helped bring back the fun with his nonprofit group, Coney Island USA. Zigun, who was born in P. T. Barnum's hometown of Bridgeport, Connecticut, was a playwright and performer who had graduated from the Yale School of Drama when he discovered the area. He created, in 1983, the Mermaid Parade, a kick-off-the-summer event that now attracts hundreds of thousands of spectators, the Coney Island Museum, and Sideshows by the Seashore, which brings a theatrical flourish to the freak show.

The Astella Corporation, a not-for-profit housing organization, spent years in the 1980s and '90s, building over one thousand private homes, adding a new wave of working-class residents—mainly Asian and Egyptian immigrants—to the ethnic stew of African American, Latino, and longtime Italian residents. Astella, along with ANCHOR, a state- and city-funded program, also helped revive commercial development. New stores arose on empty lots along Mermaid Avenue. "Astella has done a wonderful job stabilizing the community," Zigun says.

In the mid-1990s, the city stepped up police patrols and repaved streets, while the federal government rehabilitated eroded beaches. And Nathan's Famous annual July 4th hot-dog-eating contest turned itself into a media extravaganza with plenty of meat-in-cheek international media coverage. The famed Coney Island Boardwalk and beach were enhanced with sprinklers, gazebos for shade, and even a splash of color on the garbage cans, with each one featuring a colorful ocean-themed painting by children.

The newly redesigned subway terminal at Coney Island was one of the first symbols of the current rejuvenation

And the Metropolitan Transit Authority began a reconstruction of the Coney Island Terminal. The terminal, which was completed in 2005, is the largest aboveground terminal facility anywhere. Thanks to new solar panels, it is also the nation's most energy-efficient mass transit facility. It looks gorgeous, too, with a terra-cotta facade and arches designed in the style of the train sheds of Europe.

Further resurgence followed, albeit with plenty of Sturm und Drang. "There has been substantial change to the Coney Island of ten years ago," Zigun says. "And all the most radical changes were about rezoning and who owns the land."

In 2001 the Brooklyn Cyclones, a minor-league affiliate of the New York Mets, made their debut on the site of the old Steeplechase Park. (The Mets also own the club.) But Mayor Rudolph Giuliani accomplished this the only way he knew how—his way. Rather than have the Mets pay for the construction, the mayor used city money to build the stadium. He simultaneously displaced a long-planned indoor amateur athletics complex that would have provided the area with much needed year-round recreation and jobs, killing it off. And after Jeff Wilpon, the son of Mets owner Fred Wilpon, complained that the defunct Thunderbolt roller coaster, just beyond the ballpark's fence, was an eyesore, the mayor had it illegally demolished without the owner's permission. (Kansas Fried Chicken magnate Horace Bullard had been sitting on this lot, along with the Shore Theater property, since 1985, without developing it, always saying his plans were being thwarted by the city.) And the Mets allowed Brooklyn only a short-season single-A club that would play just thirty-eight home games, despite a market that could easily have supported a Double A team. Despite all this, the Cyclones have proved a hit, still drawing well a decade into their run.

"The ballpark and the subway terminal put Coney Island back on the map," says Charles Denson, executive director of the Coney Island History Project.

Meanwhile, a developer named Joe Sitt and his company, Thor Equities, began buying up parcel after parcel in the area. This led to a major real-estate war as Sitt was alternatively cast as a hero for planning to bring new life to the amusement area and a villain for his plans to build high-rises and to destroy historic buildings for ticky-tack arcades. He took particular heat for buying out and closing down the Astroland amusement park and nearby go-karts and batting cages. Mayor Michael Bloomberg and the city, in turn, developed alternate plans and worked to push Sitt aside. The battle ended when the city paid Sitt about $95 million—which was a profit for him of about $55 million—for the Astroland site and other spots. (Sitt still owns about eight acres in the area.)

Charles Reichenthal, the local community board's district manager, agrees that the picture became hopelessly muddled for most of the public as the fight dragged on. "Sitt brought hope then became the bad guy," says Judi Orlando, Astella's executive director, adding that both "Sitt and the Mayor confused the community" about what was being planned for Coney Island.

A nonprofit organization called Save Coney Island worked futilely to stop Sitt from razing buildings like Henderson's Music Hall, where Al Jolson performed and Harpo Marx supposedly joined his brothers onstage for the first time. Founder Juan Rivero blasts Sitt as "unpredictable and erratic," saying he's not only demolishing history but also undermining the potential for long-term growth.

But Sitt, a Brooklynite who feels "picked on," defends his actions, saying the old buildings were decrepit (his critics say he neglected them until they were) and long ignored. "No one cared about these properties till I came along," he says.

He also says he deserves credit for luring Ringling Bros and Barnum & Bailey Circus to Coney Island—a big hit in 2009 and 2010—although the circus didn't perform on his property. And while most of his other announced construction plans have fallen by the wayside, he still sees himself as "a savior of Coney Island" because "I forced the administration to pay attention to Coney Island."

At various times Sitt's plans have featured hotels, timeshares, and luxury condos; under the city's plan, condos will be built, with the first one rising on W. 32nd Street in the summer of 2011. (That building, however, is more than a half-mile from the entertainment area and sits across from the daunting housing projects. Future plans call for more condos just west of the ballpark.) Orlando says the city will need to ensure not only that affordable housing is included but also that it provides the necessary new schools, traffic patterns, and improved infrastructure. Although she's opposed to skyscrapers, she says some high-rises can stabilize the community, filling in empty lots and creating a need for services that will bolster existing merchants and bring out new ones, which in turn creates much-needed jobs. One plan already approved is Coney Island Commons, which will have five thousand housing units, with 180 set aside for affordable housing, and a forty-thousand-square-foot YMCA. "It'll be different, but it'll be good," says Orlando. "I'm very optimistic,"

Today, the Coney Island amusement area is revitalized. The city leased the 3.5-acre Astroland site to Central Amusement International (CAI), an offshoot of Zamperla USA, an amusement ride manufacturer. Zamperla launched its brand-new Luna Park in 2010 with $15 million worth of new rides. It surpassed even its own internal projections, celebrating its millionth rider before August was over and welcoming well over four hundred thousand visitors by season's end. The season was such a smash that instead of closing in September, Luna Park stayed open on weekends through Halloween, which in turn led to Coney Island's first Halloween parade. For 2011, Zamperla will open the Scream Zone, featuring the latest in daredevil rides, on an adjoining site, and it signed on to operate and spruce up the historic Cyclone for 2011 before the city puts out a bid for a long-term lease for 2012.

Zamperla also stirred some controversy with its plan to improve the Boardwalk area near its parks. To create an upscale sit-down restaurant and a sports bar, CAI tried evicting eight of the ten tenants along that stretch, including the beloved Ruby's, which had been a popular bar since

1934 and Ruby's since 1975, and "Shoot the Freak," a game in which customers shot paintball "bullets" at a man in protective gear dancing among debris in an alley. The Coney Island Eight, as they dubbed themselves, fought back in court, and won the right to operate for one more season in 2011. (Shoot the Freak, however, was forced to move from its location.)

Thanks to the new Luna Park, in 2010 Coney Island's amusement area had its best year in nearly four decades.

Meanwhile, the city is developing Steeplechase Plaza near the ballpark. The 2.2-acre site will include a performance green and possible space for other amusement rides. Its centerpiece will be the restored fifty-horse B&B Carousell, which moved from New Jersey to Coney Island in 1932—in an era when there were as many as two dozen carousels in the area—and which the city bought to preserve in 2005. William Mangels created the carousel's mechanical workings at his Surf Avenue workshop in 1919, while forty-nine of the horses were among the last carved by Charles Carmel, the master carver credited with devising Coney Island style. (Marcus Charles Illions, another top carver of the day, produced the lead horse, cloaked in armor.) This is one of only twelve surviving Carmel carousels and one of only sixteen left where riders can "grab the brass ring."

Like the soon-to-be-reincarnated carousel, "Coney Island basically died and came back to life," says Dianna Carlin, owner of Lola Star boutique on the Boardwalk.

"This is more rides than Coney Island has had since the days of Stee-plechase," Zigun says.

Skeptics argue that the city, instead of buying the Astroland site from Sitt, should have purchased the old Thunderbolt site, thereby linking the stadium to the amusement area. Then when Sitt or someone else redeveloped the Astroland site, the overall amusement area would have been larger. But Zigun argues that while he would have done things differently, that's no longer the point. In his 2010 "State of Coney Island" speech, Zigun said "there is no return to the past," and implored those who care about the area to stop being "constant critics" and to instead encourage the city to fulfill its promises and do more. Among the items he still sees on the city's to-do list: make the circus a permanent addition instead of a year-to-year guest; acquire Bullard's properties for amusement rides to balance out Sitt's plans; pour resources into enhancing the New York Aquarium; and build a new proposed amphitheater for concerts in the community's Asser Levy Park.

Reichenthal hopes to add express trains to lure more people to the area and change the perception that "we're the outer part of the outer boroughs." But his main goal is to make Coney Island a year-round destination, pointing to Luna Park's successful extended season in 2010 as an important first step. "There's no reason we can't have more things going on from November to March," he says, pointing to the thousands of people who pour onto the beach each New Year's Day to participate in and watch the famous Polar Bear Club swim.

While all those plans will take years—and more political battles—to sort themselves out, Coney Island's 2010 season was, with fourteen million visitors, its best since 1964. With all the excitement over the new attractions, Coney Island is finally enjoying another moment in the sun.

Exploring the Island

Coney's island days are long gone, but the peninsula remains a cherished destination for anyone pursuing simple, often hedonistic, pleasures. The major attractions are the beach and two neighborhoods—Coney Island and Brighton Beach. To fully embrace Coney Island, cast off your inhibitions, disregard decorum, and celebrate the tacky. (Call ahead between Labor Day and Memorial Day, as many attractions close or operate only on weekends during the off-season.)

"Our beach is exceptional," says Zigun. "It's the largest public beach on the East Coast, and it has southern exposure. Plus, it's full of half-naked New Yorkers."

Coney Island doesn't have much in the way of shopping, but the **Coney Island Beach Shop**, which is open year-round, does have "everything you forgot that you need for the beach—and with prices that won't kill you," says Maya Haddad, whose family owns the store at 3018 Stillwell Avenue, 718-333-1110. In addition to carrying everything from bathing suits to suntan lotion to smash balls and string for kites, the store has a vast collection of creative T-shirts. "We try to bring out the history of Coney Island," Haddad says, with designs illustrating the B&B Carousell or the Elephant Hotel.

The other hot spot for souvenirs is **Lola Star Boutique** on the Boardwalk, which also has a kiosk inside the Stillwell Avenue Subway Station (www.lolastar.com). Owner Dianna Carlin, a.k.a. Lola Star, designs and prints her own Coney Island T-shirts and also created the only Coney Island snow globe on the market. Along with a Nathan's outpost, Lola Star was the only Boardwalk vendor invited to stay by Zamperla.

Beyond the beach, the heart of Coney Island is the amusement area. The new centerpiece is **Luna Park**, which brings a bright and shiny polish to an amusement area that, for all its appeal, felt ragged and worn for decades. Rides like Surf's Up, which glides back and forth with only moderate rotations, are fun but relatively tame; others like Hang Glider generate more of an adrenaline rush, while the Air Race and Electro Spin, which go higher, faster and with more revolutions, are for real adventure seekers. The success of the first season extended well beyond summer as the park stayed open through Halloween with a "Nights of Horror" special haunted house throughout October; Coney Island also hosted its first Halloween Parade to cap off the year.

For 2011, Zamperla, the company behind Luna Park, expands its footprint with the Scream Zone. Plans for this four-acre park include possible rides such as "Screaming Eagle," a new roller coaster, a reverse bungee ride called the "Sling Shot" that catapults riders thirty stories into the air, a double-decker go-kart track, and a new Steeplechase ride.

The soul of Coney Island's amusement area remains the **Cyclone**, 718-265-2100. When it opened in 1927 on Surf Avenue and West Tenth Street, the Cyclone's 110-second ride over nine hills rocked the senses in unforgettable style. It still does. One of the few wooden-track roller coasters around, the rattling Cyclone—with its first drop of eighty-five feet at a sixty-degree angle—nearly jolts you out of your body. According to legend, a man who lost his voice due to trauma in World War II rode the Cyclone five years later and staggered off saying, "I feel sick." From then on, he could speak. Don't worry, the rickety feel is merely part of the ambience—the wooden tracks on this landmark are periodically replaced.

The Cyclone, a New York landmark and one of the world's great roller coasters, remains the area's star attraction.

Besides the Cyclone, the area's other ageless classic is the **Wonder Wheel**, a twenty-four-car Ferris wheel weighing two hundred tons and standing 150 feet high. It was built of steel forged right on the spot. The only time this New York City landmark stopped rotating was during the 1977 blackout when it had to be cranked by hand to let riders out. It opened as an independent ride in 1920. Denos Vourderis bought it in 1983 and surrounded it with Deno's Wonder Wheel Park, 718-372-2592, which includes several other rides, the Spook-A-Rama haunted house, and a kiddie park. Deno's sponsors fireworks every Friday night at 9 PM in-season.

Beneath the Wonder Wheel is the **Coney Island History Project**'s exhibition center, 718-266-0012, which is open on summer weekends and is free of charge. (It moved from underneath the Cyclone after Zamperla took that ride over.) It offers new exhibits each season—the original Luna Park was the 2010 headliner, but the small space also has other gems like the area's oldest artifact, a Coney Island Toll House sign dating to 1823. The organization, founded in 2004 by the Albert family, which then owned Astroland, also sponsors readings, movie nights, treasure hunts, and other events, which are posted on its website (www.coneyislandhistory.org). Visitors are also encouraged to record their Coney memories for the organization's oral history archive.

Coney Island also has independent operators with other rides and attractions. One highlight is **El Dorado**, a bumper car extravaganza at 1216 Surf Avenue off West Twelfth Street, 718-946-6642. Outside, the prerecorded barker invites passersby to "bump, bump, bump yo' ass off." Inside, blasting music, flashing lights, and slamming cars bring you to the zenith of mindless merriment on which Coney Island has built its reputation. It also hosts an arcade and leads out to a narrow block with the types of midway games usually found at carnivals.

Sideshows by the Seashore is run by Dick Zigun, the "mayor" of Coney Island and the founder of the annual Mermaid Parade.

Down the block is the **Sideshows by the Seashore** freak show run by Dick Zigun, a modern-day George Tilyou, and his not-for-profit group, Coney Island USA, 1208 Surf Avenue, 718-372-5159, www.coneyislandusa.com. (The entrance is on West Twelfth Street.) Although the delightfully gauche barker outside lays it on thick, this is less of an excursion into seamy voyeurism than its historical predecessors since societal changes have shifted the emphasis from people with deformities, like Pinhead Boy, to stupid human tricks, like the fire eater, the glass chewer, or the guy who lies on a bed of nails while audience members stand on him. The group even offers a Sideshow class to teach the secrets of skills like sword swallowing and snake charming, which may lead to a spot onstage.

Upstairs from Sideshows by the Seashore is Coney Island USA's overlooked **Coney Island Museum**. Although not the full-fledged museum Coney deserves, the displays are charming. There are old Boardwalk rolling chairs, funhouse mirrors, and dozens of antique artifacts like a Steeplechase horse with a TWO ON A HORSE sign, a wooden milk bottle from an impossible-to-win midway game, and photos of early freaks like Seal Boy. Old documentary footage of Coney Island runs continuously. Coney Island USA also sponsors numerous cultural events, including a tattoo and motorcycle show each September and a movie and a concert series during the summer.

Next door the **Shmaltz Brewing Company** has set up the world's smallest brewery, producing two gallons at a time of experimental beer flavors. They provide tastings and give "tours," informal conversations that explain their brewing process. They sell bottles of Coney Island Craft Lagers inside Coney Island USA.

Coney Island USA's highlight is undoubtedly the **Mermaid Parade**, which has inaugurated each summer on the season's first Saturday since 1983. The parade is raucous and flamboyant in grand Coney Island tradition, kind of like a summertime version of the Greenwich Village Halloween parade. Riding in floats or marching along Surf Avenue and the Boardwalk are thousands of King Neptunes and mermaids, with many of the latter topless but for some pasties. You might also *see* tentacled silver Mermaids from Mars, an S&M mermaid, or even a dachshund dressed as a mermaid. Each year celebrities serve as the merman and mermaid King and Queen. Past guests of honor include David Byrne, Lou Reed, Harvey Keitel, Queen Latifah, and Laurie Anderson. The parade's most regal Neptune is crowned king and presented with a cardboard thermometer to turn up the temperature and usher in summer. Neptune and Zigun then plunge, fully clad, into the Atlantic Ocean and declare the season open. "I'm astonished and honored that this has become a New York holiday with 100,000 people there," says Zigun. "It's something I made up out of my head."

While the Mermaid Parade kicks off summer, the **Coney Island Polar Bear Club**—founded in 1903 and the nation's oldest winter bathing club—knows how to celebrate the off-season with élan (www.polarbearclub.org). While they swim the Atlantic every Sunday from November through April, their biggest event is its New Year's Day swim, which attracts hundreds of people. However, the main off-season attraction for folks not looking to jump in the ocean is ice-skating at the **Abe Stark Skating Rink**,

718-946-6536, at West Twentieth Street and the Boardwalk.

If warm weather is your preference, however, there are plenty of other events worth checking out. The circus comes to town each summer when **Ringling Brothers and Barnum & Bailey** sets up their big tent for a one-ring show that's much more intimate than their annual Madison Square Garden extravaganza (www.ringling.com/coneyisland).

Wistful for your pail-and-shovel days? Then check out the **Sand Sculpture Contest** in late July as part of the Astella Development Corp community group's "Unity Day" festival (www.astelladevelopment.org). If you're nostalgic for some golden oldies, then try the **Seaside Summer Concert Series** at Asser Levy Park, West 5th Street and Surf Avenue (www.brooklynconcerts.com/seaside.html). Performers in 2010 included Neil Sedaka, Aretha Franklin, the Beach Boys, George Thorogood, and the B-52s. (Controversy has dogged the popular series, however, as two synagogues across the street have brought legal action, forcing performers in 2010 to turn down their volume to barely audible levels.)

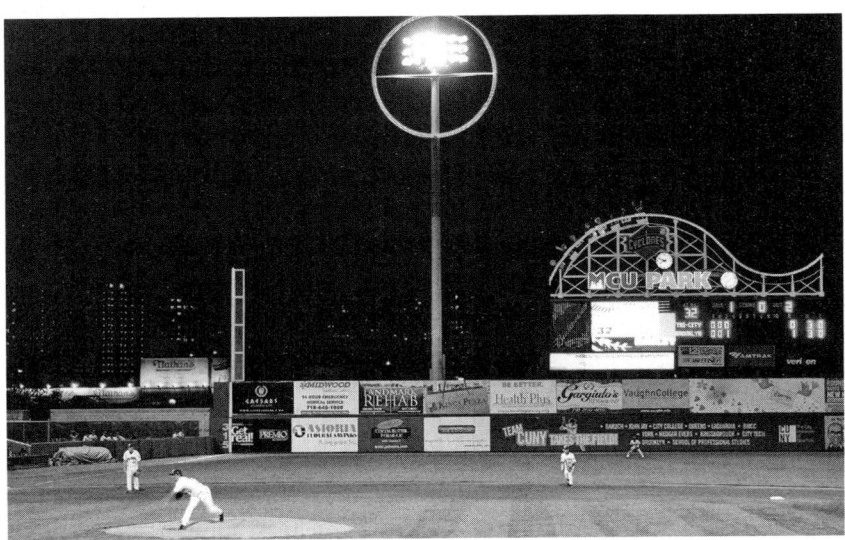

Since 2001, Brooklynites have been flocking to see the Cyclones, the borough's first professional baseball team since the Dodgers left town

The *Village Voice* brings a more contemporary sound with its annual **Siren Festival** by the Boardwalk from West 10th Street to Stillwell Avenue each July.

And for baseball fans, there's the **Brooklyn Cyclones** at MCU Park, on the site of the former Steeplechase Park, Surf Avenue at West 19th Street, 718-449-8497. Fans sitting along the first-base line gaze out at the Cyclone,

Wonder Wheel, and Luna Park while spectators along the third-base side gaze upon the Parachute Jump just beyond the stadium's walls. The Jump, brought over to Coney Island from the 1939–40 World's Fair, closed in 1963. It slowly deteriorated and was to be dismantled by the city until locals fought for its preservation. Affectionately called the Eiffel Tower of Brooklyn, it has a fresh coat of paint, brightly colored base panels, lights . . . and national landmark status. A concourse connects the stadium directly to the Boardwalk. (If you leave the ballpark via the Boardwalk and head down to the beach, you'll find Steeplechase Pier, a popular fishing spot.)

The New York Aquarium, a Coney Island staple since 1957, is undertaking a major expansion that will feature a huge new shark exhibit.

The ballpark marks the westernmost entertainment to be had; toward the eastern end of the amusement area is the **New York Aquarium,** Surf Avenue and West Eighth Street, 718-265-3474 (www.nyaquarium.com). The aquarium has been in Coney Island since 1957 and is the oldest continuously operating aquarium in the country. Like the amusement area, the aquarium, run by the Wildlife Conservation Society (which also runs the Bronx Zoo), is undergoing a face-lift.

Dubbed Sea Change, a ten-year, public-private initiative (with an initial investment of $100 million) includes a major renovation of the aquarium's open-air Aquatheater, which has featured trainer-led California sea lion demonstrations. (Aquatheater is expected to reopen in late 2011.) The aquarium will also build a new, inviting exterior along the Boardwalk and Surf Avenue to physically connect the aquarium to the Boardwalk and the neighborhood. The marine conservation program will expand, with a special emphasis on the water surrounding New York City. And the shark exhibit will be quadrupled in a massive exhibit called Ocean Wonders, expected to open in 2013. Three new exhibitions scheduled for the main hall include freshwater fish of Africa, fish of the Amazon, and a coral exhibition.

While the expansion is under way, there is still plenty to *see* from walruses and sea otters (public feedings daily) to sharks and penguins. Check out **Sea Cliffs**, a Pacific Coast replica, where you'll learn that sea otters eat the human equivalent of eighty hamburgers a day; **Explore the Shore**, a coastal exhibit that features a four-hundred-gallon tidal wave that you can stand under and not get wet; and **Alien Stingers**, a dark exhibit space featuring mesmerizing, glowing jellyfish species.

For an additional fee, take a seat and experience Planet Earth—Shallow Seas, an eight-minute digital adventure in 4-D that envelops viewers in special effects such as wind, mist, scents, and dramatic lighting.

Continue down Surf Avenue until you reach Ocean Parkway. Across the other side is Brighton Beach, which takes you into a totally different world . . . one revolving around Russia and the Ukraine. Brighton Beach Avenue is filled with clothing, jewelry, and gift shops, but two stores stand out. **Kids' World**, 605 Brighton Beach Avenue, 718-332-7502, is also a superb book and toy store. It features imported merchandise from stuffed animals that "speak" in Russian to models of Soviet-era tanks and planes to puzzles featuring Russian artwork. It also has an impressive selection of toys, games, and books catering to English speakers, including children's versions of Russian literature. Its sister store, **St. Petersburg Trade and Publishing**, 230 Brighton Beach Avenue, 718-361-4128, sells Russian-language CDs, DVDs, and books and a large collection of translated Russian literature. There's also a wide array of souvenirs: silk shawls; handsome boxes, some lacquered, some made of birch bark but all with intricate designs; Russian china; Soviet-era winter hats; and nesting dolls—both the classic Matryoshka and those featuring American politicians (including President Obama) and Soviet leaders like Lenin and Stalin.

Where to Eat

A Coney Island parable tells of a couple of starving cabaret performers who, in 1916, complained to a Feltman's delivery man/roll slicer about the frankfurter's ten-cent price tag. Heeding the cries of these struggling entertainers—Jimmy Durante and Eddie Cantor—young Nathan Handwerker took his $300 life savings and opened a stand selling hot dogs for a nickel.

Another myth: To quell public fears concerning the quality of these cheap dogs, Handwerker gave free hot dogs to doctors, who chomped away while clad in their reassuring white coats and stethoscopes. Some say Handwerker actually hired bums and dressed them up as physicians.

A fact: The spiced-meat formula devised by Nathan's wife, Ida, had sold a hundred million hot dogs by 1955 and still sells nearly a million a year from this site alone.

Nathan's remains a year-round staple at Coney Island, but it becomes an international attraction on July 4th, when it hosts its hot-dog-eating contest

Nathan's, 1310 Surf Avenue, 718-946-2202, serves corn, barbecued chicken, and fried seafood (including frog legs), but its hot dogs and fries remain the quintessential Coney dining experience. According to legend, Babe Ruth once consumed twenty-four Nathan's franks and two gallons of lemonade in a single sitting. But for the record books, Nathan's sponsors a hot-dog-eating contest every July 4. (Another legend: the contest was started on Independence Day in 1924 by four immigrants who staged a contest among themselves, believing that winning this would demonstrate the ultimate in patriotism.) The contest itself and the top mark have grown exponentially over the last two decades. What once attracted small crowds and then the local press is now a major media event covered live on ESPN and around the world. The restaurant now even has a giant outdoor Wall of Fame on its Stillwell Avenue side, with a clock counting down the minutes till next July 4th as well as a list of the annual winners, from Jay Green, who ate 14 in 1988; to Ed Krachie who swallowed 22¼ in 1996; to Takeru

Kobayashi, who won six straight years, peaking with 54 in 2006; to Joey Chestnut, who won four straight times after Kobayashi and set a hard-to-fathom new record by inhaling 68 hot dogs . . . with buns . . . in twelve minutes.

For dessert, try **William's Candy Shoppe**, 1318 Surf Avenue, 718-372-0302, which opened in 1926 and seems oblivious to these health-conscious times: jelly apples, cotton candy, giant swirl lollipops, and candied marshmallows whisper sweet nothings from large storefront windows. Or walk down to **Denny's Delight** at 1212 Surf Avenue, 718-266-9371, where the soft-serve ice cream flavors extend to include banana and pistachio.

Don't worry, Coney Island also has food your mother would let you eat, and some of it comes with a healthy side portion of history. In 1965, after buying fifty-eight-year-old **Gargiulo's**, 2911 West 15th Street, 718-266-4891, three Russo brothers revived its flagging reputation. Since then Gargiulo's has been one of Brooklyn's, make that the city's—most popular Italian restaurants (with space for private parties of twenty to four hundred people). It has simple yet tasteful décor, and its dishes are moderately priced and made with exquisite ingredients—one of the Russos makes fresh mozzarella each morning. From the pennette pasquiline to the creamy chocolate mousse cake, the food will have you sighing softly in appreciation. And you'll be squealing with excitement when they bring the lottery shaker to your table afterward—if you guess the right number, the meal is on the house.

In 1924 Totonno Pero, who got his start at Lombardi's—New York's first pizzeria—opened **Totonno's**, 1524 Neptune Avenue, 718-372-8606. Today, Totonno's coal-fired brick ovens are in good hands with the third generation of the Pero family. The service is brusque at best, but they make fresh dough daily and turn out some of the city's finest pies.

Another sign of the area's revival is the appearance of new restaurants. **Coney Island Surf and Turf Grill**, 1315 Surf Avenue, 718-513-6491, offers little in the way of ambience, but serves snow crabs, pulled pork, and other goodies that won't be found in the fast-food eateries. **Footprints Café**, 1521 Surf Avenue, 718-265-2530, brings delicious Caribbean food to the neighborhood (albeit with music at unnecessarily high volumes). The restaurant, a spin-off of the Flatbush original, serves up jerk and curry dishes as well as the zesty Roy's Honey Garlic Wings and its signature Rasta Pasta dishes in a spicy, creamy sauce.

Brighton Beach's food options are plentiful, though the focus is almost exclusively on Russian and Ukrainian cooking. Brighton Beach Avenue, the neighborhood's main strip, features several fascinating markets. The most famous is **M & I International Foods**, 249 Brighton Beach Avenue,

718-615-1011, but there are other options, like **Gold Label Supermarket**, 281–285 Brighton Beach Avenue, 718-743-3900; **Exclusive Deli**, 411 Brighton Beach Avenue, 718-368-3001; and **Brighton Bazaar**, 1007 Brighton Beach Avenue, 718-769-1700. All sell copious amounts of meat, fish, pickled foods, chocolates, and traditional dishes like stuffed cabbage.

One of the more unusual restaurants is **Café Kashkar**, 1141 Brighton Beach Avenue, 718-743-3832, a little storefront eatery that serves up food from Uzbekistan's Uighur community—the Uighurs are Muslim Turks from China and other parts of Asia, so there are plenty of noodle and rice dishes alongside sizzling kebabs and lamb dishes. The appetizer portions are large, but the kebab meat is of varying quality. Specialties include *samsa* (hand-chopped lamb inside flaky pastries), Chinese-style *lagman* noodles, and salad *langsai*.

Perhaps the most notable of the more typical Russian restaurants is **Café Glechik**, 3159 Coney Island Avenue, 718-616-0494. It serves a wide array of traditional dishes, but specializes in two types of stuffed dumplings—the *vareniki* and the *pelmeni*. The *New York Times* once observed that the restaurant's potato *vareniki* "are as light as carbs stuffed into carbs drenched in melted fat can be."

Many of the neighborhood's other restaurants also double as nightclubs, with dance floors and live music to draw weekend crowds. These include **Cafe Arbat**, 306 Brighton Beach Avenue, 718-332-5050; **Pastorale Restaurant**, 410 Brighton Beach Avenue, 718-648-5484; and **Primorski**, 282 Brighton Beach Avenue, 718-891-3111.

The most mind-blowing experience in Brighton Beach is at the granddaddy of them all. The National, 273 Brighton Beach Avenue, 718-646-1225, with a main dining room seating 450 people, offers a prix fixe, multicourse meal and live entertainment. A cross between a wedding celebration and Disneyland's It's a Small World ride, a night here is not so much a true Russian experience as it is a Russian interpretation of American self-indulgence and European glamour. So get a group of friends together, dress up, and prepare for a surreal night of partying. The food is traditional Russian fare and ranges from decent to delicious but the emphasis is more on excess than ethnicity—herring, caviar, and pickled tomatoes to go with the endless supply of meat in all shapes and sizes. A bottle of vodka is included, and you are allowed to bring your own alcohol, too.

The evening's real treat, however, is the surreal floor show, which is the wackiest cabaret show imaginable: a broad, colorful spectacle with acts that might include gymnasts, dancers, drag queens, or singers in bumblebee outfits or other dresses that might make Cher jealous. Then it's time to dance, with the music going till 3 AM.

There are also several hybrid Russian eateries along the Brighton Beach boardwalk, offering French dishes and hamburgers along with chicken Kiev and *kostiza moldavien* (marinated pork chops). But the emphasis at the outdoor cafés is often on vodka, cigarettes, and vibrant conversation. They're ideal places for people-watching, since the boardwalk is a veritable mob scene on summer nights—people of all ages chat in a Babel of languages as they drink or stroll or simply relax on benches.

Island Hopping

By bus: Many buses travel to Coney Island. The B29, B36, B64, B74, and X29 all go to the western half, while the B1, B36, B68, and B49 all go to the eastern portion.

By train: The B, Q, F, and N trains all stop in Coney Island at Stillwell Avenue. The D and Q stop in Brighton Beach.

By car: Take Coney Island Avenue or Ocean Parkway south to the peninsula or take the Belt Parkway to exit 7 and get on Ocean Parkway.

19. Forgotten Islands of South Brooklyn
Plum Island – White Island

Forgotten Islands of South Brooklyn

Plum Island

LONG BEFORE THE UNITED STATES invaded Grenada or Panama, American troops were called in to protect vital interests and establish order at a troublesome spot much closer to home.

The brief story of Plum Island is one of the stranger chapters in New York history, in which this 150-acre strip just east of Coney Island was invaded twice within a year by the U.S. Army.

Plum (or Plumb) Island blossomed after the United States purchased a portion of it in 1891 to build a fort. When the plans fell through, enterprising Brooklynites set up tent camps and shacks and, later, bars and inns on this federal land, because alcohol and tobacco could be sold without local excise taxes. By 1907 there was a five-cent ferry to Sheepshead Bay and nearly a hundred homes in this poor man's resort, including one owned by sixty-six-year-old John Greenwood, who had grown up on Plum Island when it supported nothing but three shacks. (His father helped capture the notorious pirate Charles Gibbs.)

Thousands of mating horseshoe crabs arrive at Plum Beach in late spring each year.

Anxious to turn a profit from the land, the federal government dispatched army troops in May 1908 to clear out the squatters and leased the property to Winfield Overton, a former judge. When the Plum Island squatters returned, Overton allowed them to stay, but began acting as if he were the czar of Plum Island. He established his own police force, and in August nearly provoked an armed confrontation with New York police by declaring that during an upcoming carnival he would hold boxing matches—illegal in New York at the time—and would use force to defend his federal land rights.

Overton eventually backed down, but in April 1909 the government revoked his lease, organized the Plum Island Association, and put new leaders in power. When rumors of Overton's return circulated, the army sent in soldiers, this time to defend residents from the ruler the government had originally installed.

Overton never returned, and islanders lived in peace for nearly three decades. Even after New York City bought the island from the federal government in 1924, hundreds of Brooklynites summered there, with grocery peddlers and icemen bringing supplies across at low tide.

A new overlord, Robert Moses, arrived in 1937, kicking out the last squatters and shutting down the beach so he could build the Belt Parkway over the land. By 1940, landfill linked the island to Brooklyn, and it was renamed Plum Beach. Moses, who had cut off the residents from their local swimming spot, opened a picnic area there for Belt Parkway drivers. Today this forgotten chunk of land, east of exit 9B, is part of the Gateway National Recreation Area.

Exploring the Island

Plum Island (today called Plum Beach) becomes a lover's paradise in late May and early June as dozens and sometimes hundreds of horseshoe crabs emerge from the ocean and climb onto the sand in their annual mating ritual. The spectacle is most amazing at high tide and when there is a new or full moon. Large females, with smaller males literally in tow, dig into the sand, where they deposit tiny, bluish-green eggs. Fertilizing males are then dragged across the eggs and the deed is done.

Physically unchanged for 500 million years (and related to trilobites), horseshoe crabs often get stranded on the beach by the tide. So if you *see* one of these harmless critters, gently pick it up and return it to the sea.

To get to Plum Island, drive along the Belt Parkway Eastbound. After passing Exit 9B/Knapp Street, look for a right-hand turnoff into the Plum Beach parking lot. Both the National Park Service (212-318-4340; www.nps

.com/gateway) and the American Littoral Society (718-318-9344; www
.alsnyc.org) lead free horseshoe crab walks in season.

White Island

When Alfred Tredway White and a friend donated 150 Brooklyn acres to
New York for parkland, White had no inkling that an island in Gerritsen
Creek would one day be named for him. Of course, that's because there was
no island in the creek in 1917.

White, a philanthropist and staunch education and housing advocate for
the poor, and Frederic B. Pratt, son of Standard Oil magnate Charles Pratt
and himself president of Pratt Institute for forty-four years, were concerned
that the rapidly developing borough would soon lose all its waterfront property and rich marshlands to development. In fact, their land was so valuable that businessmen pressured the city not to accept the men's offer, and
it took the city seven years to embrace the deal.

Then, in 1934, the Supreme Court ordered New York City to stop dumping garbage in the ocean, so Parks Commissioner Robert Moses used trash
to fill in marshes and create Marine Park. Over the next quarter century,
trash was also dumped onto and around several marshy islands in Gerritsen Creek, and White Island was born.

For years afterward, White Island's innards—banana peels, pieces of
concrete, discarded chicken dinners, and newspapers referring to Dwight
D. Eisenhower—leached into the creek. Plans to build an executive golf
course on the island were proposed, but by the time funds were raised to
build a permanent bridge to the island (a temporary bridge was used to
transport trash to the island), White Island had come under the protection
of the National Park Service. Except for the occasional squatter or fisher-
man who would row past dozens of wrecked boats to try his luck from the
island's edge, White Island sat undisturbed. (Local residents and fishermen often didn't even call the island by its given name, adorning it with
monikers like Mau-Mau Island, Golf Course Island, or Gilligan's Island—
the latter in homage to a former squatter.)

Then in 1995 it was announced that White Island would receive an environmental makeover as mitigation for the destruction of an eighty-acre
grassland known as Vandalia Dunes. These grasslands—rare in the city
and an important habitat for certain bird species—were destroyed to make
way for the massive Gateway Mall, which opened near Starrett City in
2002. "Several million dollars was supposed to have been set aside for the

work, but for over ten years, nothing happened," says Ida Sanoff, an environmental advocate and the Natural Resources Protective Association chairperson. In 2007, "we started complaining about this at Jamaica Bay Task Force meetings and asking what happened to the money [\$1.5 million had been set aside for mitigation by the mall developer] and all of a sudden, the Parks Department woke up and started to actually do some work." The cost of the project has skyrocketed to \$60 million, with much of it coming from the city. But when all is said and done, and White Island is returned to nature, the legacy of Alfred Tredway White will be fully realized.

Exploring the Island

White Island may be inaccessible, but it can easily be seen from a gravel trail at the **Salt Marsh Nature Center at Marine Park**, 718-421-2021. The one-mile loop begins at the back of the nature center, meandering through a protected salt-marsh environment, much like what Alfred T. White wanted preserved. The trail, rich with salt-marsh hay, salt-marsh cord-grass, and the wildlife that calls this ecosystem home, features several viewing spots along the way. Lookout Hill offers an excellent chance to *see* the marsh and White Island from a perch perspective. The view of the island is even better once you round the bend en route back to the nature center.

The Urban Park Rangers (www.nycgovparks.org) offer free, guided tours along the trail that passes White Island as well as canoeing along Gerritsen Creek.

Island Hopping

By car: Take the Belt Parkway east to exit 11-N. Take Flatbush Avenue to Avenue U and turn left. Take Avenue U to East Thirty-third Street. Parking is across from the nature center.

By subway: Take the D train to Avenue U, then transfer for the B3 bus toward Kings Plaza, getting off at East Thirty-third Street.

By bus: The B3 bus stops right by the nature center on Avenue U at East Thirty-third Street.

Part VII

The Kills

PRALL'S ISLAND • SHOOTER'S ISLAND • ISLE OF MEADOW

The Kills separate Staten Island from New Jersey. The Arthur Kill winds its way up Staten Island's western shore, while the Kill Van Kull wends between Staten Island's northern shore and Bayonne, New Jersey, before flowing into Upper New York Bay.

20. Prall's Island, Shooter's Island, and Isle of Meadow

"For the average citizen and even for the weathered naturalist, the finding that nature survives and, at times, even thrives in an urban matrix can be a revelation,"

FROM *An Islanded Nature*, a 2000 report by the Trust for Public Land and New York City Audubon

Prall's Island, Shooter's Island, and Isle of Meadow

IN 1974, A LOCAL LONGSHOREMAN AND AVID BIRDER NAMED SCOTTY JENKINS spotted a beautiful egret with a twig in its mouth on Prall's Island in the Arthur Kill just west of Staten Island. Neither Jenkins nor the bird could have known it, but that was the start of something big.

Prall's Island (eighty acres), along with Shooter's Island (forty-three acres), and Isle of Meadow (101 acres), its neighbors in the Arthur Kill and nearby Kill Van Kull, was, to say the least, an unlikely starting point for anything to do with nature. Since the 1880s, the waters surrounding these islands have been home to heavy industry—especially oil refineries on the New Jersey side—and more ship traffic than the Panama Canal. By the late 1960s the kills were so polluted that the water couldn't sustain the fish and other marine life that many of the birds eat. The Clean Water Act of 1972, however, improved conditions enough to support some aquatic life. This in turn, attracted glossy ibis, black-crowned night herons, yellow-crowned night herons, snowy egrets, great egrets, and cattle egrets, all of them building nests and nurturing their young amid these green patches along the periphery of this industrial area.

Today, these islands are bereft of birds—predators, human disturbances and Asian longhorned beetles are among the contributing factors—but the homes they provided gave these waders a foothold in the city. They've since spread their wings and moved on to islands in Lower New York Bay, the East River, and the Hutchinson River. The city lies along the Atlantic Flyway, one of four North American bird migration routes. This rookery—the most significant in the state—now welcomes as many as two thousand nesting pairs each year from March to September. They are protected by the Harbor Herons Project, which is run by the New York City Department of Parks and Recreation and the New York Audubon Society, along with other state and city agencies and nonprofits like Trust for Public Land.

Historical Detour: Ruthless People

Nothing much ever happened on Prall's Island. The quiet salt meadow once fed livestock that sloshed over from Staten Island. In 1910, it was a depository for dredge spoils scooped from the Arthur Kill. That was about it.

Then, in 1916, the city proposed building a garbage facility there. Virtually overnight, Prall's became the subject of a bitter debate over its ownership, prompting opposing interests to seize the island with little regard for the law.

While Staten Island and Queens processed their own garbage, refuse from other boroughs was treated on Brooklyn's Barren Island, until complaints from Brooklynites forced Mayor John Mitchel to close the plant. Without any public notice, Mitchel won approval for a new garbage facility on Staten Island at a special board of estimate meeting on April 10.

Needless to say, Staten Islanders were not happy. "The Garbage War" dominated the front pages of the *Staten Islander* and *Staten Island Register*, inspired formation of the Staten Island Vigilance Committee and the Women's Anti-Garbage League, and provoked thousands of Staten Islanders to denounce Mitchel at city-hall protests.

When Prall's Island, just off Staten Island's west shore, was selected as the plant site, the island's ownership quickly became a matter of dispute. As Manhattan real-estate man J. Sterling Drake prepared to sell Prall's to the plant's builders, Edward P. Doyle, a leader of the antigarbage movement and a real-estate man himself, claimed he held the title.

Doyle secured the island with a barbed-wire fence, built a shack, and hired twin seventy-one-year-old watchmen, James and William Farmer, to keep the contractors out. On May 18, under cover of darkness, fifteen men raided Prall's Island, kidnapped the lookouts, and confiscated the controversial land. The Farmers were taken by launch to Brooklyn, where they were freed but warned that returning to Prall's Island might result in death. The old men notified the police, who stormed the island and arrested the group, found huddled around the shack's stove. The island-snatchers had been employed by Drake, who was later indicted for the kidnapping.

Two days later, Edward Doyle took out a full-page ad in the *Staten Islander*, defending the validity of his title and stating that in order to stop the plant he would take possession of any site by "any title available and by any means necessary." Doyle claimed to own not only Prall's Island but also other local properties delineated in a land grant made in the early eighteenth century by Queen Anne. Drake countered that his title had been undisputed for a century and that Doyle's claim would destroy the local real-estate market. Drake even said he worked on Prall's Island, cutting salt hay.

When the plant's builders became frustrated by Drake's inability to sell them Prall's Island, they took possession of a marshy hummock near the Fresh Kills called Lake's Island. The city approved the relocation, but the facility operated for less than two years before being abandoned. Lake's Island later became home to the city's notorious landfill, while Prall's Island slipped back into anonymity.

Back in 1974, Jenkins had reported his discovery to the Staten Island Institute of Arts and Sciences, which kept records of avian breeding, and the National Audubon Society. The birds were not only attracted to these rare strips of green in the city but also found delightful the remains of wooden pilings and ships around Shooter's Island. But Representative John Murphy, a Staten Island Democrat, was attempting to blow Shooter's Island and its ship graveyard out of the water, claiming it would make navigation easier for ship traffic and create jobs in the region. Fortunately, a study by the Army Corps of Engineers concluded that Shooter's Island was not hazardous to navigation and recommended against spending $60 million to obliterate it.

The threat of destruction helped galvanize concern among environmentalists, especially at the newly founded New York City Audubon. By the mid-eighties, Prall's Island was under the protection of the Parks Department, and New York Audubon took responsibility for Shooter's Island as a wildlife refuge. In 1988, waders were spotted on Isle of Meadow. Soon after, the Harbor Herons Project was started to preserve the birds' fragile wetlands habitat. While Prall's, Shooter's and Isle of Meadow are collectively part of the Harbor Herons Project, each possesses a distinct history.

Situated in the Kill Van Kull across from Mariner's Harbor on the north shore of Staten Island, Shooter's Island was a popular colonial hunting preserve. During the Revolution, agents for General George Washington used the island as a drop-off point for delivering messages.

Shooter's Island was home to shipyards from 1865 to 1920.

Until industry arrived in the mid-nineteenth century, the area surrounding Shooter's Island was known for its thick, tasty oysters. In the early 1860s, David Decker—whose ancestors were among the earliest Dutch settlers on Staten Island—had a small shipyard on what was then an eleven-acre island. The Shooter's Island Petroleum Refining & Storage Company bought the island in 1865 and added a new dock and huge buildings. At the turn of the twentieth century, the Townsend-Downey Shipbuilding Company built cruising and racing yachts there.

The island's most spectacular event occurred on February 25, 1902, when two thousand invited guests, including President Theodore Roosevelt, witnessed the launching of *Meteor III*, a magnificent racing yacht built for the emperor of Germany, Kaiser Wilhelm II. The *New York Times* called the affair "the most distinguished gathering ever assembled to witness the naming of a vessel in American waters." The yacht featured a majestic eagle figurehead on its prow; a main saloon with fireplace, grand piano, and mahogany bar with silver handrails; and a dining table that seated twenty-four.

Mostly, however, the workers at Shooter's Island toiled on projects with more grit than glamour. During World War I, the Standard Shipbuilding Company employed nine thousand men who churned out steel cargo ships for the war effort. When operations ended in 1920, the island became a dumping ground for derelict vessels. Today, the landscape is littered with rotting dry docks, piers, and pilings.

It was during the shipbuilding days that about thirty acres of fill were added to Shooter's Island to accommodate the massive shipyards. Most of the expansion was on the island's north side, enlarging it beyond its New York border and into New Jersey. Today, Shooter's Island is forty-three acres, thirty-four of them in New York City. Two New Jersey cities—Bayonne, which owns seven and a half acres, and Elizabeth, which owns one and a half acres—have granted New York conservation easements, allowing it to manage the entire island as a wildlife refuge. If the island is not used for this purpose, the properties revert back to New Jersey.

Prall's Island, in the Arthur Kill just south of the Goethals Bridge, has minimal documented history. It was known as Dongan's Island when New York governor Thomas Dongan took title in 1688. The name was later corrupted to Duncan's Island. The name Prall's Island, which took hold in the late nineteenth century, is likely derived from a prominent local family who lived on Staten Island just across from the marshy island.

During the two world wars, locals, who often rowed out to investigate the military leftovers, dubbed surplus ships anchored off the island's shores the Prall's Island Fleet. Through the centuries, however, Prall's Island was generally ignored—until the birds were discovered nesting there.

Isle of Meadow, less than two miles south of Prall's Island and at the intersection of the Arthur Kill and the Fresh Kills, was dubbed Dead Man's Island in the eighteenth century after a deadly accident occurred there. A ferry crossing the Arthur Kill was blown off-course in 1768, forcing ashore nine men, two slaves, and a boy. A sharp wind and lack of shelter killed one man and the boy; the others lost fingers and toes from frostbite.

Ten years later, three boats with American soldiers landed on the island, catching off-guard British sentries posted there. By the late 1790s, the island was referred to as Ye Island of Meadow or Island of Salt Meadows.

A rickety wooden footbridge connected the island to Staten Island until a storm destroyed it in 1929. The Department of Sanitation proposed joining the island to the mainland in 1940, but instead developed land east of the island and created the world's largest landfill, the Fresh Kills Landfill. Ironically, before the landfill closed in 2001, Isle of Meadow was the only spot in the Harbor Heron Project to play home to cattle egrets. Cattle egrets traditionally live near cows and other animals that attract bugs for them to eat. There are no bovines in Staten Island, but the machines served in their place, moving garbage around and thus churning up ample meals of bugs.

The Harbor Herons Project seeks to ensure that the entire urban estuary complex is protected from further degradation. Numerous agencies and not-for-profits help, including the Trust for Public Land, the National Park Service at Gateway, and the Urban Park Rangers, as well as ordinary citizens like Scotty Jenkins, who started it all, or residents of Co-op City in the Bronx who report sightings from their windows of life on nearby Goose Island.

Despite ecosystem improvements, this extraordinary avian haven is still extremely vulnerable. "The birds are vulnerable to human disturbance during the breeding season," says Susan Elbin, director of conservation for New York City Audubon. "They are vulnerable to habitat degradation, loss, or fragmentation. Contaminants in the harbor, ingested by fish and crustaceans and then subsequently ingested by harbor herons, lead to impaired growth, reduced or halted reproduction, and reduced survivorship. Predators like raccoon and feral cats are a threat."

In 1990, a series of spills dumped nearly 1.6 million gallons of oil into the harbor's waterways and wetlands. The gravest peril came when Exxon's underwater pipeline between Linden and Bayonne burst, pouring 567,000 gallons of fuel oil into the Arthur Kill. About seven hundred waterfowl and gulls died (the waders had gone south for the winter) and nearly two hundred acres of salt marsh were damaged, killing the organisms at the bottom of the food chain.

Nesting patterns for the waders suffered for several years, with snowy egrets and glossy ibis—dependent on the salt marshes and tidal mudflats for food—reproducing less and losing many chicks in infancy. Exxon pleaded guilty to criminal charges and paid $15 million in criminal and civil penalties to an array of city, state, and federal government agencies. That money was spent on cleanup and research into the effects of the spill as well as rehabilitating the contaminated areas by hand-planting salt-marsh cordgrass and other native plants.

In recent years, other seemingly less dramatic threats have driven thousands of birds from these islands. By the mid-1990s, invasive ailanthus trees had grown taller than the island's other tree species. Herons don't like nesting so high up for fear of becoming easy prey. In 2000, the parks department's natural resources group received city and state money and began replacing the ailanthus with gray birch, red maple, and hackberry saplings. But before the gray birch could get established, the voracious Asian longhorned beetle (ALB) was discovered on the island. In 2007, three thousand trees were removed from the island, with another eight thousand trees removed from nearby parts of Staten Island as part of the precautionary protocol. "It was not only a terrible problem, it was a huge piece of work," says parks commissioner Adrian Benepe, explaining that his staff made a "military-style landing" on the island, bringing gear and equipment needed for the project.

In a recent Harbor Heron Project report, the idea of a new approach to dealing with ALB was raised out of concern that other infestations could lead to the decimation of the habitat not only for these waders but also for other wildlife. But Benepe says there was no choice—three thousand acres of mostly native woodland in the nearby Staten Island Greenbelt had to be protected.

The aggressors on Shooter's Island were of a different species: human partiers. Campfires and liquor bottles indicated the presence of this destructive force—visitors even tore down NO TRESPASSING signs explaining the presence of nesting birds in flagrant disregard for their survival. Even though enforcement was stepped up and there has been no evidence of humans in recent years, the waders have not returned—although a colony of double-crested cormorants continues to nest on the dry docks and other wreckage west of the island.

To educate the public about the islands' importance, the Harbor Herons Project is using volunteers to help with observational studies and other conservation projects and offering eco-cruises to some of the nesting islands in the East River.

And more research needs to be done on the birds themselves.

"We need to have a better understanding of how birds are interacting and communicating with each other," says Elbin. "That is, do birds from different colonies forage at the same sites?" And, she adds, "We would like to do a decoy study to *see* if we can bring some of the harbor herons backs to the islands of the Arthur Kill and Kill van Kull."

The battle has certainly come a long way from the turn of the twentieth century, when herons and egrets were almost extinct because of the demand for their gorgeous feathers in decorating women's hats. While these three islands are not currently home to the waders, they remain beacons of green in this urban environment for osprey, red-tailed hawks, northern harriers, wild turkeys, and smaller birds like warblers, wrens, flycatchers, and Eastern towhees.

And the herons, egrets, and ibises that first arrived here as immigrants in the 1970s continue to flourish on the other islands of New York City, in new "in" neighborhoods like Hoffman Island in Lower New York Bay, Goose Island in the Hutchinson River, and Canarsie Pol in Jamaica Bay. These birds serve as a reminder of the vitality and importance of urban nature, of how we can and must protect the environment even here. And in their ability to find a more desirable piece of real estate and willingness to tough things out and adapt to change in the city, these waders have proven themselves to be true New Yorkers.

EXPLORING THE ISLAND

For information on volunteering in the Harbor Herons Project, call 212-691-7483 or go to www.nycaudubon.org/getinvolved/volunteer.

Acknowledgments: No Author Is an Island

For this third edition of the book, we'd like to start by thanking our boys, Caleb and Lucas, for making our visits to these islands more fun than ever before and for putting up with all the extra hours that Mom and Dad were busy writing.

And, of course, we want to express our appreciation for Kermit Hummel at Countryman Press for giving us the go-ahead on this revision and for Lisa Sacks and Susan Barnett for shepherding the book through the editing process.

We interviewed many people for this new edition and almost all ended up in the pages you've just read. But a few must be singled out for the extra help they provided in terms of providing background information, steering us in the right direction and checking to make sure everything in here is accurate.

Several are fixtures in their island communities: Ron Terner and Tommy Nye of City Island; Dan Mundy (from Ecowatchers) and Don Riepe (from the northeast chapter of the American Littoral Society), both of Broad Channel; Dick Lutz (editor of the Main Street WIRE) of Roosevelt Island; and Dick Zigun of Coney Island USA.

There are others who have worked at institutions to make these islands what they are today: Aimee Boden and Eric Peterson at the Randalls Island Sports Foundation; Susan Elbin of New York City Audubon; Elizabeth Rapuano at the Trust for Governors Island; Darren Boch at the National Park Service; Peg Zitco at the Statue of Liberty–Ellis Island Foundation; Dorothy Hartman of Save Ellis Island; Kathy Krause of the Gateway National Recreation Area; and Ida Sanoff of the Natural Resources Protective Association.

We'd also like to thank everyone who helped us with the first two editions but they are too lengthy to list by name. We'd like to at least highlight the research institutions that receiving public funding and that were so pivotal in our original historical research: the New York Public Library; the Brooklyn Public Library; the Long Island Room of the Queens Public Library; the Bronx Historical Society; the New-York Historical Society; the Queens Historical Society; the New York City Municipal Reference Library; the Staten Island Institute of Arts and Science; the National Park Service; the Harbor Defense Museum; and the South Street Seaport Museum.

Selected Bibliography

We wish we could have listed every research source, but that would have doubled the length of the book. What follows, therefore, is a partial bibliography. These books not only provided historical perspective but in many cases also led us to contemporary sources—newspapers, magazines, memoirs, and personal papers (including those of City Island forefather Benjamin Palmer), government reports, maps, and journal articles—that also helped us in the writing of this book. Some newspapers worth mentioning are the *Staten Island Advance, Brooklyn Eagle, Newtown Register,* and City Island's *Island Current.* Not included in this research inventory are those books already cited in the text, such as *The Iconography of Manhattan Island* by I. M. Phelps Stokes and *The Power Broker* by Robert Caro.

Barlow, Elizabeth. *The Forests and Wetlands of New York City.* Boston: Little, Brown, 1971.

Berengarten, Sidney. *Ellis Island.* Unpublished, 1932.

Black, Frederic. *Jamaica Bay: A History.* Washington, D.C.: Gateway National Recreation Area, 1981.

Duffy, Francis J., and William H. Miller. *The New York Harbor Book.* Falmouth, Maine: TBW Books, 1986.

Flood, Allen and Robert Mullen. *City Island: Her Voyage Through History.* City Island: Self-published, 1949.

Gschedler, Andre. *True Light on the Statue of Liberty and Its Creator.* Narberth, Penn.: Livingston Publishing, 1966.

Holliman, Jennie, and Regina Maria Hughes. *The Statue of Liberty,* Parts I and II. Unpublished, 1934.

Homberger, Eric. *The Historical Atlas of New York City.* New York: Henry Holt and Company, 1994.

Kraut, Alan. *Silent Travelers.* New York: Basic Books, 1994.

Kroeger, Brooke. *Nellie Bly: Daredevil, Reporter, Feminist.* New York: Times Books, 1994.

McCullough, Edo. *Good Ol' Coney Island*. New York: Scribner, 1957.

McNamara, John. *History in Asphalt: The Origins of Street and Place Names*. New York: Harbor Hill Books with Bronx Historical Society, 1978.

Payne, Alice. *Tales of the Clam Diggers*. City Island: Self-published, 1969.

Pisciotta, Alexander. *Theory and Practice of the New York House of Refuge*. Thesis, Florida State University, 1979.

Pitkin, Thomas. *Keepers of the Gate: A History of Ellis Island*. New York: New York University Press, 1975.

Reitz, Conrad. *Fort Lafayette: Civil War Prison 1861–1864*. Unpublished, 1962.

Richmond, John. *New York and Its Institutions, 1609–1872*. New York: E. B. Treat, 1872.

Rothman, David. *Discovery of the Asylum: Social Order and Disorder in the New Republic*. Boston: Little, Brown, 1990.

Smith, Thelma E. Knickerbocker. *Scrapbook: The Islands of New York City*. Municipal Reference Library, Notes: Volume XXXVI, Number 6, June 1962.

Stiles, Henry. *The History of Kings County*. Brooklyn: W. W. Munsell and Co., 1884.

Toward North Brother Island. New York: Institute of Man and Science, 1978.

The WPA Guide to New York City. New York City: The Federal Writers' Project, 1939.

Van Wyck, Frederick. *Keskachauge, or the First White Settlement on Long Island*. New York: Putnam, 1924.

Index